Getting Started with LetterPerfect®

Steven J. Bennett

Brady

New York ■ London ■ Toronto ■ Sydney ■ Tokyo ■ Singapore

BRADY

Simon & Schuster, Inc.
15 Columbus Circle
New York, NY 10023

Manufactured in the United States of America

10 9 8 7 6 5 4 3 2 1

Library of Congress Cataloging-in-Publication Data

Bennett, Steven J., 1951-
Getting Started with LetterPerfect/by Steven J. Bennett.
p. cm.

Includes index.
1. Desktop publishing. 2. LetterPerfect. I. Title.
Z286.D47B45 1990
686.2'2544--dc20 90-47500
CIP

ISBN 0-13-805615-3

Production Note

This book was produced on a Apple LaserWriter II NTX at PageWorks, Inc, in Cambridge, MA,. All figures were created with HOTSHOT Graphics, manufactured by Symsoft, Inc, Incline Village, NV.

Disclaimer

Trademark Acknowledgments

Contents

Section II: LetterPerfect Fundamentals

Section III: Document Processing

Section IV: Printing

Section V: File Maintenance

Section VI: Special Features

Appendices

Acknowledgments

First and foremost, I'd like to thank Burt Gabriel, my editor, and Michael Mellin, Publisher, for their support and encouragement in the project. Thanks also go to Paul Eddington of WordPerfect Corporation, for his help in arranging for pre-release copies of LetterPerfect. Beth McMacken of PageWorks, Inc., did a splendid job of designing the book and laying out the pages. Geraldine Albert, production manager for Brady Books, was also extremely helpful in getting the book to press on time. Marcy Ketcham worked hard to prepare the manuscript for desktop publishing. And once again, I'd like to thank my friend and agent, Mike Snell, for helping to make this project possible.

Introduction

An Old Truism Revisited

Two thousand years ago, the Chinese philosopher Lao Tzu wrote the memorable phrase, "Reversal is the movement of the Way." Far from being mystical gibberish, this phrase has a simple meaning: when anything reaches its maximal state, any further change to it will be in the opposite direction. For instance, the peak of daylight means that the next moment will symbolize an inevitable movement toward darkness. Similarly, the moment of greatest darkness heralds a steady movement toward the light of dawn.

The same principle applies to software. The trend in just about every category has been toward increasing complexity and size. With word processing, for example, many packages began as simple programs occupying a single disk. Today's word processors are monsters, with their advanced features and desktop publishing capabilities, and now gobble up as much as four or five *megabytes* of precious hard disk space (that's 11 to 14 low-density 5 1/4 disks!). Manuals, too, have ballooned in size, with some tomes having as many as 1,000 pages or more. How much more weight can our bookshelves stand?

The good news is that a "reversal of the Way" seems to be in the wind, at least in terms of word processing software. As evidence there is WordPerfect Corporation's simplified program, LetterPerfect. If you're the kind of person who needs to type memos, letters, basic reports, etc., and has no need to create multi-column newsletters, generate tables of authorities for legal briefs, or index a 300-page document automatically, then LetterPerfect is the answer to your prayers. This simple, but feature-laden program will take care of just about all of your word processing needs. You'll find its learning curve short, and best of all, you'll only need a minimum of computer horsepower to use it. You can even run it on a single-drive floppy system (see the chapter on installing LetterPerfect on a floppy-based system).

LetterPerfect is also the ideal word processor for battery-powered laptops; the program was designed to minimize how often the computer needs to read the floppy or hard disk for key files, thereby reducing power consumption.

Far more than a stripped-down version of its big cousin, the best-selling WordPerfect program, LetterPerfect contains an intelligently organized set of features and functions. (By the way, LetterPerfect and WordPerfect 5.1 files are interchangeable, so if your office uses WordPerfect 5.1, you can still use LetterPerfect at home and bring in your disks for additional formatting and printing.) Be assured that LetterPerfect is by no means lacking in power. Among other features, it offers:

Extensive formatting and editing functions (such as cut and paste, search and replace).

Extensive font support (including bold and underline, as well as soft fonts and PostScript fonts).

Support for more than 600 printers.

The ability to incorporate graphics into documents.

Mail merge functions.

A built-in outliner.

A comprehensive spell-checker.

To make LetterPerfect as easy to use as possible, WordPerfect Corporation equipped the program with a "pull-down" menu system that enables you to access all key functions with a minimum of effort (you can also use the mouse to select options from the menu system). In addition, you'll find a set of "Fast Keys," (combinations of (Alt) plus a designated key) that enable you to perform certain functions without breaking your typing stride.

In short, LetterPerfect is a program whose time has come. It represents an admirable attempt to bring word processing capabilities to those who don't have the hardware or patience for programs designed with the "power user" in mind.

A Jump Start

Getting Started with LetterPerfect was written to guide you through the essential LetterPerfect functions. While it's not designed to be a complete substitute for the package's manual, the book's organization models the mental processes you'll probably go through from the moment you open the program's box to the first time you print a document. As you read along with these instructions, you can experiment with your own text and create documents relevant to your own pursuits. Here are the topics we'll cover, in order:

Installing the program and a printer

Finding your way around the keyboard

Learning to use the menu system, function keys, and fast keys

Personalizing the program

Creating and formatting text

Editing text

Using fonts

Using the thesaurus, checking your spelling

Adding graphics

Printing your document

Saving and retrieving your document

Using special features—mail merge, outliner, utilities

Now that you're familiar with the logic flow of *Getting Started with LetterPerfect*, let's see how it translates into the content of individual chapters—this will help you decide what portions of the book are most relevant to your needs.

Section I: Getting Started

Chapter 1: Installing a Hard Disk System, Starting, and Exiting LetterPerfect

Version 1.0 has an automated installation routine. This chapter explains how and when to use the routine, as well as how to avoid cluttering your hard disk with unnecessary files. It also lists the minimum hardware requirements for running the program. In addition, step-by-step instruction is provided for installing a printer. Proper start-up and exit routines are also discussed.

Chapter 2: Installing a Floppy Disk System, Starting, and Exiting LetterPerfect
This chapter explains the various types of floppy installation that you can perform. It shows you how to run LetterPerfect on systems with four different disk types, and provides step-by-step instruction for installing a printer. The chapter concludes with a discussion of the proper ways to start and exit LetterPerfect.

Section II: LetterPerfect Fundmentals

Chapter 3: Navigating through LetterPerfect: the Keyboard and Screen Display
There are many ways to move the cursor in LetterPerfect: by space, by word, by screen, by page, and by document. You also have a number of options for deleting words, lines, and pages. You'll find all of the cursor and editing key movements described in this chapter.

Chapter 4: The Menu System
The pull-down menu system allows you to see all key functions at a glance, and then "point and shoot" at the desired option, making it very easy to use LetterPerfect's most powerful commands. This chapter describes how to use the menu system, and describes each menu option.

Chapter 5: The Function Keys and Fast Keys
If you prefer a function key approach to the menu system, LetterPerfect lets you have it your way. By combining the 10 special function keys with the (Ctrl), (Shift), and (Alt) keys, LetterPerfect allows you to access many built-in functions. In addition to discussing the pull-down menus and function keys, this chapter also covers the use of the "Fast Keys," which are yet another way of accessing certain major functions.

Chapter 6: Personalizing LetterPerfect
Using the Setup Options. LetterPerfect allows you to personalize a number of program aspects, such as screen colors, and backup options.

Section III: Document Processing

Chapter 7: Creating Documents with LetterPerfect
Once you know the keyboard layout and understand the concept behind the function keys, you're ready to create a document. This chapter covers how to use LetterPerfect 1.0's powerful formatting features to set margins and tabs, choose line spacing, assign page numbers, etc.

Chapter 8: Editing Tools
The main advantage of a word processor over a typewriter is that it allows you to revise your work continually without retyping or cutting and pasting scraps of paper together. LetterPerfect allows you to manipulate your document electronically through a number of editing functions, such as electronic "cut and paste" and "search and replace." In this chapter, you'll learn how to use these and other features to alter the content and appearance of your documents quickly.

Chapter 9: Changing Fonts
If you've installed a printer that has built-in fonts or uses plug-in font cartridges or soft fonts, you can use LetterPerfect to create professional-looking documents with a typeset look. This chapter covers the basics of changing fonts for new and existing text.

Chapter 10: Fine Tuning Your Document
LetterPerfect includes an extensive thesaurus to help you find synonyms, and a spell-checker for picking up and correcting typographical errors. In this chapter, you'll learn how to use both features to make your final documents as creative and professional as possible.

Chapter 11: Adding Graphics
With LetterPerfect's built-in graphics functions, you can incorporate certain types of graphic images directly into your document for a more polished look. This chapter tells you everything you need to know about the program's graphic functions.

Section IV: Printing

Chapter 12: Printing Your Document
LetterPerfect offers excellent printer control, allowing you to print a

whole document, a single page of a document, or a series of non-continuous pages. You can specify how many copies are to be printed, and even let the program adjust for the binding width of the document. All key printer functions are discussed in this chapter.

Section V: File Maintenance

Chapter 13: Storing and Retrieving Your Document
Built into LetterPerfect 1.0 is a sophisticated file manager that allows you to retrieve, rename, and delete files. All of the file management functions are explained in this chapter, along with tips for backing up your work—just in case...

Section VI: Special Features

Chapter 14: Other LetterPerfect Functions
LetterPerfect makes it easy to send personalized letters through its “mail merge” function. This chapter explains how to set up and use a merge quickly. It also covers the use of the outliner, which enables you to sketch the main points of a document. Finally, the chapter describes three special LetterPerfect programs that you can install optionally. These include the “Shell” and two conversion programs. The Shell is a memory manager that allows you to run more than one program at the same time, or return to DOS to format a disk without leaving LetterPerfect. One conversion program enables you to convert your LetterPerfect files to or from a number of other word processing formats. A graphics conversion program makes it possible to convert many common graphic formats into ones that LetterPerfect can use.

Appendices

Appendix A: Installing an HP LaserJet Series II or III Printer
The LaserJet Series II or III makes an ideal companion for LetterPerfect 1.0. Whereas Chapter 1 provides a simple installation for any printer, this Appendix describes options for specifying optional font cartridges and soft fonts.

Appendix B: Summary of LetterPerfect Commands
This alphabetical listing gives you the key combinations for each function.

Appendix C: Summary of LetterPerfect Codes
LetterPerfect places hidden codes in your document whenever you issue a formatting command (bold, center, etc.). As explained in Chapter 8, these codes can be seen and edited with a special command. This appendix provides a complete list of all the hidden codes you might encounter.

Typographical Conventions

Throughout this book, you'll be shown various combinations of keystrokes used to activate LetterPerfect commands. Here's a summary:

1. Special keys that do not represent characters are enclosed in parentheses and are abbreviated as they are on the keyboard. The Delete key, for example, appears as:

   (Del)

2. Some keys have symbols, but are spelled out with the name of the function.

   a. The four keys with arrows on the numeric keypad move the cursor. In this book, they are referred to as:

   (Right Cursor)

   (Left Cursor)

   (Up Cursor)

   (Down Cursor)

   b. The key located in the upper right portion of the keyboard, designated by a large arrow pointing left, is referred to as:

   (Backspace)

   c. The long key at the bottom of the keyboard is referred to as:

   (Spacebar)

   d. The key marked by a "hooking" left arrow (↵) is referred to variously by people as "enter," "return," or "carriage return" (a holdover from the days of manual typewriters). In this book it is referred to as:

(Enter)

3. When a special key must be pressed and held while a second key is pressed, the two keys are separated by a hyphen. For example:

   (Shift-F1)

   which means you are to press and hold the shift key, then press the key marked F1, and finally release both keys. Another example would be:

   (Ctrl-Left Cursor)

   which means press the key marked "Ctrl," then press the left cursor once, and release both keys.

4. When keys are to be pressed one at a time in sequence, they are separated by a plus (+) sign, as in:

   (Home) + (Home) + (Up Cursor)

   which means to press the key marked home two times, then press the key with the arrow pointing up.

5. When commands are listed, such as,

   "Type CD \LP10 (Enter)"

   they are listed in upper case for clarity only; you can enter all commands in lower- or uppercase, as you please.

6. Finally, when commands sequences are provided, they consist of two parts: a series of letters that represent the menu system, followed by keyboard equivalents using the function key combinations. For example,

   L,L or (Alt-F6)

   means either press Alt to activate the menu system, then "l" followed by another "l," or press the Alt-F6 key combination. (You can type lowercase menu letters).

   In some cases, the letter and function key combinations will be followed by a series of numbers, indicating that you are invoking a menu with suboptions. For instance:

   L,F + 6 + 1 + 2 or (Shift-F8) + 6 + 1 + 2

means, press Alt to activate the menu system, then type "l" followed by "f" followed by 6, followed by 1 followed by 2, or press the Shift-F8 key combination and then enter the sequence 6,1,2. (By the way, both sequence are used to create a header or footer in your documents.)

Regardless of your previous computing experience, this book can quickly help you take full advantage of the simple yet powerful functions that LetterPerfect places at your fingertips. As Lao Tzu put it: "The wise person avoids excess, extravagance, and arrogance." Be proud to be among those who support a return to simpler software. After all, it's the movement of the Way.

Section I

Getting Started

Place First Class
Postage Here
Post Office
Will Not Deliver
Without Postage

Brady Books
15 Columbus Circle
New York, NY 10023

ATT: J. Padlad

Chapter 1

Installing a Hard Disk System, Starting, and Exiting LetterPerfect 1.0

Highlights

- Installation considerations
- Required RAM
- Required disk space
- Printer
- Automated install routine
- Starting LetterPerfect from data directories
- Safe exiting procedure

Preinstallation Inventory

Few things are more annoying than opening a new software package only to be told you must first stop and assess all possible alternatives for setting up the program on your system. In contrast, LetterPerfect does not make you jump through any major installation hoops, because most of the options are set later, via an internal set-up option. (More on that in Chapter 6.)

Nevertheless, there is some information you must gather before installation. This includes:

the amount of available memory (RAM).

the size of your hard disk.

the type of printer you're using.

Each topic is discussed below.

Available RAM Memory

LetterPerfect 1.0 requires a minimum of 330K of memory; that is, *available* RAM memory or memory not already used for DOS or

RAM resident programs, such as Sidekick. (Programs like Sidekick can always "pop up" for use because they reside in RAM. The trade-off: they reduce the amount of available RAM.) Remember that DOS alone uses 40K of memory or more, depending on the version you're using. WordPerfect Corporation recommends a minimum of 512K of RAM to allow for DOS and any RAM resident programs.

The easiest way to determine how much RAM you have left on your system available for LetterPerfect is to run the CHKDSK utility from DOS. This program lists the total amount of disk storage you have left on the specified disk, and also lists the amount of total RAM on your system and the amount of RAM still available. To run the CHKDSK program:

1. Turn on your computer and load all the RAM resident programs that you plan to be using when you run LetterPerfect 1.0.
2. If you are using a hard disk system, make sure you have the C> prompt; if you are using a floppy-disk-based system, you will be at the A> prompt. Either way, type:

   ```
   CHKDSK (Enter)
   ```

   The system response will look something like this:

   ```
   31768576     bytes total disk space
   165888       bytes in 9 hidden files
   137216       bytes in 55 directories
   20858880     bytes in 1548 user files
   20480        bytes in bad sectors
   10586112     bytes available on disk
   655360       bytes total memory
   524288       bytes free
   ```

(**Note:** The actual numbers displayed on your screen will undoubtedly differ, as they will reflect the particular memory situation of your computer.) The last line indicates the amount of available RAM. If you do not have at least 330K of available RAM, you will have to either reduce the number of RAM resident programs loaded with LetterPerfect, or add more memory to your computer in order to run this program. Contact your dealer or the person responsible for configuring computers in your company for information about increasing your available memory.

Required Hard Disk Space

If you do have a hard disk, be aware that the complete LetterPerfect package (minus the tutorial) requires about 1.5 megabytes (M) of hard disk space. If you do not have at least 1.5 megabytes of free space, you will not be able to perform a complete installation. (You also won't have any room to create new files of your own!) To find out how much space you have left, repeat the CHKDSK command described above. This time, you're interested in the last line of the top set of numbers, which indicates:

```
[X]            bytes available on disk
```

To make additional space available, you have two options: eliminate obsolete files from your disk (or transfer them to floppies to clear up the space); or install only the program files. By skipping the utility, Help, speller, and Shell files, and by eliminating "drivers" for hardware that you don't use, graphic samples, and the learning files, you can reduce the program's hard disk requirements to about 800K.

Printer

Before you can print with LetterPerfect, you must tell the computer what printer you're using, even if you do not have one connected to your computer at this time. You can always change your printer selection later.

Using the Automated Installation Program

At this point, your preinstallation "inventory" should be complete and you'll be ready to begin installing the program. The automated installation program included with LetterPerfect guides you along all key steps in this process. Whenever the install program prompts you for a Yes/No choice, you can type either Y or N, or press (Enter) to accept the first choice. Be aware that you don't have to install all the files now; you can always restart the install program and choose the files you wish to add to your program directory.

IMPORTANT!!! You cannot simply copy the files from your distribution disks (the ones supplied with your LetterPerfect program). The files are in a special compressed format, and must be uncompressed with the built in installation program. Also, before running the automated installation program, you should back up your distribution diskettes. Refer to your DOS manual if you do not know how to use the COPY or DISKCOPY commands.

Take Care of Preliminaries

If you have a hard disk, you must decide where you want to keep your program files and data files. A hard disk has so much storage space that you cannot simply scatter files anywhere and then expect the computer to find them instantly. Instead, hard disks are organized by areas, called *directories*. Every hard disk must contain a *root directory*. The root directory, like the root system of a tree, branches into other directories (see Figure 1.1). Directories themselves can be split into *subdirectories*. You can create and name any directory or subdirectory you wish, as explained below. The key concept, however, is that LetterPerfect files should be kept in one directory, spreadsheet or database files in another, communication programs in another, etc. Each program should have its own special place on the hard disk. This helps you organize what would otherwise be an impossible mess, and helps the computer find your files more quickly.

Figure 1.1 Hard disk concept—each directory is like a location on a map where files are located.

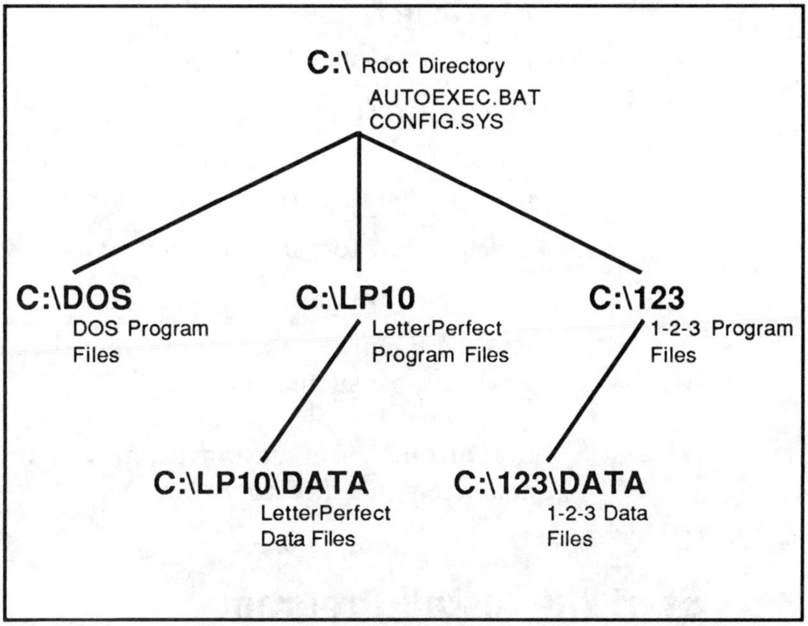

With LetterPerfect, it's important to separate the program files (the actual word processing files) from your data files (letters, reports, and other documents that you create). There are two reasons for this hard disk strategy. First, it makes it easy to back up your data files, which change frequently, without wasting time and space to back up the program files, which only change when WordPerfect Corporation issues a new release. If your data resides by itself in its own directory, you can copy the entire directory with one command. Second, when you want to list the files in your directory to retrieve a document on which you've been working, you don't want to search for your letter to Joe among program files with names like {LP}SPC.FRM or LP{LP}US.LCN.

You are therefore well advised to install your program files in a separate directory, called LP10 (for LetterPerfect, Version 1.0) or some other appropriate name. Set up another separate directory called WORD or LPDATA or any other name you choose as a subdirectory of the program file directory, or as a totally independent directory branching from the root directory. To create a new directory, use the following procedure.

1. Make sure you are in the root directory of the hard drive on which you wish to install the program files (C,D,E, etc) by typing:

CD \ (Enter)

2. Create a directory for the program files by typing:

   MD \ LP10 (Enter)

   (or whatever name you choose). Alternately, wait and let the installation create the directory for you.

3. Create a directory for your own word processing files by typing:

   MD \WORD (Enter)

   Hint: You can have many different data directories for specific applications, such as LETTERS, REPORTS, etc. When you create directories, use names that make sense so that they're easy to remember. You may have a maximum of eight alphanumeric characters in a directory name.

Start the Install Program

Insert the disk marked Install/Utilities 1 in your A drive. Type:

A:INSTALL

You could also start the installation from your B drive, in which case you would type:

B:INSTALL

The title screen shown in Figure 1.2 will appear.

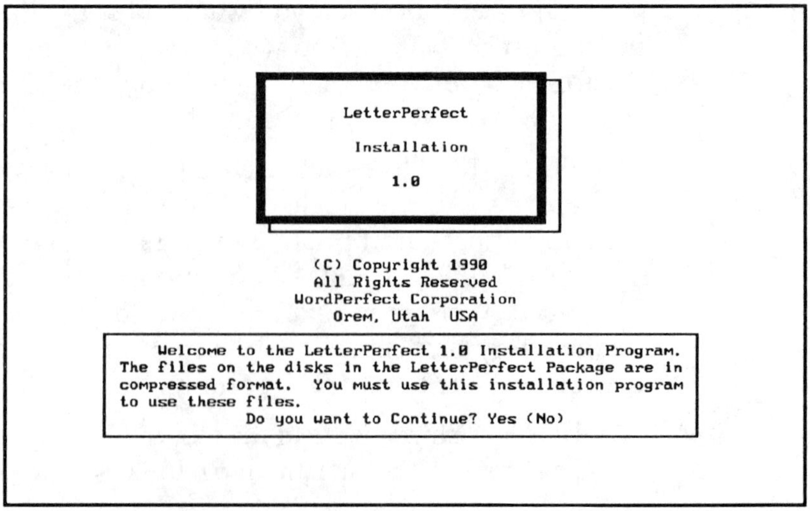

Figure 1.2 Installation title screen.

When the program asks whether you wish to continue, select Y for yes.

Note: You can abort the installation procedure at any time by pressing (Esc). Also, at times you may be prompted to insert your Program 1 disk into the A drive.

Indicate Whether You Have a Color or Monochrome Monitor

Next, LetterPerfect will ask whether you can see the colors red, green, and blue. If so, type Y, and the rest of the installation screens will appear in color; if you indicate No, the screens will appear in monochrome.

Indicate the Type of Disk Drive You are Installing To

After you've indicated whether you have a color or a monochrome display, LetterPerfect will ask if you are installing to a hard disk. Answer Yes.

Choose the Type of Installation

LetterPerfect now displays an installation menu with four options:

1 Install—copies and expands word processing files for a single computer.

2. Network—installs LetterPerfect on a network. This should be done by the person who maintains your company's computers.

3. Printer—installs additional printers.

4. Exit—returns you to the DOS prompt.

Select 1 to install LetterPerfect on your computer.

Specify the Source Drive

Before it actually transfers the files to your hard disk, LetterPerfect must know the drive from which your program will be copied. If the letter in the lower-left corner of the screen does not correspond to the drive in which you placed the install disk, change it now (make sure you put a colon after the letter, as in "B:". Press (Enter) to continue).

Indicate the Target Directory on Your Hard Disk

LetterPerfect assumes that you will want to install the program files to a directory called C:\LP10. If you want to install the program files in this directory, press (Enter). If you haven't already created C:\LP10, LetterPerfect will ask if you want it to create the directory for you. Type Y. If you've created a directory with a different name and would like to install your LetterPerfect program files there, type the name and press (Enter).

LetterPerfect will now ask you to accept or reject the installation of various types of files. Simply indicate Yes or No for each grouping.

Indicate Whether You Want to Install the Utility Files

LetterPerfect will now ask whether you want to install the utility files (see Figure 1.3). Unless you're strapped for space, these files should be copied. They allow you to convert from LetterPerfect to other formats (CONVERT.EXE), and to convert various types of graphic images into files that LetterPerfect can use (GRAPHCNV.EXE). If you find that, over time, you're not using these utilities, you can remove them with the DOS DELETE command or LetterPerfect's built in file delete command (see Chapter 13).

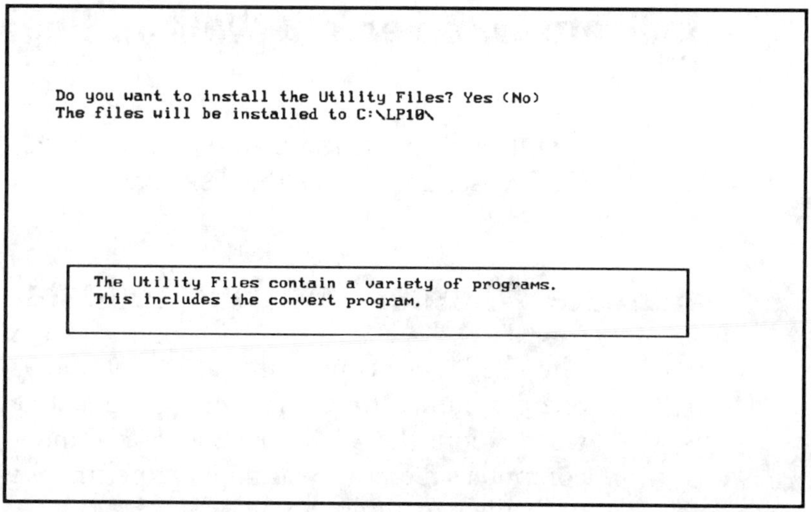

Figure 1.3 Utility file installation prompt.

Note: The next steps use a screen identical to the one shown in Figure 1.3. Each one prompts you as to whether you want to install a particular type or group of files.

Indicate Whether You Want to Install the Graphic Images

The Graphic Images are predrawn illustrations, such as a computer, a clock, and other simple images that you can incorporate into your documents. If you have the disk space and want to experiment, go ahead and indicate Yes at the prompt.

Indicate Whether You Want to Install the Thesaurus

If you've never used an electronic thesaurus before, try it (assuming you have the space) by indicating Yes at the prompt. While some users (the author included) find WordPerfect's thesaurus too clumsy to be practical, you may find it useful (see Chapter 10). Since it is a large file (172K), definitely remove it from your system if you decide not to use it.

Indicate Whether You Want to Install the Learning Files

If you plan to use the LetterPerfect tutorial, you'll need these files. Otherwise, don't waste the disk space.

Indicate Whether You Want to Install the Shell Files

The Shell is a memory manager that allows you to run more than one program at the same time. If you're a new computer user, don't worry about the Shell for now. If you know your way around your computer's memory, you might experiment with it. In any case, you probably won't miss it.

Install the LetterPerfect Program

No choice on this one, at least for the first-time installation. Select Yes. Note: If you decide, at a later time, to install the graphics, utility, or other files that you didn't install the first time around, you don't need to reinstall the program files.

Install the Language Resource File

The Language Resource file contains a number of conventions such as number and date formats. It is worthwhile installing, so you can set your style preferences.

Install the Speller

This is a "must," from a professional word processing point of view. LetterPerfect is equipped with a superb speller; once installed, there's no excuse for sloppy spelling in documents. Chapter 10 describes how to use the speller.

Install the Help file

Your LetterPerfect program includes a comprehensive help system. You might find it a useful adjunct to this book and the manual. Later, you can remove it to save hard disk space.

Check Your CONFIG.SYS File

In order for LetterPerfect to use your computer's memory, a special start-up file, called CONFIG.SYS, must exist, and it must contain the line "FILES=20". If you don't have a CONFIG.SYS file, LetterPerfect will ask if you want one created for you (see Figure 1.4). If you don't know how to do that yourself, answer Yes.

Figure 1.4 Create CONFIG.SYS prompt.

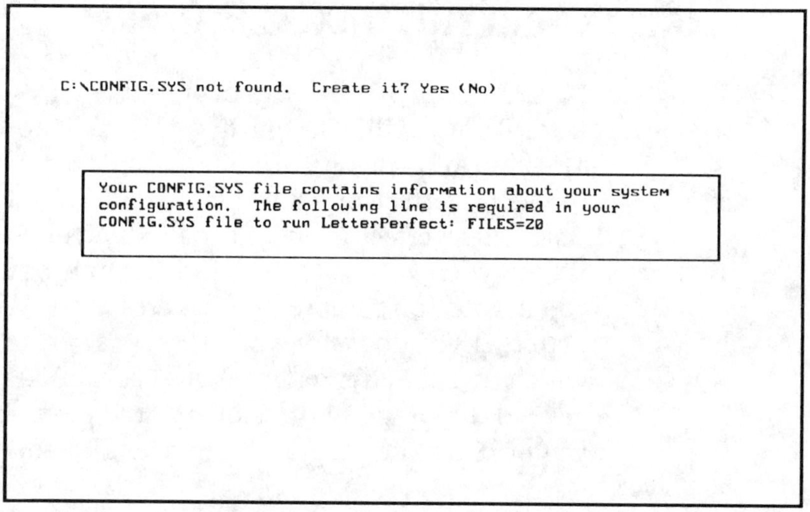

If you do have a CONFIG.SYS file, but it does not specify enough files, the installation program will ask you if you want it to increase the number of files (see Figure 1.5). Again, answer Yes, unless you know how to do it yourself from DOS. After you indicate Yes, LetterPerfect will prompt you to "Press any key to continue."

Figure 1.5 Modify CONFIG.SYS prompt.

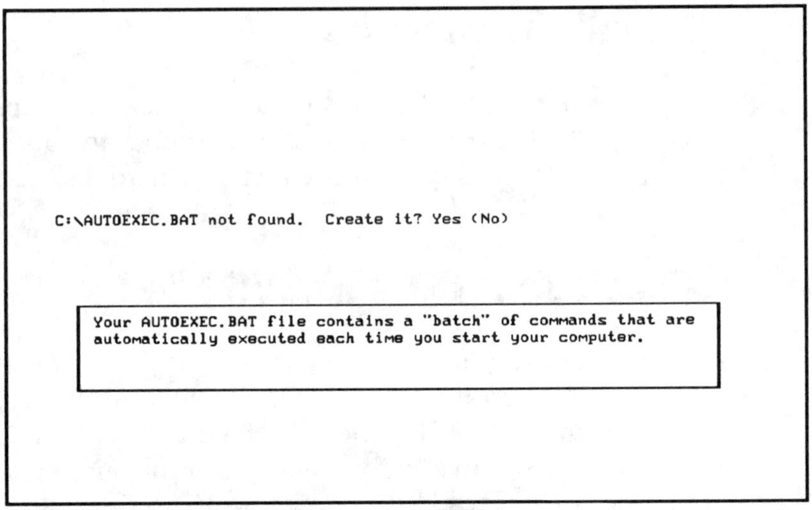

Check Your AUTOEXEC.BAT File

If your computer does not have an AUTOEXEC.BAT file, LetterPerfect will ask you if you want it to create one (see Figure 1.6). An AUTOEXEC.BAT file is necessary to indicate the "path" of the LetterPerfect program files. The PATH command allows you to start LetterPerfect from your data directories. The advantage of this is that when you go to retrieve files, only your data files will be listed. If you don't know how to create an AUTOEXEC.BAT file, let LetterPerfect do it for you. Also answer Yes to the next prompt, which asks if LetterPerfect should add LP10 (or whatever name you gave to the program directory) to the path—this is necessary if you want to start the program from data directories, as just described.

1.6 Prompt to create AUTOEXEC.BAT

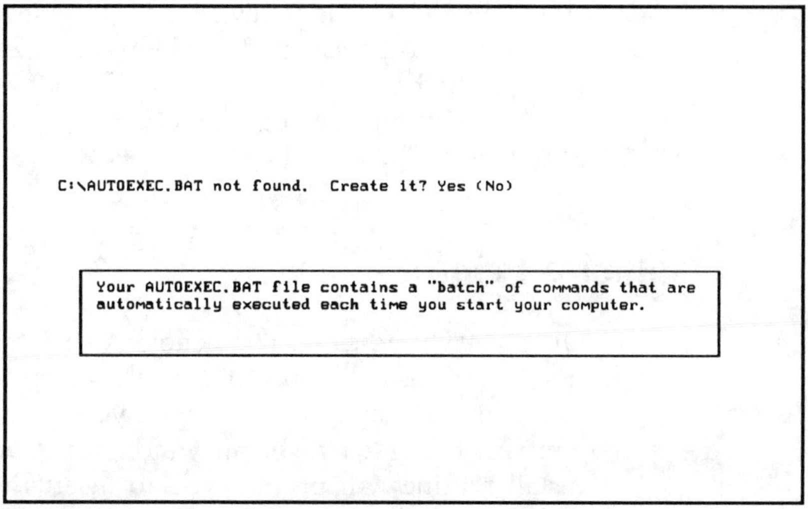

If you already have an AUTOEXEC.BAT file, but it does not contain LP10 (or whatever name you assigned to the program directory), LetterPerfect will ask if it should make the addition (see Figure 1.7). Say Yes unless you plan to do it yourself at the DOS level.

Figure 1.7 Modify AUTOEXEC.BAT prompt.

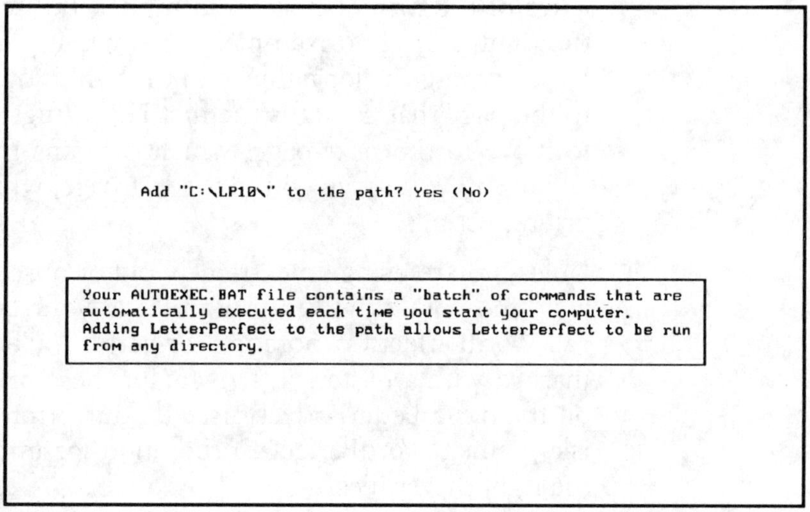

Assign the F1 Function Key

In a gesture of civility rare these days, WordPerfect Corporation. gives you the option of making the F1 key the Help key or the Cancel function key. The default for the F1 key is Cancel function

(F3 is the default Help key). Many programs use F1 for help, so if you're used to pressing F1 for help, press 2, and LetterPerfect will reassign the F1 key as the help key. If you want to leave the default arrangement in place, just press (Enter), and the F1 key will remain as the Cancel function key.

Select a Printer

Once you've indicated your choice of F1 assignment, the installation routine asks if you want to select a printer. If you say No, you can install one at a later date. But you might as well do it now so you will be all set to begin word processing. If you say Yes, the install routine will prompt you to insert the Printer disk in your disk drive and press ENTER. You will then see the first 22 lines of an extensive list of printers—see Figure 1.8 (LetterPerfect supports over 600 different printing devices). Use the cursors, or page down through the alphabetical list until you find the make and model of your printer. You can also search by name. Press the N key, and the menu will clear from the bottom of the screen. As you type each letter of the printer make and model, the screen will "zero in" on the right page. For example, let's say that you have an HP LaserJet III. By typing "n" for name, and then "h", you tell the screen to shift to the page that contains the first HP listings. Just hit the PgDn key to move to the next page, which contains the LaserJet III listings. Typing "x" will move you to the last page, which contains the Xerox printer listings.

Unless you're using an extremely old or obscure brand, you'll probably find your printer. If not, refer to your LetterPerfect manual or call WordPerfect Corporation for help. You'll also see some printers marked with an asterisk. Drivers for these printers are not included on the basic LetterPerfect disk. If your printer's name has an asterisk, contact WordPerfect Corporation for information on obtaining the right driver files.

Figure 1.8 Listing of printers.

```
 1 *Acer LP-76
 2 *AEG Olympia Compact RO           Printers marked with '*' are
 3 *AEG Olympia ESW 2000             not included with shipping
 4 *AEG Olympia Laserstar 6          disks.  Select printer for
 5 *AEG Olympia Laserstar 6e         more information.
 6  AEG Olympia NP 136-24
 7  AEG Olympia NP 136 SE            If you do not see your printer
 8  AEG Olympia NP 30                listed, press F3 for Help.
 9  AEG Olympia NP 80-24
10  AEG Olympia NP 80 SE
11  AEG Olympia NPC 136-24
12 *AEG Olympia Startype
13 *AGFA Compugraphic 9400PS
14  Alphacom Alphapro 101
15  Alps Allegro 24
16 *Alps Allegro 24 (Additional)
17  Alps ALQ200 (18 pin)
18  Alps ALQ200 (24 pin)
19  Alps ALQ224e
20 *Alps ALQ224e (Additional)
21  Alps ALQ300 (18 pin)
22  Alps ALQ300 (24 pin)

N Name Search; PgDn More Printers; PgUp Previous Screen; F3 Help; F7 Exit;
Selection: 0
```

Assuming that you've found your printer, type in the number and press (Enter). LetterPerfect will ask you to confirm your choice. Press (Enter) to continue.

Next, LetterPerfect will copy the file containing your printer files to your hard disk. When that task is completed, you will be asked if you want to install a second printer. Enter Yes if you do and repeat the process, and you will again be asked if you want to install yet another printer. When you finally enter No at the "install another printer" prompt, the main LetterPerfect program will start. The title screen will be displayed, and you will be asked to enter your registration number (located on the registration card included with your disks and manuals).

When you press (Enter) after typing your registration number, LetterPerfect will install the printers you selected. When it's finished with the printer installation, you will return to the DOS prompt. And you will be ready to begin using the program with no further installation tasks. The following sections describe how to start and exit properly from LetterPerfect.

Note: To install other printers later on, you may have to restart the installation program. LetterPerfect installs driver files for some printers related to the ones you selected. For example, if you selected an HP LaserJet III, you will be able to select several other HP LaserJet models from within LetterPerfect. If you wanted to add a QMS laser printer, or an Alps dot matrix printer, though, you would have to use the install routine. At the installation menu (see step 5, above), you would select option 3, Printer.

Starting LetterPerfect on Hard Disk Systems

Since you created a PATH to the LetterPerfect program directory as part of the installation procedure, you can start LetterPerfect from any subdirectory simply by typing:

LP (Enter)

at the DOS prompt. As explained earlier, you should set up a separate directory for your LetterPerfect data, either as a subdirectory of the LP10 directory or as a separate directory off the root directory.

To start LetterPerfect from the data directory, type:

CD \[DIRECTORY NAME] (Enter)

Then type:

LP (Enter)

HINT:If you plan to keep all your documents in the directory called LPDATA (or any other name of your choosing), create a batch file to facilitate switching directories and starting LetterPerfect. (A batch file executes a sequence of steps with just one command from the keyboard.) Here's how:

1. Type:

   COPY CON:LP.BAT (Enter)

   CD\LP10DATA [or whatever name you gave your data directory] **(Enter)**

   LP (Enter)

   CD \ (Enter)

2. Press (F6) and the computer will display:

   ```
   ^Z
   ```

   Press (Enter) and the computer will display:

   ```
   1 file copied
   ```

3. The next time you enter LP, the computer will make your data directory the current directory and call up LetterPerfect. Since the system is PATHed to the directory containing the LetterPerfect program files, it will have no trouble finding the necessary start up files. Once LetterPerfect is loaded, your data files will be available immediately, without your having to change directories. When you exit LetterPerfect, the batch file will return you to the root directory.

Exiting LetterPerfect

When you are finished with a LetterPerfect session, press (F7) to exit. The system will ask you if you wish to save the current document. Enter Y, type a name and press (Enter) if you want to save it to disk, or N, if you want to abandon it. The system will ask you if you are sure that you want to exit LetterPerfect. Enter Y to confirm your exit, or N to return to a blank document.

CAUTION: You must exit LetterPerfect by the proper method. Simply turning the computer off may cause you to lose data. If you do "crash out," the next time you run LetterPerfect, the logo screen will ask:

```
Are there other copies of LetterPerfect running
(Y/N)
```

Type N, and LetterPerfect will continue.

Chapter 2

Installing a Floppy Disk System, Starting and Exiting LetterPerfect 1.0

Highlights

- Installation considerations
- Required RAM
- Floppy disk drive options
- Printer
- Automated install routine
- Starting up single and dual drive floppy systems
- Proper exiting technique.

Preinstallation Inventory

Make sure you have the following information before you begin installing your computer:

the amount of available memory (RAM).

the density and number of floppies needed.

the type of printer you'll be using.

Each topic is discussed below.

Available RAM Memory

LetterPerfect 1.0 requires a minimum of 330K of memory; that is, available RAM memory or memory not already used for DOS or RAM resident programs, such as Sidekick. (Programs like Sidekick can always "pop up" for use because they reside in RAM. The trade-off: they reduce the amount of available RAM.) Remember that DOS alone uses 40K of memory or more, depending on the version you're using. WordPerfect Corporation recommends a minimum of 512K of RAM to allow for DOS and any RAM resident programs.

The easiest way to determine how much available RAM you have left on your system available for LetterPerfect is to run the CHKDSK utility from DOS. This program lists the total amount of disk storage you have left on the specified disk, and also lists the amount of total RAM on your system and the amount of RAM still available. To run the CHKDSK program:

1. Start up your computer and load all the RAM resident programs that you plan to be using when you run LetterPerfect 1.0.
2. At the A> prompt, with your DOS disk in the A drive, type:

   CHKDSK (Enter)

The system response looks something like this for a 720K disk:

```
724480        bytes total disk space
52736         bytes in 3 hidden files
546304        bytes in 56 user files
125440        bytes available on disk
654336        bytes total memory
524288        bytes free
```

(**Note:** The actual numbers displayed on your screen will undoubtedly differ, as they will reflect the particular memory situation of your computer.) The last line indicates the amount of available RAM. If you do not have at least 330K of available RAM, you will have to either reduce the number of RAM resident programs loaded with LetterPerfect, or you must add more memory to your computer to run this program. Contact your dealer or the person responsible for configuring computers in your company for information about increasing your available memory.

Disk Drives

LetterPerfect will run on any IBM or 100 percent compatible computer with any of the following floppy disk configurations:

Single 720K or 1.44 Megabyte (M) (3 1/2") floppy drive

Single 1.2 M (5 1/4") floppy drive

Dual 360K (5 1/4") floppy drives

Many word processors run poorly on floppy disk systems, because they are constantly seeking "overlay" files that contain menus and other key files. LetterPerfect's structure reduces the number of times that it must access the disk for files, so that floppy performance is quite acceptable. As mentioned in the introduction, this makes the program well suited for battery-powered laptops.

Printer

Before you can print with LetterPerfect, you must indicate to it what printer you'll bee using, even if you do not have one connected to your computer at this time. You can always change your printer selection later.

Using the Automated Installation Program

At this point, your preinstallation inventory should be complete and you'll be ready to begin installing the program. The automated installation program included with LetterPerfect guides you along all key steps. Whenever the install program prompts you for a Yes/No choice, you can type either Y or N, or press (Enter) to accept the first choice. Finally, be aware that you don't have to install all the files now; you can always restart the install program and choose the files you wish to add to your program directory.

IMPORTANT!!! You cannot simply copy the files from your distribution disks (the ones supplied with your LetterPerfect program). The files are in a special compressed format, and must be uncompressed with the built in installation program. Also, before running the automated installation program, you are advised to back up your distribution disks. Refer to your DOS manual if you do not know how to use the COPY or DISKCOPY commands.

Format the Necessary Number of Disks

Use the DOS FORMAT command to format enough disks for the installation. You will need:

Density	Capacity	Size	# disks required
Low	360K	5 1/4"	7
Low	720K	3 1/2"	4
High	1.2 M	5 1/4"	3
High	1.44 M	3 1/2"	3

Start the Install Program

Insert the disk marked Install/Utilities 1 in your A drive. Type:

A:INSTALL

You could also start the installation from your B drive, in which case you would type:

B:INSTALL

The title screen shown in Figure 2.1 will appear.

Figure 2.1 Installation title screen.

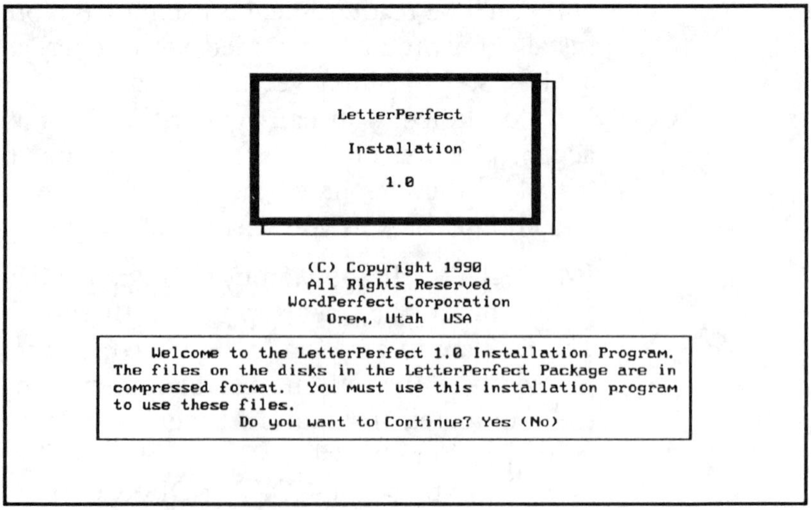

When the program asks whether you wish to continue, select Y for Yes.

Note: You can abort the installation procedure at any time by pressing (Esc). Also, at times you may be prompted to insert your Program 1 disk into the A drive.

Indicate Whether You Have a Color or Monochrome Monitor

Next, LetterPerfect will ask whether you can see the colors red, green, and blue. If so, Type Y, and the rest of the installation screens will appear in color; if you indicate No, the screens will appear in monochrome.

Indicate the Type of Disk Drive You are Installing To

After you've indicated whether you have a color or a monochrome display, LetterPerfect will ask if you are installing to a hard disk. Answer No.

Indicate the Number of Floppy Drives

Type 1 for a single floppy system, or press (Enter) to accept the default of 2 drives.

Indicate the Density of the Drive You Are Using

The installation routine gives you the option of using a number of different floppy disk drive densities.

Single Drive

Low density, 720K (3 1/2")

High density, 1.2 M (5 1/4")

High density, 1.44 M (3 1/2")

Note that you cannot use a single 360K 5 1/4" floppy drive.

Dual Drive:

Low density, 360K (5 1/4")

Low density, 720K (3 1/2")

High density 1.2 M (5 1/4")

High density 1.44 M (3 1/2")

What happens next depends on whether you selected a single or dual drive installation. For single drive installations, you will have the option of choosing between normal and minimal installations. Minimal installations allow you to run LetterPerfect with only a single 720K disk. But you will not be able to use the speller, thesaurus, or install your printer, because you'll need the space to save your data files. That's the tradeoff. A single high-density disk will enable you to install a printer as well. To carry out a minimal installation, follow the prompts for labeling and inserting your formatted disks into the drive as requested.

To carry out a normal installation, you will need multiple disks. In each case, the installation routine will tell you how many blank formatted disks to have on hand, and how to label them. When you select a two-drive installation or a single drive normal installation, a menu with the following options will be displayed:

1. Install—copies and expands word processing files for a single computer.
2. Network—installs LetterPerfect on a network. This should be done by the person who maintains your company's computers.
3. Printer—used to install additional printers.
4. Exit—returns you to the DOS prompt.

Follow the prompts for inserting the disks supplied with the program and the disks you have labeled. The normal installation will ask you whether you want to install the following types of files, in the following sequence (these file installation options won't be displayed if you're installing a LetterPerfect on a single 720K floppy):

Utility files

These files allow you to convert from LetterPerfect to other formats (CONVERT.EXE), and to convert various types of graphic images into files that LetterPerfect can use (GRAPHCNV.EXE).

Figure 2.2 Utility file installation prompt.

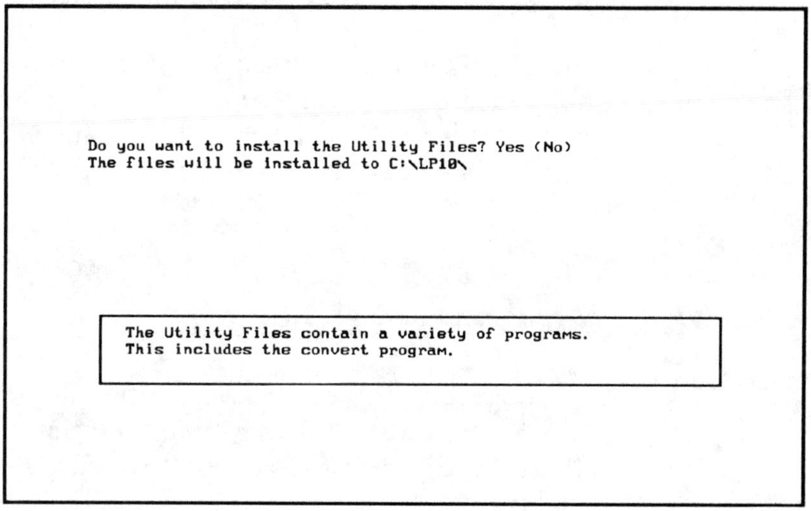

Note: The next steps use a screen identical to the one shown in Figure 2.2. Each one prompts you as to whether you want to install a particular type or group of files.

Graphic Images

The Graphic Images are predrawn illustrations, such as a computer, a clock, and other simple images that can insert into your documents. If you want to experiment, go ahead and indicate Yes at the prompt.

Thesaurus

If you've never used an electronic thesaurus before, try it (assuming you have the space) by indicating Yes at the prompt. While some users (the author included) find LetterPerfect's thesaurus too clumsy to be practical, you may find it useful (see Chapter 10).

Learning Files

If you plan to use the LetterPerfect tutorial, you'll need these files.

Indicate Whether You Want to Install the Shell Files

The shell is a memory manager that allows you to run more than one program at the same time. If you're a new computer user, don't worry about the Shell for now. If you know your way around your computer's memory, you might experiment with it. In any case, you probably won't miss it.

The LetterPerfect Program

No choice on this one, at least for the first-time installation. Select Yes. If you decide, at a later time, to install the graphics, utility, or other files that you didn't install the first time around, you don't need to reinstall the program files.

Language Resource File

The Language resource file contains a number of conventions, such as number and date formats. It is worthwhile installing, so you can set your style preferences.

The Speller

This is a "must," from a professional word processing point of view. LetterPerfect is equipped with a superb speller; once installed, there's no excuse for sloppy spelling in documents (Chapter 10 describes how to use the speller).

The Help File

Your LetterPerfect program includes a comprehensive help system. You might find it a useful adjunct to this book and the manual.

Check Your CONFIG.SYS File

When all the files have been copied, the installation will check your boot disk. In order for LetterPerfect to use your computer's memory, a special start-up file, called CONFIG.SYS, must exist on your boot disk, and contain the line "FILES=20". If you don't have a CONFIG.SYS file, LetterPerfect will ask if you want one created for you (see Figure 2.3). If you don't know how to do that yourself, answer Yes.

Figure 2.3 Create CONFIG.SYS prompt.

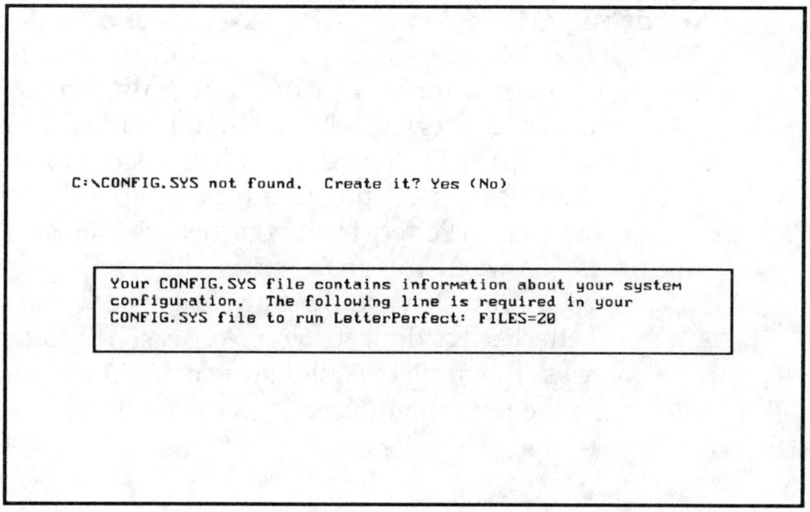

If you do have a CONFIG.SYS file, but it does not specify enough files, the installation program will ask you if you want it to increase the number of files (see Figure 2.4). Again, answer Yes, unless you know how to do it yourself from DOS. After you indicate Yes, LetterPerfect will prompt you to "Press any key to continue."

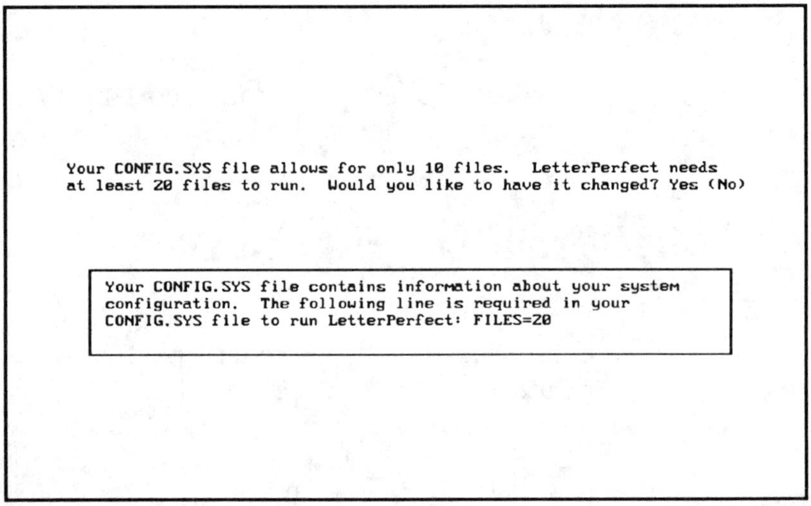

Figure 2.4 Modify CONFIG.SYS prompt.

Check Your AUTOEXEC.BAT File

If your computer does not have an AUTOEXEC.BAT file, LetterPerfect will ask you if you want it to create one (see Figure 2.5). An AUTOEXEC.BAT file is necessary to indicate the "path" of the LetterPerfect program files. The PATH command allows you to start LetterPerfect from your data directories. The advantage of this is that when you go to retrieve files, only your data files will be listed. If you don't know how to create an AUTOEXEC.BAT file, let LetterPerfect do it for you. Also say Yes to the next prompt, which asks if LetterPerfect should add LP10 (or whatever name you gave to the program directory) to the path—this is necessary if you want to start the program from data directories, as just described.

Figure 2.5 Create AUTOEXEC.BAT prompt.

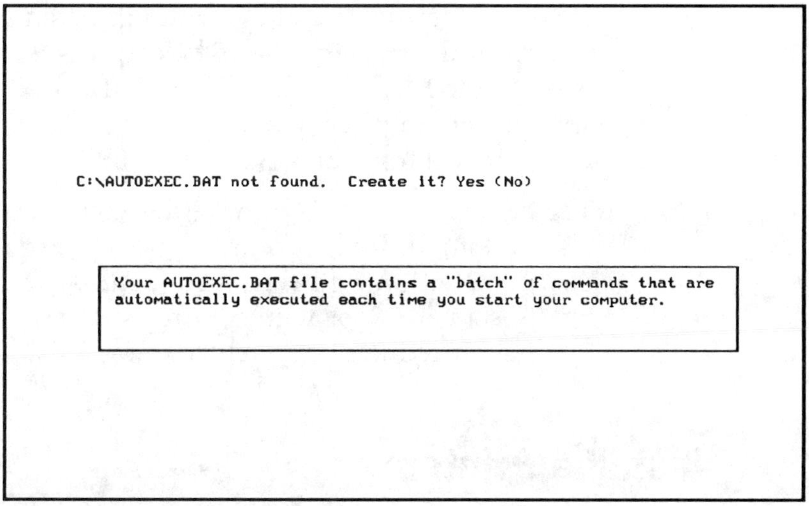

If you already have an AUTOEXEC.BAT file, but it does not contain LP10 (or whatever name you assigned to the program directory), LetterPerfect will ask if it should make the addition (see Figure 1.13). Say Yes unless you plan to do it yourself at the DOS level.

Figure 2.6 Modify AUTOEXEC.BAT prompt.

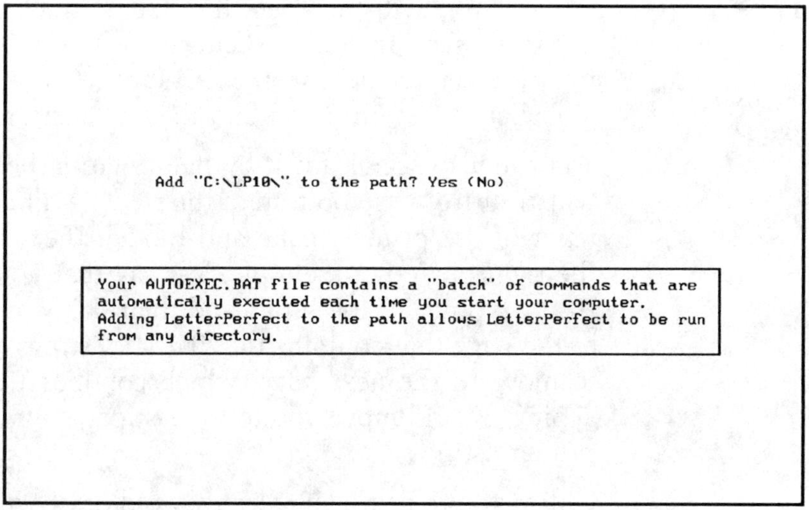

Assign the F1 Function Key

In a gesture of civility rare these days, WordPerfect Corporation gives you the option of making the F1 key the Help key or the Cancel function key. The default for the F1 key is Cancel function

(F3 is the default Help key). Many programs use F1 for help, so if you're used to using F1 for help, press 2, and LetterPerfect will reassign the F1 key as the Help key. If you want to leave the default arrangement in place, just press (Enter), and the F1 key will remain as the Cancel function key.

The next step depends on whether you selected a one or two-drive installation, and what density you selected. A single-drive, 720K disk installation will terminate at this point—LetterPerfect will briefly start, prompt you for a registration number, perform a few internal procedures, then return to the DOS prompt.

Install a Printer

If the configuration that you've chosen allows it, LetterPerfect will ask if you want to install a printer. If you say No, you can install one at a later date. But you might as well do it now so you're all set to begin word processing. If you say Yes, the install routine will prompt you to inset the Printer disk in your disk drive and press (Enter). You will then see the first 22 lines of an extensive list of printers—see Figure 2.7 (LetterPerfect supports over 600 different printing devices). Use the cursors, or page down through the alphabetical list until you find the make and model of your printer.

You can also search for it by name. Press the N key, and the menu will clear from the bottom of the screen will clear. As you type each letter of the printer make and model, the screen will "zero in" on the right page. For example, let's say that you have an HP LaserJet III. By typing "n" for name, and then "h", you tell the screen to shift to the page that contains the first HP listings. Just hit the PgDn key to move to the next page, which contains the LaserJet III listings. Typing "x" will move you to the last page, which contains the Xerox printer listings.

Unless you're using an extremely old or obscure brand, you'll probably find your printer. If not, refer to your LetterPerfect manual or call WordPerfect Corporation for help. Also, you'll see some printers marked with an asterisk. Drivers for these printers are not included on the basic LetterPerfect disk. If your printer name has an asterisk, contact WordPerfect Corporation for information on obtaining driver files.

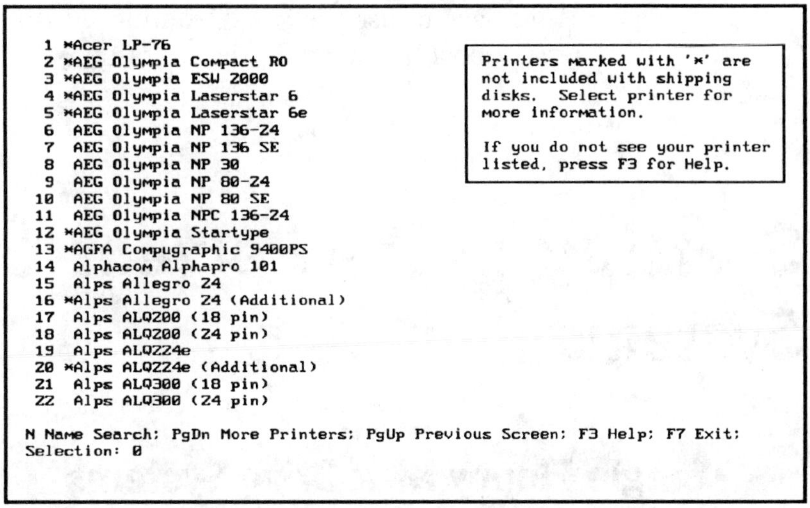

Figure 2.7 Listing of printers.

Assuming that you've found your printer, type in the number and press (Enter). LetterPerfect will ask you to confirm your choice. Press (Enter) to continue.

Next, LetterPerfect will copy the file containing your printer files to your hard disk. When that task is completed, you will be asked if you want to install a second printer. Enter Yes if you do and repeat the process, and you will again be asked if you want to install another printer. When you finally enter No at the "install another printer" prompt, the main LetterPerfect program will start. The title screen will be displayed, and you will be asked to enter your registration number (located on the registration card included with your disks and manuals).

When you press (Enter) after typing your registration number, LetterPerfect will install the printers you selected. When it's finished with the printer installation, you will be returned to the DOS prompt. And you will be ready to begin using the program with no further installation tasks. The next sections describe how to start and properly exit from LetterPerfect.

Note: To install other printers later on, you may have to restart the installation program. LetterPerfect installs driver files for some of the printers related to the ones you selected. For example, if you selected an HP LaserJet III, you will be able to select several other HP LaserJet models from within LetterPerfect. If you wanted to add a QMS laser printer, or an Alps dot matrix printer, though, you would have to use the install routine. At the installation menu (see step 6, above), you would select option 3, Printer.

Starting LetterPerfect on Floppy Systems

Single Floppy Disk Drive Systems

The procedure for starting with a single 3 1/2" disk is as follows:

1. Start your computer with your DOS disk.
2. After the computer displays an A> prompt, insert the disk you labeled LetterPerfect (minimal installation) or LetterPerfect 1 (normal installation) in the A drive.
3. Type:

   LP

4a. If you have carried out the minimal installation, LetterPerfect will load without any further prompts.

4b. If you have performed the normal (full) installation, you will be prompted to insert the disk labeled LetterPerfect 2. When the second disk loads, you can begin word processing.

Note: With a single disk drive and minimal installation on one disk, you will store your data files on your LetterPerfect program disk. With a full installation, you will store your data files on LetterPerfect 2. Either way, you can't remove the program disk to store files on another data disk. That means that the floppy containing your data files is bound to fill up over time. You will then have to use the DOS COPY command to copy noncritical data files to other disks.

Dual Floppy Disk Drive Systems

1. Start your computer with your DOS disk.
2. After the computer displays an A> prompt, insert the disk you labeled LetterPerfect (minimal installation) or LetterPerfect 1 (normal installation).
3. Insert your data disk into the B drive.
4. Type:

   B: (Enter)
5. The prompt will now read "B:>". Type:

   A:LP
6. The program will prompt you to insert LetterPerfect 2. When the program finishes loading, you can begin word processing. Data will be stored on the disk in the B drive.

Exiting LetterPerfect

When you are finished with a LetterPerfect session, press (F7) to exit. The system will ask you if you wish to save the current document. Enter Y, type a name and press (Enter) if you want to save it to disk, or N, if you want to abandon it. The system will ask you if you are sure that you want to exit LetterPerfect. Enter Y to confirm your exit, or N to return to a blank document.

CAUTION: You must exit LetterPerfect by the proper method. Simply turning the computer off may cause you to lose data. If you do "crash out," the next time you run LetterPerfect, the logo screen will ask:

```
Are there other copies of LetterPerfect running (Y/N)
```

Type N, and LetterPerfect will continue.

Section II

LetterPerfect Fundamentals

Chapter 3

Navigating in LetterPerfect 1.0

Highlights

- Screen layout—the menu bar and status indicator
- Keyboard arrangements
- Special navigation keys
- Editing keys

The Screen

Menu Bar and Status Indicator

When you start LetterPerfect, your screen displays the program's logo, which contains the program name and version number. The screen then appears to be blank. Why such a plain screen, when many word processor screens are festooned with rulers? LetterPerfect's philosophy is that an uncluttered mind works better with an uncluttered screen. Rulers are merely distractions, and the blank screen allows you to focus on your writing. And writing is, after all, what word processing is all about.

Actually, the screen isn't totally blank—along the top you'll see the Menu Bar (which you can also turn off—see Chapter 6), and in the bottom right-hand corner, you can see the Status Line, which gives you the following information (refer to Figure 3.1).

Figure 3.1 Status line (lower right-hand corner)

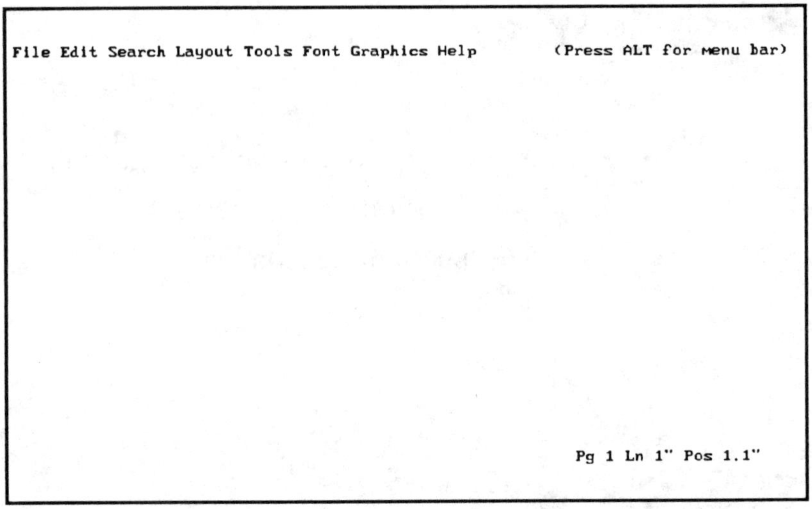

Pg: LetterPerfect "knows" how many lines of type to put on a page, depending on the type font and paper size you're using. Pages are separated on screen by a dotted line, as shown in Figure 3.2. (The number following Pg indicates the assigned page number of the current page.)

Ln: This indicator shows the vertical position of the cursor on the current page. For example, if you set up LetterPerfect in inches, a Ln 9.16 means that the cursor is 9.16 inches from the top of the page.

Pos: The Pos(ition) indicator shows the horizontal location of the cursor. A horizontal position of 5.1 means that the cursor is 5.1 inches from the left edge of the page.

Figure 3.2 Page break (dotted line)

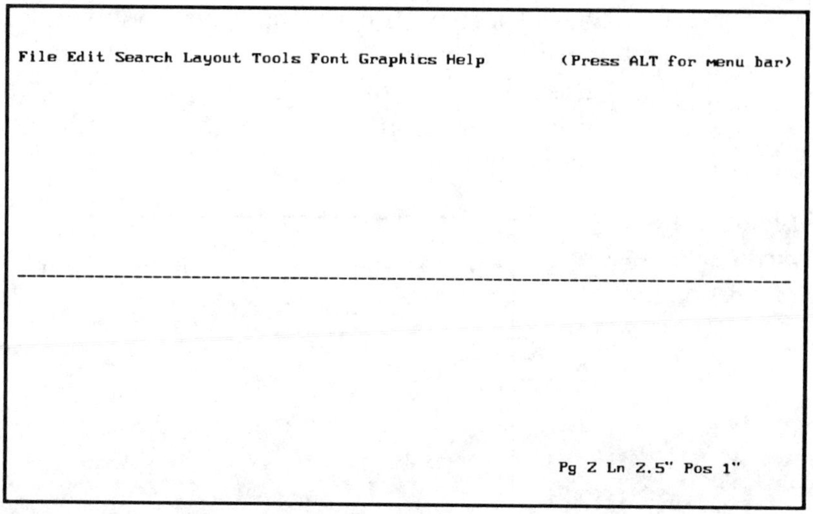

After you save a file (see Chapters 4 and 5), when you then work on it later, the name of the file also appears in the left-hand corner of the screen, as shown in Figure 3.3.

Figure 3.3 File indicator (lower left hand corner)

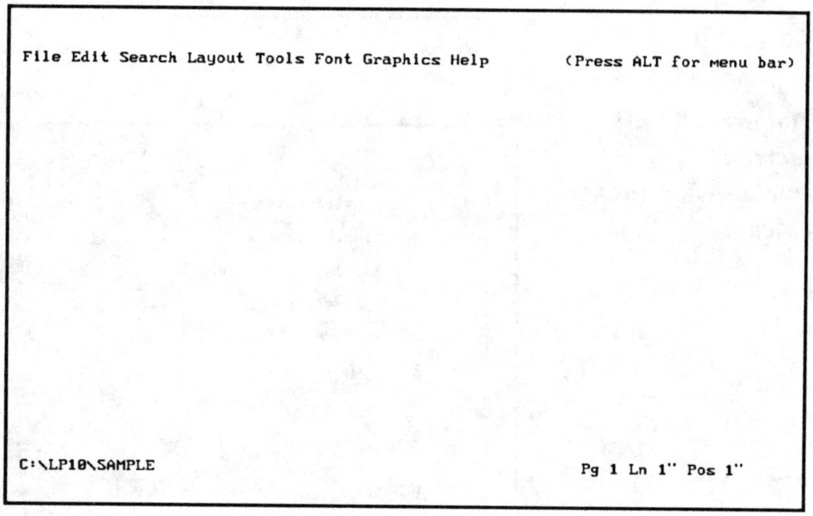

When you select a feature that presents several options, such as Format-Page and Type Font-Select (see Chapters 4 and 5), LetterPerfect displays two types of menus. Menus allowing you to select from among five or fewer options are usually displayed along the bottom of the screen, underneath your text, as shown in Figure

3.4. Those with more than five options fill the whole screen, lying on top of your text, as shown in Figure 3.5. When LetterPerfect does display a full-screen menu, it occupies the screen only temporarily; as soon as you are finished with a menu, it clears and your text reappears.

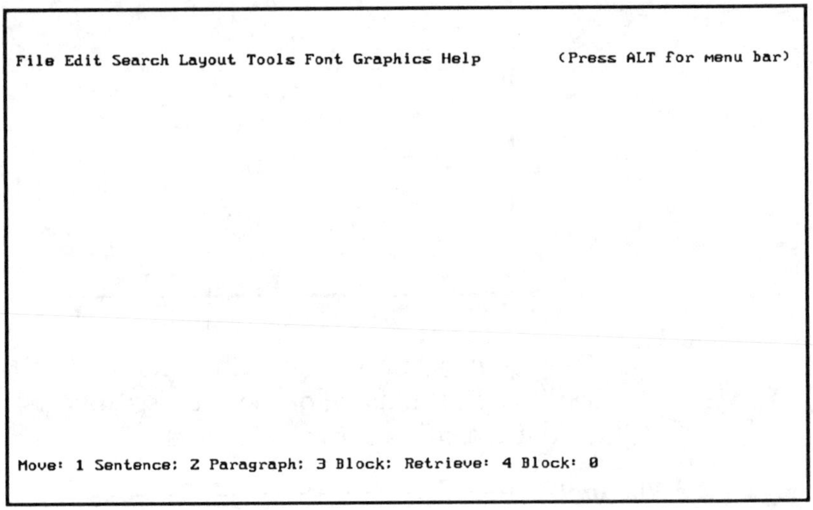

Figure 3.4 Bottom menu style—Move Menu.

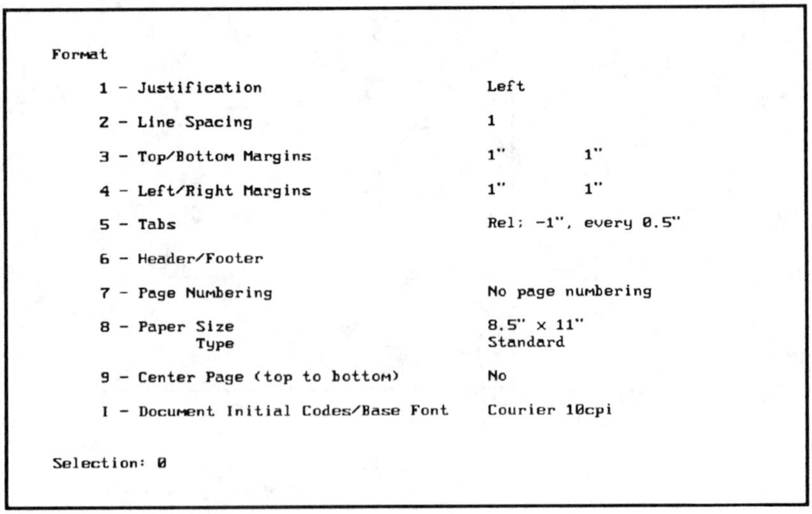

Figure 3.5 Full screen menu—Format Menu.

Now that you know how LetterPerfect displays information on the screen, let's consider how the program uses the keyboard to move the cursor around the page and through the document.

The Keyboard

The cursor is the blinking dash on the screen, probably in the upper left hand corner if you have just started LetterPerfect and haven't entered any text or commands through the keyboard yet. The cursor shows where a character will be placed on the screen when you press a key on the keyboard. It automatically moves one space to the right automatically each time you press a key. You can also move it along without entering any characters by pressing the (Spacebar)—the large key at the bottom of the keyboard.

Try typing several sentences. When you get to the right margin, the cursor jumps down to the leftmost edge of the next line. This action is called Wrapping, and eliminates the need to press a carriage return, as you would with an electric typewriter (or to push the bar on the carriage as you would with a manual typewriter). LetterPerfect may or may not try to break up and hyphenate the last word on the line, depending on the built-in hyphenation rules it uses.

Notice that the cursor will move across space created by the (Spacebar). When you encounter "uncharted territory," however, where the (Spacebar) has never roamed, where you have never entered text, or placed a hard (carriage) return (by pressing the (Enter) key), the cursor will not move, no matter how many times you press the cursor key. This is because LetterPerfect "sees" spaces as characters, and hard returns as hidden codes, even though they appear on the screen as blanks. In Chapter 8, you'll learn how to display all the hidden codes LetterPerfect actually stores as part of your document, which is a useful way of altering the screen.

Once you enter some text, you can use the cursor keys to move the cursor to any character appearing on the screen.

Unfortunately, not all microcomputer keyboards position the keys in the same locations, so the placement of your cursor key is dependent on the type of computer you have. The following discussion refers to the standard IBM PC keyboard (there are three common IBM keyboards, and several that are less widely used).

IBM PC/XT

On an IBM keyboard, the four cursor keys, which have arrows pointing up, down, left, and right, are located on the far right side. The "classic" 88-key keyboard combines the cursor keys and the numeric keypad, which contains keys for the numbers zero through nine. Normally, the keys function in cursor movement mode; that is, when you press them, the cursor moves in the direction of the arrow along the characters you've typed, or the spaces you've created by pressing the (Enter) key (see below). If you press the (Num Lock) key, however, the numeric keypad is activated, so pressing 8 places an "8" on the screen, rather than moving the cursor up one space.

As a convenience, when (Num Lock) is activated, the Pos indicator on the status line blinks. Press the (Num Lock) key and see for yourself what happens. Press (Num Lock) again and control returns to the cursor keys.

IBM AT

The original IBM AT keyboard is identical to that of the "classic" PC/XT, with the addition of a green light that glows when Num Lock is activated. The Pos indicator still blinks when (Num Lock) is activated.

IBM Enhanced AT and PS/2

The "enhanced" AT-style keyboard, also standard with the PS/2 line, has an additional set of cursor keys independent of the numeric keypad. These always move the cursor, regardless of whether the (Num Lock) key is pressed. (Num Lock) also causes Pos to blink. Because the dedicated cursor keys are always available, IBM switched the action of the (Num Lock) on its PS/2 line so that it is automatically activated automatically when the computer is turned on.

IBM PC Desktop and Laptop Compatibles

If you have an IBM PC-compatible computer, check your manual for information regarding the use of the cursor and (Num Lock) keys. Laptops may also vary, depending on their keyboard layout.

Special Cursor Movements

As you've probably discovered by now, each time you press the cursor key, the cursor moves one character or space up, down, left, or right, depending on its position. If you hold the cursor key down, the cursor zooms along without stopping. This is not always the most efficient way to get the cursor to where you want it, and LetterPerfect offers a number of interesting alternatives for moving the cursor by more than one space at a time. The following "express" cursor options are arranged by increasing size of cursor movement, starting with movement by words and ending with movement by document.

Move by Word

If you place the cursor anywhere within a word and press:

(Ctrl + Right Cursor)

the cursor jumps to the first character of the next word.

Press:

(Ctrl + Left Cursor)

and the cursor moves backwards to the first character of the previous word. If you hold down either the right or left cursor keys while also pressing (Ctrl), the cursor moves repeatedly word by word until you release the key or it reaches the end of document.

Move by Line

The (Home) key, located in the upper left corner of the numeric keypad, is a powerful way to navigate around the document. (On the enhanced AT/PS/2 keyboards there's also a dedicated (Home) key located above the dedicated cursor keys.) Press:

(Home) + (Home) + (Left Cursor)

and the cursor moves to the beginning of the current line. Press:

(Home) + (Home) + (Right Cursor)

or

(End)

and the cursor moves to the end of the current line. (Note: the (End) key is located at the lower left hand corner of the numeric keypad.)

Move by Screen

Sometimes it is convenient to move by "screenfuls," 25 lines at a time. For example, when you're reading a document on screen, it is convenient to be able to read a screen, then display the next screen. Note: this is different from moving by document pages with (PgUp) and (PgDn) keys, which move by printed pages, as described below. To move down one screen at a time, press:

(+) key

or

(Home) + (Down Cursor)

The (+) key is located next to the numeric keypad. Note that the plus sign accessed by pressing (shift) + (=) does not achieve the desired action.

To move back up a screen, press:

(-) key

or

(Home) + (Up Cursor)

The minus key is located above the (+) key, next to the right of the numeric keypad.

Holding down the plus or minus keys repeatedly moves the screen until you release the key, or the cursor reaches the top of the document or the last screen with text.

Move by Page

To move down one page, press:

(PgDn)

To move up one page, press:

(PgUp)

On the classic PC/XT keyboard, the (PgDn) and (PgUp) keys are located on the numeric keypad, sharing space on the 3 and 9 keys, respectively. They are normally active unless (Num Lock) is pressed. On the enhanced AT/PS/2 keyboards, the (PgDn) and (PgUp) keys are dedicated and are located above the dedicated cursor keys. If you press and hold the (PgDn) or (PgUp) keys, the cursor moves down by pages until you reach the end of the document, or up by pages until you reach the beginning of the document.

Move by Document

To move to the very last character of a document, press:

(Home) + (Home) + (Down Cursor)

To move to the very beginning of a document, press:

(Home) + (Home) + (Up Cursor)

These two cursor movements are very useful for traversing a large document. Perhaps you want to get a quick page count, or move to the end of the document to do some editing. The (Home) + (Home) + (Down Cursor) combination makes this a breeze to do. Alternately, if you're working on the ending of a document, and need to zip back up to the beginning to check something, (Home) (Home) + (Up Cursor) is like taking an express elevator.

At this point you should be familiar with the LetterPerfect display, and know the primary cursor movements. The best way to get the keystrokes ingrained in your mind is practice. So before going any further, you might want to type several pages. Then experiment with all of the "express" options just described. Don't worry about making or correcting mistakes—you'll learn about that in the next section, which explains how to use the various editing keys.

Editing Keys

As you enter or proofread your text, you'll undoubtedly want to make changes in characters, words, or sentences. LetterPerfect uses several of the standard keyboard keys to make the task easy. These are described below. (Note that while LetterPerfect provides many ways to do the same word processing tasks, it is not necessary to learn them all. Pick out the ones that are easiest for you to remember and use, and develop a repertoire of basic skills. The goal is to develop familiarity with the smallest subset of features that will accomplish your task as quickly as possible. As you need to learn new ones, you can easily pick them up and add them to your knowledge base.)

Deletion Keys

LetterPerfect allows you to delete in a number of ways. Use the one most convenient for your text.

Delete by Character

Move the cursor underneath the character you want to delete. Press the (Del) key, (located below the numeric keypad) once and the character is deleted. Try it. Notice that if you hold the (Del) key down, all characters to the right of the cursor are "sucked into the void." Eventually you could delete an entire page or even a 200 page document this way. But that would be highly inefficient and time consuming. As you'll see in Chapter 8, LetterPerfect provides powerful functions for altering and deleting large blocks of text.

An alternative way of deleting characters is to use the (Backspace) key, which is marked with a heavy left arrow and located in the upper right hand corner of the keyboard, above the (Enter) key. Each time you press (Backspace), one character to the left of the cursor is deleted. As in the case of the (Del) key, if you repeatedly held down the (Backspace) key, LetterPerfect would delete characters continually until the cursor "bumped" up against the beginning of the document.

Delete by Word

LetterPerfect allows you to delete by words as well as characters. Try this. Place the cursor anywhere in the word you wish to delete. Then press:

(Ctrl-Backspace)

Shazam! The word and the space following it are gone. If you place the cursor in the space before the word, however, LetterPerfect deletes the word to the left of the cursor. If you hold down the (Ctrl - Backspace) key combination, LetterPerfect deletes words to the right of the cursor continually until you release the keys or there are no more words left to delete. Note: LetterPerfect defines a "word" as any contiguous string of characters or numbers, including hyphenated strings; any breaks in the string indicate to the program that the word has ended.

Two alternate ways of deleting words are also available. To delete a word to the left of the cursor, place the cursor in the space just after the word and press and release:

(Home)

then press and release:

(Backspace)

The alternative for deleting a word to the right of the cursor is to place the cursor under the first letter of the word to be deleted, and press and release:

(Home)

then press and release:

(Del)

The word to the right of the cursor will be deleted.

Delete to End of Line

To delete from the cursor position to the end of the line, press:

(Ctrl - End)

The text from the cursor to the end of the line is removed from the screen.

Delete by Page

To delete the remainder of a page below the cursor, press:

(Ctrl - PgDn)

Since this command has dangerous consequences, LetterPerfect asks you to confirm your choice by asking:

`Delete remainder of page (Y/N) No`

If you enter N or press enter (to accept the default of No), LetterPerfect cancels the command. If you enter Y for Yes, everything beneath the cursor on to the page break is deleted.

CAUTION: "Delete remainder of page" means delete from the current cursor position to the end of the printed page, which means that you might delete material not shown on the screen, because the screen only shows a portion of the printed page. For example, if you are displaying the first 25 lines of a 54 line page on the screen, and select Delete to end of page, you will delete all 54 lines, including the 29 lines that you can't see. Therefore use this option with extreme care.

Note: Even if you decide that you really didn't want to delete the page, all is not lost; LetterPerfect has an undelete feature, described in the next two chapters, which enables you to undo your last three deletions.

Inserting Characters

LetterPerfect defaults to Insert mode. In other words, if you place the cursor in the middle of a word, then enter text, LetterPerfect inserts whatever characters you type at the cursor location, spreading the text as necessary to accommodate them. You've probably discovered this already as you've experimented with the keyboard.

The alternative is Typeover mode, in which your keystrokes overwrite existing text. To switch into Typeover mode, press the (Ins) key. The word "Typeover" appears in the lower left hand corner of the screen to remind you of the current mode (see Figure 3.6). To return to Insert mode, press the (Ins) key again. This dual action, in which one key switches between two functions, is called Toggling; you "toggle" the key between the two modes.

You can use either Insert or Typeover as your predominant mode, although most people prefer Insert mode, because it's generally more efficient to insert text and then delete unwanted text. Besides, Typeover is sometimes hard to control—you might find yourself overwriting and recreating text you had wanted keep. Nevertheless, the choice is yours.

Figure 3.6 Typeover indicator, lower left-hand corner.

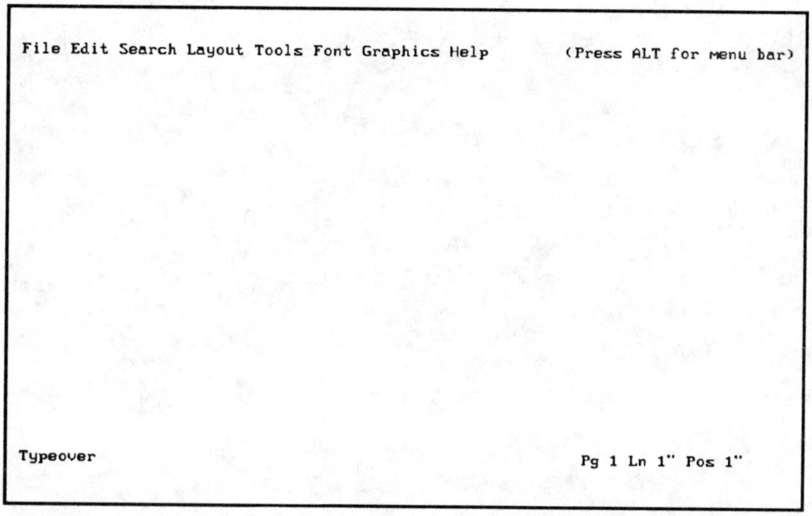

At this point, stop and experiment with the various key movements described above. Again, when several commands achieve the same results, you don't have to learn them all. The goal is to assemble a collection of usable skills that meet your needs quickly. In the following chapters, you'll learn about the commands issued through the menu system (Chapter 4) and special function keys (Chapter 5), which lie at the heart of LetterPerfect's power.

Chapter 4

The Menu System

Highlights

- The Menu bar
- The File menu
- The Edit menu
- The Search menu
- The Layout menu
- The Tools menu
- The Font menu
- The Graphics menu
- The Help menu

Have It Your Way

LetterPerfect allows you to access its functions (centering, bolding, cutting and pasting, etc.) by using the menu system or by function key combinations. You will probably end up using one method in favor of the other, rather than mixing the two. If you opt for the function key approach, you can turn off the menu display (see Chapter 6). A third way of performing certain important functions is by using the Fast Keys (Ctrl plus a specified key).

This chapter describes the menu approach, while Chapter 5 describes the function and fast keys. The menu explanations in this chapter are organized according to the order in which they appear on the LetterPerfect screen.

For some items, such as passwords, you'll find complete descriptions, since they are not mentioned elsewhere in the text. For other features, such as formatting, only a brief description is provided, since you'll find lengthy discussions of the topics in various chapters of the book.

About the Menu System

The Menu Bar

Unless you've changed your setup preferences (Chapter 6), the menu bar at the top of the screen will be displayed each time you start LetterPerfect (See Figure 4.1). If you have turned off the menu bar, just press the (Alt) key, and it will be displayed.

The mouse is also useful in controlling the menu bar. If the menu bar is displayed (but now pull-down menus are on the screen), clicking on the right button will clear it from the screen. Click again on the right button and the menu bar will reappear.

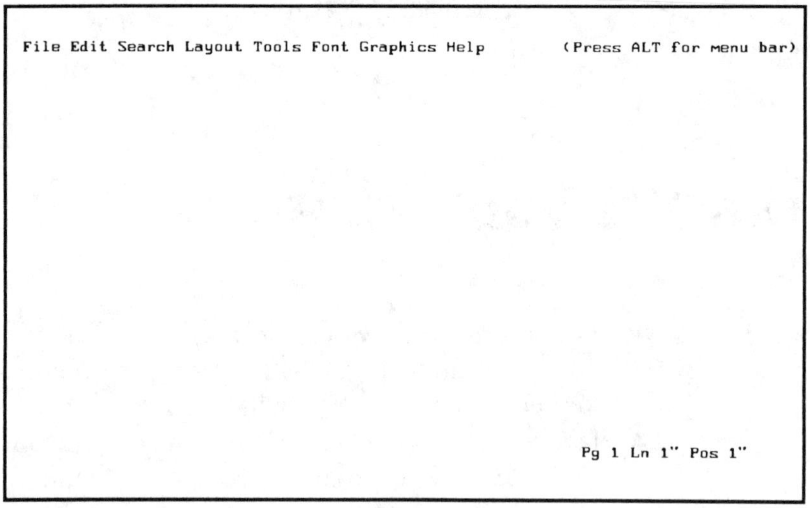

Figure 4.1 Menu bar (top of screen).

As you can see in Figure 4.1, the menu bar contains six categories of functions: File, Edit, Search, Layout, Tools, Font, Graphics, and Help. (Each one is described at length in the upcoming sections.) You can select a category in one of three ways:

1. Type the highlighted letter:

   f = File

   e = Edit

   s = Search

   l = Layout

   t = Tools

   o = Font

   g = Graphics

   h = Help

2. Use the left and right cursors to highlight the category. If you press the right cursor when the last category, Help, is highlighted, the cursor will "loop" around to the first category on the left, File. The reverse holds true as well.

3. Use the mouse—place the rectangular cursor on any letter of the category name and press the left button. This has the same effect as using the cursors and pressing (Enter).

Whichever method you use, selecting a category will cause a pull-down menu to appear on the screen, as shown in Figure 4.2. (They're called "pull-down" because they're literally dropped from the menu bar.)

Figure 4.2 Pull down menu.

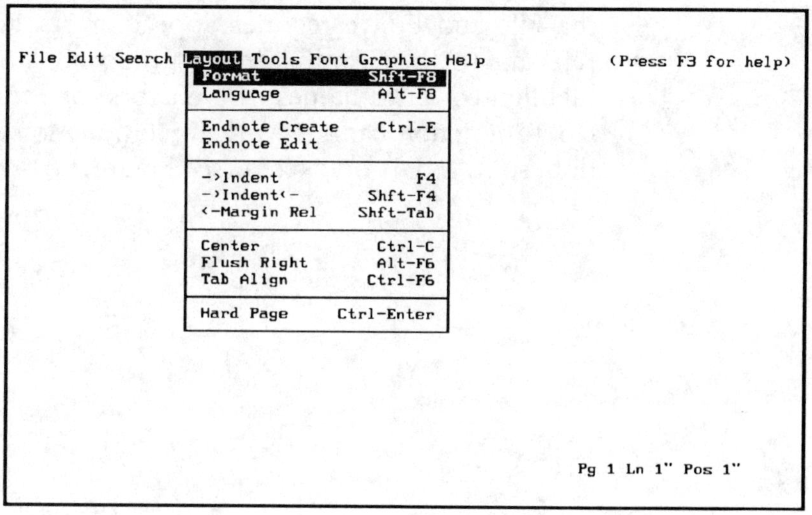

Once a menu has been pulled down from the menu bar, you can view pull-down menus from other categories simply by pressing the right or left cursor. If you use the mouse, you must reselect a main file category, then click on the left button.

To select features from a pull-down menu, you again have three choices:

1. Type the highlighted letter in the menu item name (the first item will always be covered by the highlight bar, so you won't be able to see the individually highlighted letter. That's no problem; if you want to select the first item on the pull-down menu, just press (Enter) since it's already highlighted (i.e., selected for you).
2. Use the up and down cursors to highlight the desired option, then press (Enter). If you press the down cursor when the last option is highlighted, the cursor will "loop" around to the top entry. The opposite also holds—you can loop from the top entry to the bottom one.
3. Move the rectangular mouse cursor to the desired menu item and press the right button.

In some cases, when you select a menu item and then return to the menu bar, file categories or specific menu options will be enclosed in [square brackets]. The highlight bar skips over such options, because they are not available at the time. For example, when using the Search command, if you display the menu bar Move command, the File and Edit categories appear in brackets since they are not relevant to the Search function, and are not accessible via their highlighted letter names, the cursors, or the mouse. Similarly, the Go To function cannot work in conjunction with the Search function, so it, too, is bracketed (see Figure 4.3).

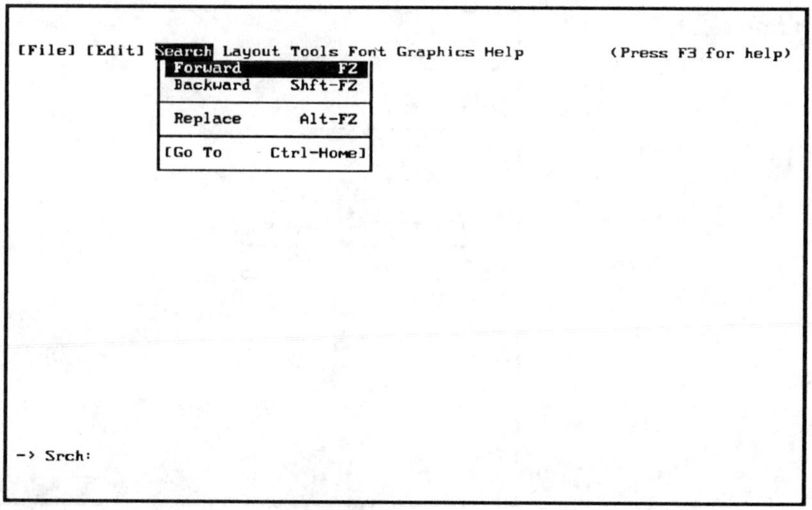

Figure 4.3 Bracketed items in the menu bar and pull-down menus are not accessible.

To abandon a pull-down menu, press the (Esc) key, or the left button on your mouse (which will also remove the menu bar from the screen). With a three-button mouse, the center button works the same as the (Esc) key.

The following discussion provides a brief description of the options available on each menu.

The File Menu

This pull-down menu contains a number of functions related to retrieving, saving, and printing files (see Figure 4-4).

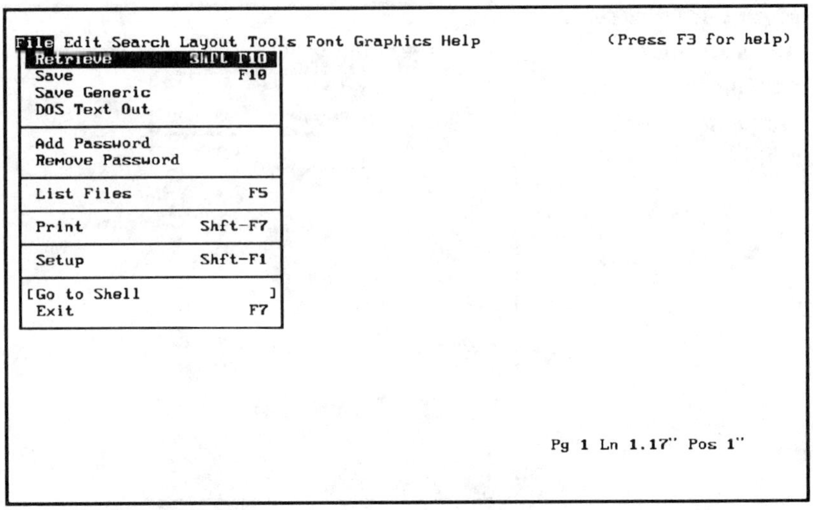

Figure 4.4 File pull-down menu.

Retrieve

The Retrieve function allows you to load a file into the current document. If you know the name of the file, Retrieve is a convenient way to load a file; if you don't remember the exact name, you're better off using the List Files option below. You can also use Retrieve to combine two files on the screen, or to bring in "boilerplate" (standard) paragraphs at a desired location in a document.

Save

This function allows you to save the current document to disk easily so you can continue editing. When you press the (F10) key, if a filename is not yet assigned to the document, LetterPerfect prompts you in the lower left corner of the screen with:

`Document to be saved:`

Enter the filename (up to eight characters in the main body of the filename, and three characters in the extension, which is separated from the main name by a period), then press (Enter) to save the file to disk. If you have already saved the file before, LetterPerfect prompts you with the previously assigned filename in the form:

```
Document to be saved: [assigned filename]
```

Press (Enter) to save the document with its current name. If you wish to save it under a different filename, edit the current name, or type a new one, followed by (Enter). Unlike the Exit function, the Save function does not ask if you would like to leave LetterPerfect; rather, it leaves you in the current document.

Save Generic

Save Generic stores your file without LetterPerfect codes while maintaining the format. For instance, centered text remains centered, but with spaces inserted instead of LetterPerfect's centering codes. This arrangement may be useful if you are transferring LetterPerfect files to another word processing program.

When you select this option, LetterPerfect prompts you with:

```
Document to be saved (Generic WP):
```

Enter the name of the file that you would like to save in generic word processing form and press (Enter). You can use the Convert utility (see Chapter 14) to convert LetterPerfect files directly to other word processing formats. The utility is run from DOS, so you would have to exit LetterPerfect first before running it, unless you are using the Shell memory manager (see Chapter 14).

DOS Text Out

DOS Text Out offers various ways of saving a file in ASCII format, so that programs other than LetterPerfect can read it. When you save in ASCII format, you lose all the LetterPerfect formatting, such as bold, underline, tabs, etc.

Add Password

Password allows you to "encrypt" a document so that no one can view, retrieve, or print it without entering the correct password. When you select the password option, LetterPerfect prompts you to:

```
Enter Password:
```

For security purposes, your keystrokes are not echoed back to the screen, so be careful. As a caution, LetterPerfect asks you to reenter the password to confirm your choice. If the password is different from your original input, LetterPerfect displays:

```
ERROR: incorrect password
```

and asks you to begin again and enter the password. The password is then added to the document on screen. You must still save it to a file on disk before password protection goes in effect.

When you go to retrieve a file with a password (see below, List Files and the F10 key), LetterPerfect will prompt you to:

```
Enter Password
```

If you enter the wrong password, it displays the message:

```
ERROR: File is locked
```

and you have to start the retrieval process again.

CAUTION: If you forget a password, there is no way to gain access to the file. Use passwords that mean something to you.

Remove Password

Remove is the only way you can get a password out of a document's file structure. To select Remove, however, you must have access to the file; you can't use the option unless the file has been "unlocked" and is on the screen. Again, you must resave the unlocked file to disk, overwriting the locked version, to deactivate the password.

List Files

This option invokes LetterPerfect's file manager, which is a very convenient way to retrieve, delete, rename, print, view, or copy a file. When you select List Files, LetterPerfect first displays the current directory in the lower left-hand corner of the screen. You can change the directory either temporarily, by editing the directory name, or for the duration of the session, by pressing the (=) key, typing in a new directory name, and pressing (Enter).

When you press (Enter) after the directory name, the file manager is displayed (see Figure 4.5). Use the cursor keys to move the highlighted bar over the file you wish to act upon. Then select an option. The various options of the file manager are discussed at length in Chapter 12.

Figure 4.5 LetterPerfect File Manager.

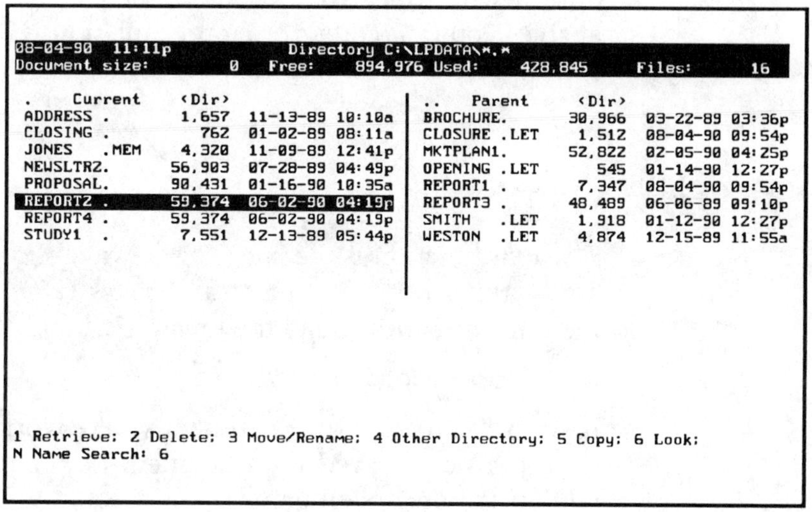

Print

LetterPerfect gives you excellent control over the printing process. When you invoke the Print function, the main print menu is displayed, providing the options of printing the full document or only the page of the document in which the cursor is currently positioned. Several other options are also available, and are discussed at length in Chapter 12.

Setup

LetterPerfect provides a number of options for customizing the program to your hardware and personal preferences. These are discussed in the next chapter.

Go to Shell

Unless you've installed the Shell files (see Chapters 1 or 2, depending on whether you performed a hard disk or floppy disk installation), and you've started LetterPerfect from the Shell file, this option will appear in brackets. Shell is a memory manager that enables you to go other programs, including DOS, without formally exiting LetterPerfect (see Chapter 14).

Exit

The Exit function is the *only* "legal" way to exit LetterPerfect. If you are working on a document and press (F7), LetterPerfect displays the following message in the lower left-hand corner of the screen:

```
Save document: (Y/N) Yes
```

If you want to save the document you're working on, press (Enter). If you've never saved the document before, LetterPerfect prompts you for the document name:

```
Document to be saved:
```

Type the name you wish to assign the file. You can use a maximum of eight characters or numbers in the main name, plus three alphanumeric characters in the extension, which is separated from the main name by a period. When you press (Enter), LetterPerfect will ask you if you want to exit the program. If you say No, then you may create a new document. In other words, Exit really means to save a document with the option of quitting LetterPerfect or starting with a blank screen. When you save via the F10 key, however, the function means only to save and continue working on whatever document is currently displayed on the screen.

The Edit Menu

This menu contains a collection of functions that can help you alter text that you've created (see Figure 4.6).

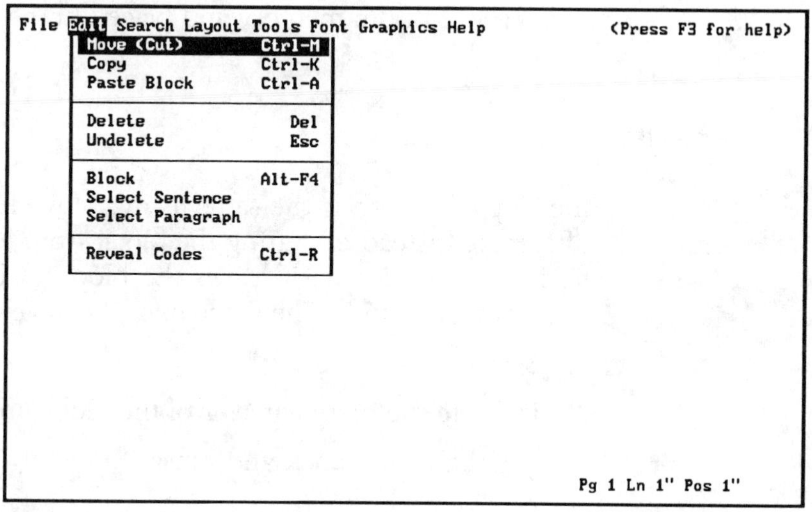

4.6 Edit pull-down menu options.

Move

This option allows you to define a block of text (anything from one character to many pages). When you select the Move option from the edit menu, LetterPerfect will display the message:

`Position to top corner of text; press Enter`

in the lower left-hand corner of the screen. This means you are to indicate the beginning of the block of text that you wish to move. After you press (Enter), LetterPerfect will then display a second message in the lower left-hand corner of the screen:

`Position to bottom corner of text; press Enter`

Move the appropriate cursor key in the desired direction. LetterPerfect will highlight the text that is to be included in the block. When you release the cursor key, the block will be highlighted. Press (Enter) to tell LetterPerfect that the block has been defined.

When you press (Enter), the block disappears (it's actually stored in a temporary RAM buffer). Another message will be displayed in the lower left-hand corner of the screen:

```
Move cursor; press Enter to retrieve.
```

This means you must move the cursor to the location where you would like to place the block. When you press (Enter), the block is then retrieved from memory and placed in the text where indicated.

Copy

The Copy function is the same as the Move function, with one key difference. Instead of cutting the block from location A and retrieving it into location B, it leaves the block in location A and duplicates it in location B. The mechanics, however, are the same:

1. Select Copy.
2. Indicate the first character of the block and press (Enter).
3. Highlight the block and press (Enter) to indicate the last character.
4. Place the cursor at the location where you want the copy of the block to appear.
5. Press (Enter).

Paste

As mentioned above, with the Move and Copy functions, the block to be moved or copied is stored in a temporary buffer. When you press (Enter), it is placed back in the text. In fact, it is *not* removed from memory until you move or cut another block. You can retrieve it again by using the Paste option. What's the use of this? For one thing, you can copy a block multiple times, without having to repeat the regular three-step procedure. For another, you can move or copy a block, save your document, retrieve a new document, and paste the block into the new document. Remember, the block stays intact in memory until you replace it with another one.

Delete

This option enables you to delete a block of characters defined by the following option, or with the mouse (see below). Since its effect is the same as pressing the (Del) key, there's not much sense in using it.

Undelete

When you delete characters (or blocks of characters—see next option), you can retrieve the text by selecting Undelete. This highlights the deleted text, and LetterPerfect displays the following two options:

```
Undelete 1 Restore; 2 Previous deletion: 0
```

Restore brings the most recently deleted text back into the document at the position of the cursor. Previous deletion shows your next-most-recent deletion. If you select the option again by pressing 2, LetterPerfect shows your third-most-recent deletion. If the text you want was zapped four deletions ago, you're out of luck. Remember, LetterPerfect considers all deletions between cursor movements as if they were a single deletion. For example, pressing the (Del) key four times without otherwise moving the cursor counts as one deletion. In contrast, deleting a space, then moving the cursor to the next character and deleting it, counts as two deletions because the cursor was moved. Therefore, even though there are three levels of undelete, as you zoom along in the course of your normal typing, fixing typos and closing spaces, you may quickly lose your three chances to undo a mistake.

Block

When you select the Block option, the words "Block on" will flash in the lower left-hand corner of the screen. As you move any cursor key, you will highlight text to be included in the block. When you have finished defining the block, you can then apply any one of a number of functions to that block. For example, you can:

1. "Block off" a whole paragraph.
2. Press the Alt key to display the menu bar.
3. Select the Font category.
4. Select the bold option.

The entire block will be bolded (although it's much easier just to press the F6 key after you define the block—see next chapter). You can also highlight a block and then underline, italicize, or center the text. You could delete, spell check, or print a block, too. In fact, you can use any function on a pull-down menu that is not in square brackets.

Once a block is defined, you can also use the Move and Copy functions described above. The only difference is that you won't have to go through the block definition phase—after selecting Move or Copy, just place the cursor where you would like the block to appear and press (Enter).

Another way to highlight a block is to use the mouse. Place the rectangular cursor at the beginning of the block. Press and hold the left button as you "drag" the mouse through your text. When you release the button, the block will be defined, and the words "Block on" will still be flashing. You can now press the (Alt) key and select available pull down menu options (or use a function key to select the desired feature—see next chapter).

To redefine the last block that you have previously edited or formatted, select the Block function from the menu, then press (Ctrl-Home) twice.

Select Sentence

This is a specialized version of the Block command that acts upon sentences. LetterPerfect defines a sentence as continuous text up to the next terminal punctuation mark (period, exclamation mark, or question mark), plus the space following the mark. When you select it, LetterPerfect will display the following menu:

`1 Move  2 Copy  3 Delete`

Option 1 allows you to move a sentence quickly to another location—simply move the cursor to the new location and press

(Enter). Option 2 allows you to copy a sentence to another location without altering the original sentence. Option 3 deletes a sentence.

Select Paragraph

The Select Paragraph option is the same as the Select Sentence option, except for its definition of the blocked text. LetterPerfect defines a paragraph as continuous text up to the next hard return. You can move, copy, or delete a paragraph in the same way as you can a sentence (see preceding menu).

Reveal Codes

This is one of the most powerful—and for some, one of the most intimidating—features of LetterPerfect. It shows you what formatting codes LetterPerfect stores in your document when you use bold or underline, or format your text in any way. Whereas your screen shows only the effect of applying bolding, underlining, and other commands, LetterPerfect is actually inserting complex codes that, if shown on the screen, would make your text illegible. Figure 4.7 shows the difference between what you see and what LetterPerfect sees. The ability to view hidden codes is extremely important for editing formatted text; in fact, in some cases it's the only way to untangle the formatting commands you've issued. Chapter 8 explains how to use Reveal Codes as an editing tool.

To exit from Reveal Codes, reselect the option from the pull down menu.

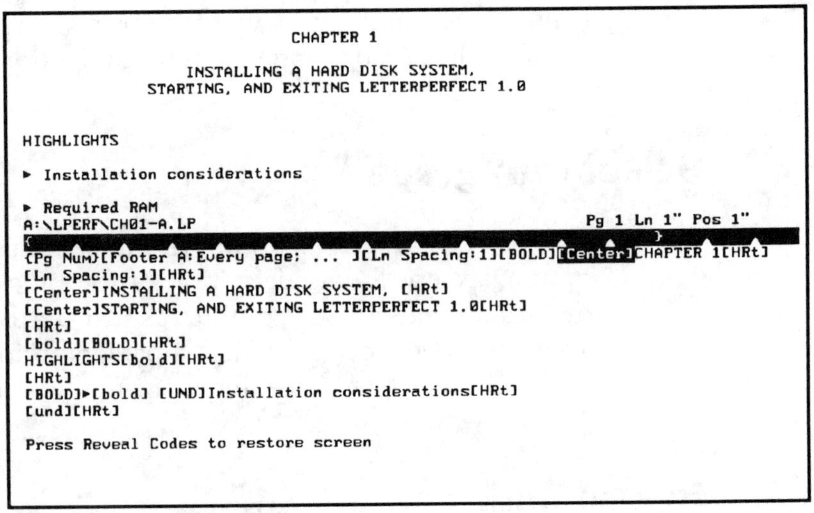

Figure 4.7. LetterPerfect inserts codes into your document when you select various formatting commands.

The Search Menu

The search menu allows you to find specific words or phrases in your document, and to replace them, if you wish, with another word or phrase (see Figure 4.8).

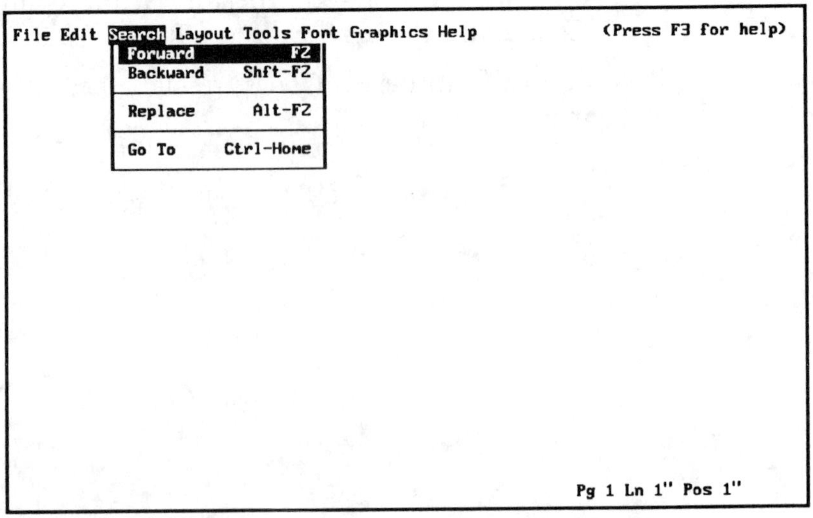

Figure 4.8. Search pull down menu options.

Forward

This option allows you to search for a word, number, or phrase, starting from the current cursor location and moving to the end of the document. Its use is also discussed in Chapter 8.

Backward

The backward search works in reverse—from the cursor location to the top of the document (see Chapter 8).

Replace

Whereas the Forward and Backward search functions enable you to locate a word or phrase, the Replace function allows you to find a word or phrase, and replace it with another. For instance, let's say that you wrote a report and used the word "individuals" throughout. Later, you decided to soften the language and wanted to use "people" instead. The Replace function locates each instance of "individuals" and replaces it with "people." This is discussed further in Chapter 8.

Go to

This function is a short cut for getting to a specific page. When you select it, LetterPerfect will prompt you in the lower left-hand corner of the screen with:

```
Go to
```

Enter the page number, and the desired page will be displayed.

The Layout Menu

As the name implies, the layout menu provides various options for formatting your pages (see Figure 4.9). These include various text placement functions, among others.

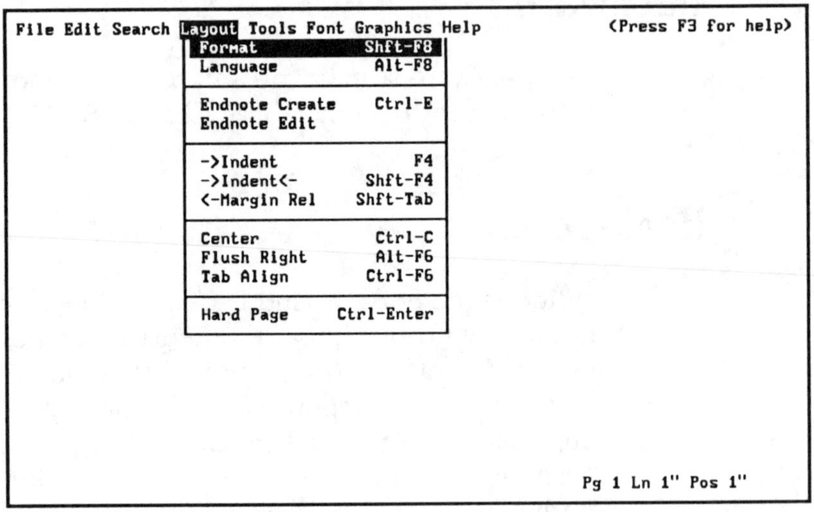

Figure 4.9 Layout pull-down menu options.

Format

This option displays LetterPerfect's main formatting menu, which allows you to control many features, such as justification, line spacing, margins, page numbering, etc. Each of these options is described in Chapter 7.

Language

The language files govern the appearance of dates, times, numbers and other entries. For example, when you choose select language, the designation US will appear in the lower left-hand corner. By changing the designation to "FR," French conventions would be used. Refer to your manual for a listing of available international formats.

Endnote Create

LetterPerfect allows you to create endnotes in your documents. The automated endnote numbering system is explained in Chapter 7.

Indent

The Indent function causes the text to left-align at the next tab and remain there until you press (Enter), which inserts a hard return. If you edit the text or insert additional text in an indented paragraph, LetterPerfect automatically rewraps the text so that it conforms to the indented margin. This feature is extremely useful for creating indented paragraphs without having to reset the left margin. Again, if you insert the Indent command in front of an existing paragraph, the text will be indented up to the next hard (carriage) return.

Indent (Left/Right)

This function creates an equal indent from the left and right margins. The left margin is indented to wherever the next tab has been set, and the right margin is automatically moved in toward the left by an equal amount. Text is indented until you press (Enter), which issues a hard (carriage) return. Indent (Left/Right) is useful for quotations and other text that needs to be set off from the rest of the text and centered. If you insert an Indent (Left/Right) command in front of an existing paragraph, all text up to the next hard (carriage) return will be indented.

Margin Release

When you select this function, you move the cursor to the left one tab stop. You can use this in conjunction with Indent to create a "hanging paragraph." To do so, first select Indent, then select Margin Release. This will cause the first line of the paragraph to begin further left than subsequent lines. In other words, the rest of the paragraph "hangs" from the first line.

Center

As the name implies, this function centers text. You can use this before you type a line, or apply it to a defined block (see above).

Flush Right

This option causes text to align with the right margin. As with the Center option, you can select the option first, and then type, or you can block text and then apply it.

Tab Align

This feature is used to align decimal points, commas, or other characters. It is useful when you are typing columns of numbers that you wish to align by decimal point, rather than by left or right edges. When you select Tab Align, you insert a Hard Decimal Tab code into the document. Everything you typed will be moved to the left of the tab. When you insert a character, such as a period or comma, normal spacing (toward the right of the screen) will resume.

Hard Page

If you want to create a new page, select this option. You can also create a new page by pressing (Ctrl-Enter).

The Tools Menu

LetterPerfect is equipped with a variety of word processing functions that will make your life easier and enhance your documents (see Figure 4.10).

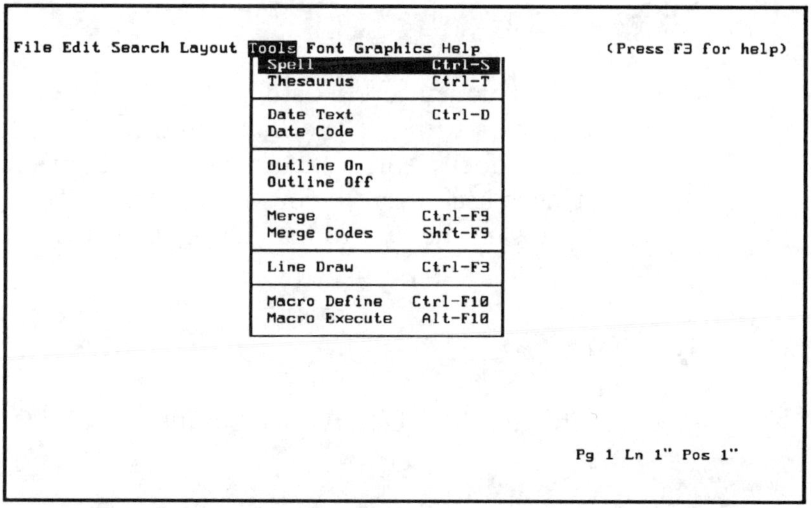

Figure 4.10 Tools pull-down menu options.

Spell

This option activates the speller, assuming that you've installed it. See Chapter 10 for details.

Thesaurus

The thesaurus will be activated (if you've installed it) when you select this option. The uses of the thesaurus are also covered in Chapter 10.

Date Text

When you select this option, LetterPerfect will insert today's date at the cursor. (The date is determined by your computer's clock. If you don't have a clock and have not set the date when you booted up, the date will be incorrect. Likewise, if your computer has a clock, but the battery is dead or it is not set correctly, the date will be wrong. To change the date format, refer to your LetterPerfect manual for instructions on how to edit the Language Resource File.)

Date Code

When you insert a date with the preceding option, it enters the date as a string of text that you can edit. This option places a code in the document, so that the date that appears will change each day. This is useful, say, if you have created a "boilerplate" memo format, and want the date to match the current date each time you use it.

Outline On

This activates LetterPerfect's built in outline. See Chapter 14.

Outline Off

Use this function to turn off the outliner.

Merge

The Merge features are used to combine two documents on the screen or as output created by the printer. For example, you can merge a letter with a list of names and addresses to create a "personalized" letter (you know, the kind you get in junk mail that appears to be individually typed with your name—see chapter 14).

Merge Codes

This feature, as explained in Chapter 14, displays a box with the codes used in setting up a mail merge.

Line Draw

The Line Draw function enables you to draw lines and boxes of various widths that can be incorporated into your document. You can print shapes created with Line Draw if your printer has the necessary line-drawing capabilities. On many printers, the line draw characters are considered a special font and may have to be added to the printer with an optional cartridge or soft font (see Appendix A).

Macro Define and Macro Execute

These functions enable you to create "macros" that automate your keystrokes. To create macros, you must install the Shell files (see Chapter 14 for a brief description).

The Font Menu

This menu allows you to alter the appearance of your document by selecting a variety of fonts (see Figure 4.11).

Figure 4.11 Font pull-down menu options.

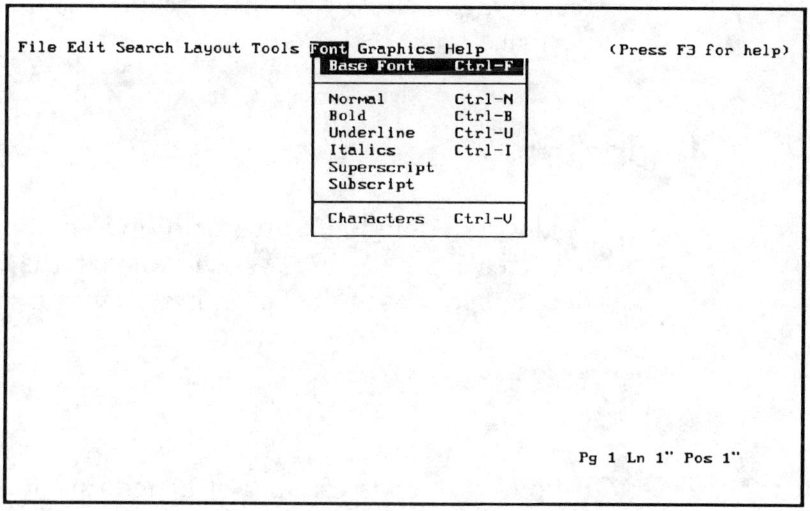

Base Font

The Base Font specifies a group of fonts built into your printer and any installed font cartridges or soft fonts. When you select this option, the available fonts will be displayed. See Chapter 9 for a complete discussion of the use of the base font concept.

Normal

This gives you "plain vanilla" type—no bold, underline, or any other attributes (see Figure 4.12).

Bold

If you select this before typing, all subsequent text will appear in bold (see Figure 4.12) until you select the option again. You can also bold an entire highlighted block by defining the block, then selecting the Bold option. Notice that when bold is in effect, the intensity of the numbers after the Pos indicator changes from normal to high. When you turn off bold, the intensity changes back to normal.

Underline

This works the same as the bold option, above, but underlines the text (see Figure 4.12). When you use the underline option, the numbers following the Pos indicator appear in a highlight block.

Italics

If your printer is capable of generating italics, you can use this option (see Figure 4.12). (Otherwise, it may underline the text.) On your screen, the italics will appear as a different shade. Use this function the same way you would Bold and Underline.

Superscript

This option is used primarily for scientific notation. When you turn it on, all text will be superscripted (placed above the text and appearing in a smaller font) (see Figure 4.12). When you turn it off, normal text will resume. Superscripted text will be highlighted on your screen. You can either turn on the Superscript function first and then type, or superscript a block of text.

Subscript

Operationally, this is the same as the preceding option, except subscripted characters are placed below the text (see Figure 4.12).

Character

This allows you to place certain characters, such as the Copyright, diacritical marks, international characters, etc. in your document. Your LetterPerfect manual provides a chart of available characters.

Figure 4.12 Font samples.

This is normal type.

This is bold type.

This is underlined type.

This is italicized type.

This is a sample of superscript: 10^2

This is a sample of subscript: CO_2

The Graphics Menu

LetterPerfect allows you to mix text and graphic images. Chapter 11 explains the process. This menu gives you access to the graphics functions (see Figure 4.13).

Figure 4.13
Graphics pull-down menu options.

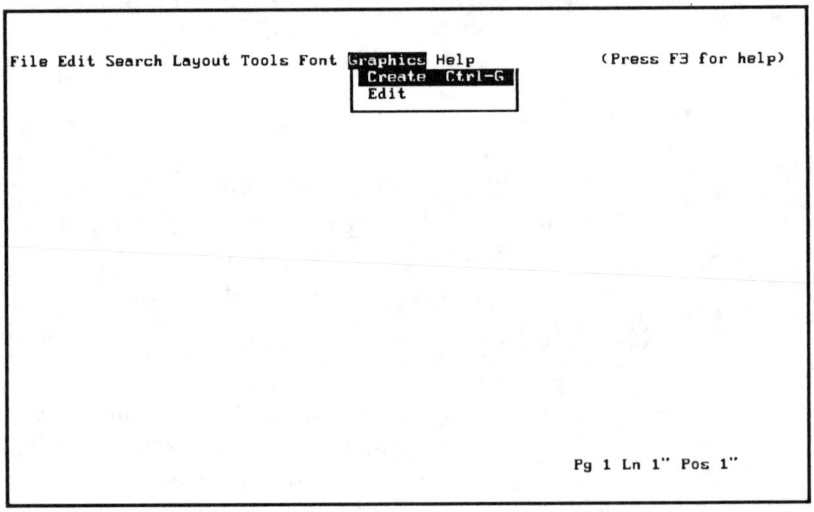

Create

This option displays the Graphics Definition menu (see Chapter 11), which is used initially to introduce a graphic element into your document.

Edit

Once you've defined a graphic element, you can edit its position and other page attributes. This option prompts you for the figure number in the lower left had corner of the screen.

The Help Menu

LetterPerfect has an extensive "context-sensitive" help system. That means whenever you press the Help key (F3, unless you changed it during installation or with the setup key), LetterPerfect will provide you with help for the function you're using. For example, if you select the Spell option from the Tools menu and then press F3, LetterPerfect will display the screen shown in Figure 4.14. (Press F7 to exit from the help screen.)

Figure 4.14 Help screen for spell-checker.

```
Speller                                      Pull-Down:   Tools, Spell
                                          Function Key:   Ctrl-F2
                                              Fast Key:   Ctrl-s

   Speller also checks capitalization errors and double words. If you use
   LetterPerfect with two disk drives, retrieve the document to check,
   insert the Speller/Thesaurus diskette into drive B, and select Spell.

   Speller highlights a word not found in its dictionary and suggests a list
   of replacement words.  To automatically replace the misspelled word,
   press the letter corresponding to the correct word in the list.  For
   information on Double Word occurrences, press D.  For information on Case
   Checking, press C.

   Skip Once - Accept the word as correct for this occurrence only.
   Skip - Accept the word as correct throughout this spell-check.
   Add Word - Add the word to the supplementary dictionary.  The Speller
   uses the supplementary dictionary as a secondary dictionary, meaning that
   the Speller will always accept the added word as correct.
   Edit - Position the cursor on the word so that you can edit it.  (You can
   also press Left or Right Arrow to begin editing).  When you are finished
   editing, press Exit (F7) to continue spell checking.
   Look Up - Look up words that match a pattern.
   Ignore Numbers - Do not check the spelling of words with numbers.
Press F7 to exit Help.
```

The pull-down menu from the Help option of the menu bar (see Figure 4.15) has three options.

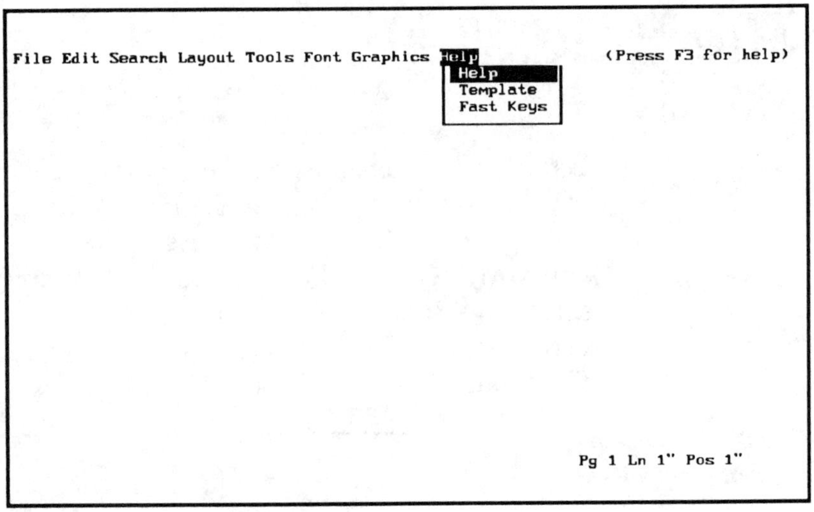

Figure 4.15 Help pull-down menu options.

Help

This displays the help index, which is organized alphabetically (see Figure 4.16). You can highlight different topics with the cursor keys, or select topics with the mouse and press the left button. (The PgDn, PgUp, and large (-) and (+) keys will also move the highlight through the list.) Then, when you press (Enter), (or quickly press the left mouse button twice), the Help screen corresponding to the topic will be displayed. When you are done reading a Help screen, press (Enter) and the Help index will again be displayed.

Another important feature of the Help index is that you can actually initiate the function that is being described simply by typing 2. For example, if you highlight Add Password from the list and type 2, LetterPerfect will prompt you to "Enter the Password," just as if you had selected the Password option from the File menu.

To exit from the index, type 3, or press (Esc), F7, or (Spacebar).

Figure 4.16 Help index screen.

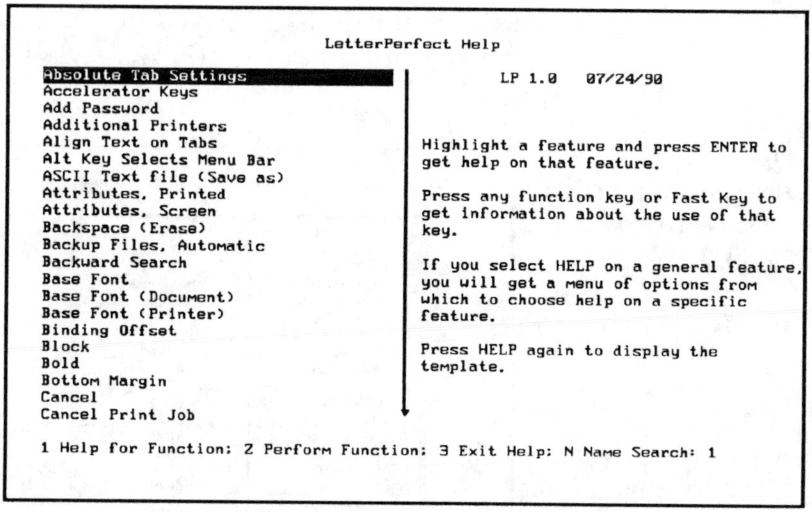

Template

When you select this option, LetterPerfect displays a pictorial layout of the function keys of the enhanced keyboard (keys across the top—see Figure 4.17. Also see Chapter 5 for a discussion of each function key).

Figure 4.17 Template of function keys—enhanced keyboard.

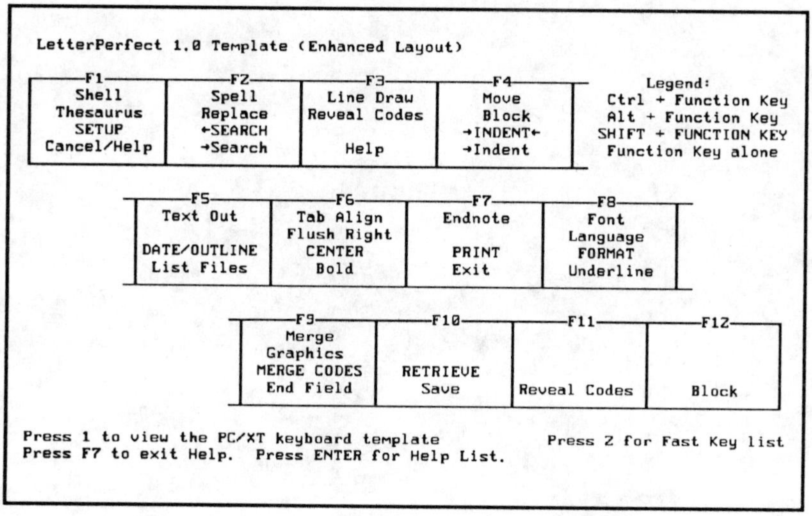

When the template is displayed on the screen and you press 1, function keys for a "classic" (PC/XT-style keyboard) are displayed (see Figure 4.18).

Figure 4.18 Template of function keys—classic keyboard.

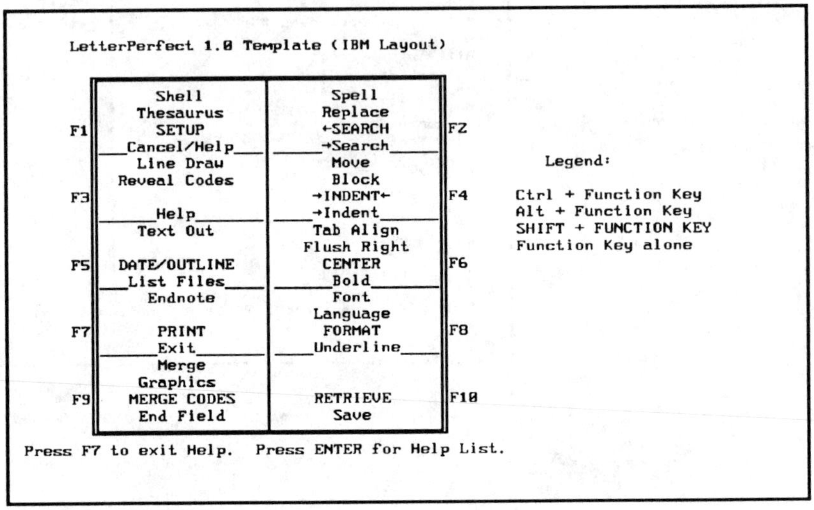

Chapter 5

The Fuction Keys and Fast Keys

Highlights

- About the Function Keys
- (F1) key
- (F2) key
- (F3) key
- (F4) key
- (F5) key
- (F6) key
- (F7) key
- (F8) key
- (F9) key
- (F10) key
- (F11) key—enhanced keyboard only
- (F12) key—enhanced keyboard only

The Menu Alternative

The function keys provide an alternative to the menu system described in the last chapter. As you pick up speed as a LetterPerfect user, you might find them a faster means of accessing LetterPerfect's functions. You might also find them less distracting than the menus, since in many cases you can execute the various functions without having your text obscured.

The fast keys are yet another way to use LetterPerfect. The fast keys allow you to access various functions with two keystroke combinations (Ctrl) plus an assigned key.

This chapter discusses the function keys and fast keys. The function key section is organized numerically, from F1 through F10. The Fast Key section is organized alphabetically, from (Ctrl-A) through (Ctrl-V).

For some items in the function key section, such as the help system and passwords, you'll find complete descriptions, since they are not mentioned elsewhere in the text. For other features, such as format, only a brief description is provided, since you'll find lengthy discussions of these topics in various chapters of the book.

About the Function Keys

So far you've used the keyboard to move the cursor, enter text, and delete text. The real power behind LetterPerfect, however, resides in the special function keys, (F1) through (F10). On "classic" PC/XT-style keyboards, the function keys are arranged in two columns located on the left side. On enhanced AT-style keyboards and PS/2 keyboards, the functions keys, also labeled F1 through F12, are arranged in a single row across the top. (F11) and (F12) duplicate certain functions of keys (F1) through (F10)—more on that later.

You have probably noticed a number of different templates packaged along with your disks. The one with the cutout is designed for the classic keyboard, while the single strip (folded in half in the packaging) is for the AT-style keyboards (other templates are for certain Compaq computers and laptops).

As you can see from looking at the templates, each key has four functions, designated by red, green, blue, and black print.

The significance of the colors is as follows:

RED means press and hold the (Ctrl) key, press the function key once, then release both keys.

BLUE means press and hold the (Alt) key, press the function key once, then release both keys.

GREEN means press and hold the (Shift) key, press the function key once, then release both keys.

BLACK means press the function key alone.

Various functions (37 in all) are activated by each function key or function key combination as explained below. For a key combination such as (Alt-F3), that means press and hold the Alt key, then press F3, and then release both keys.

The following pages have been set up like a reference manual, organized by function key. As a reminder, next to each feature the corresponding color appears in parentheses, with:

(R) = RED

(B) = BLUE

(G) = GREEN

(Bl) = BLACK

A usage comment is also given for each function, indicating whether it is universally used or generally reserved for advanced operations.

Finally, this chapter is organized by function keys, rather than by the functions themselves. Appendix B provides a table based on the functions (Center, Right Align, etc.), and should be used when you need to track down the keystrokes for a specific command.

F1 Key

Functions	Executed by	Usage
1. Shell (R)	(Ctrl-F1)	Depends on personal style
2. Thesaurus (B)	(Alt-F1)	Depends on personal style
3. Setup (G)	(Shift-F1)	Generally used once
4. Cancel (Bl)	(F1) alone	Every day

Shell

Shell is a memory manager that enables you to go into other programs, including DOS, without formally exiting LetterPerfect (see Chapter 14). You can only use it if you've installed the Shell files (see Chapter 1 or 2, depending on whether you performed a hard disk or floppy disk installation), and started LetterPerfect from the Shell file.

Thesaurus

LetterPerfect is shipped with an electronic thesaurus containing many thousands of words. You can invoke it at any time, and it will provide synonyms for whatever word is at the cursor. Some people use the thesaurus constantly, while others have no need for it at all. Try using it for a while and see if it's helpful for you. If not—and you're using a hard disk—delete it, since it consumes more than 170K of space. Use of the thesaurus is described in Chapter 10.

Setup

The Setup command, which you generally use once, allows you to personalize the program. You may choose, among other things, the screen colors, backup options, and whether the menu bar is always to be displayed. The Setup options are described in Chapter 6.

Cancel

This function is used to cancel other commands (unless you've designated it as the Help function, in which case the (Esc) key takes on the Cancel function). For example, if you invoke the thesaurus, or begin a search-and-replace operation, and then decide you don't want to do either, you can press the (F1) key to cancel whatever operation is in process. Note: If you are several layers down in a complex series of menus, you may have to press the (F1) key more than once to return to the "surface."

Another purpose of Cancel is to undo a deletion. If you make a deletion, whether it's a word or 100 pages (in one fell swoop), you can retrieve the text by pressing (F1). This highlights the deleted text, and LetterPerfect then displays the following two options:

`Undelete 1 Restore; 2 Previous deletion: 0`

Restore brings the most recently deleted text back into the document at the position of the cursor.

Previous deletion shows your next-most-recent deletion. If you select the option again by pressing option 2, LetterPerfect shows your third-most-previous deletion. If the text you want was zapped four deletions ago, you're out of luck. Remember, LetterPerfect considers all deletions between cursor movements as a single deletion. For example, pressing the (Del) key four times without otherwise moving the cursor counts as one deletion. In contrast, deleting a space, then moving the cursor to the next character and deleting it, counts as two deletions because the cursor was moved. Therefore, even though there are three levels of undelete, as you zoom along in the course of your normal typing, fixing typos and closing spaces, you may quickly lose your three chances to undo a mistake.

F2 Key

Functions	Executed by	Usage
1. Spell (R)	(Ctrl-F2)	Every day
2. Replace (B)	(Alt-F2)	Every day
2. (Backward) Search (G)	(Shift-F2)	Every day
4. (Forward) Search (Bl)	(F2) alone	Every day

Spell

LetterPerfect's spell-checker is a superb tool and should be used whenever you complete a document. It is easily invoked to check a word, a page, or a whole document. Spell is covered in detail in Chapter 10.

Replace

This function enables you to locate a word or phrase and replace it with another. For instance, let's say that you wrote a report and used the word "individuals" throughout. Later, you decided to soften the language and wanted to use "people" instead. The Replace function locates each instance of "individuals" and replaces it with "people." This is discussed further in Chapter 8.

(Backward) Search

The Backward Search allows you to search from the current cursor position back to the beginning of the document for a specific word, number, or phrase. Searching techniques are discussed extensively in Chapter 8.

Forward Search

This command allows you to search for a word, number, or phrase, starting from the current cursor location and moving to the end of the document. Its use is also discussed in Chapter 8.

F3 Key

Functions	Executed by	Usage
1. Line Draw (R)	(Ctrl-F3)	Occasional
2. Reveal Codes (B)	(Alt-F3)	Every day
3. Not used	(Shift-F3)	
4. Help (Bl)	(F3) alone	Depends on personal style

Line Draw

As the name suggests, Line Draw enables you to draw lines and boxes of various widths for incorporation into your document. You can print shapes created with line draw if your printer has the necessary line drawing capabilities. On many printers, the Line Draw characters are considered to be a special font and may have to be added to the printer with an optional cartridge or soft font (see Appendix A).

Reveal Codes

This option shows you what formatting codes LetterPerfect stores in your document when you use bold or underline, or format your text in any way. Whereas your screen shows only the effect of applying bolding, underlining, and other commands, LetterPerfect is actually inserting complex codes that, if shown on the screen, would make your text impossible to edit. Figure 5.1 shows the difference between what you see and what LetterPerfect sees. The ability to view hidden codes is extremely important for editing formatted text; in fact, in some cases, it's the only way to untangle the formatting commands you've issued. Chapter 8 explains how to use Reveal Codes as an editing tool.

To exit from reveal codes, press (Alt-F3) again.

Figure 5.1
LetterPerfect inserts codes into your document when you select various formatting commands.

```
      running the program. In addition, step-by-step instruction

      is provided for installing a printer. Proper startup and

      exit routines are also discussed.


      Chapter 2: Installing a Floppy Disk System, Starting, and

      Exiting LetterPerfect. This chapter explains the various
A:\LPERF\INTRO-A.LP                                  Pg 5 Ln 2.33" Pos 1.5"
{                                                 }
is provided for installing a printer. Proper startup and[SRt]
exit routines are also discussed.[HRt]
[HRt]
[→Indent][UND]Chapter 2: Installing a Floppy Disk System, Starting, and[SRt]
Exiting LetterPerfect[und]. This chapter explains the various[SRt]
types of floppy installation that you can perform. It shows[SRt]
you how to run LetterPerfect on systems with four different[SRt]
disk types, and provides step[-]by[-]step instruction for[SRt]
installing a printer. The chapter concludes with a[SRt]
discussion of the proper ways to start and exit[SRt]

Press Reveal Codes to restore screen
```

Help

When you press the Help key, LetterPerfect will display a Help index, which is organized alphabetically (see Figure 5.2). You can highlight different topics with the cursor keys or select topics with the mouse and press the left button. (The PgDn, PgUp, and large - and + keys will also move the highlight through the list.) Then, when you press (Enter), quickly press the left button twice, or type 1, the Help screen corresponding to the topic will be displayed (see sample, Figure 5.3). When you are done reading a Help screen, press (Enter) and the Help index will again be displayed.

Another important feature of the Help index is that you can actually initiate the function that is being described by typing 2. For example, if you highlight Reveal Codes from the list and type 2,

LetterPerfect will immediately shift into Reveal Codes mode, just as if you had pressed (Alt-F3).

To exit from the index, type 3, press (Esc), F7, or (Spacebar).

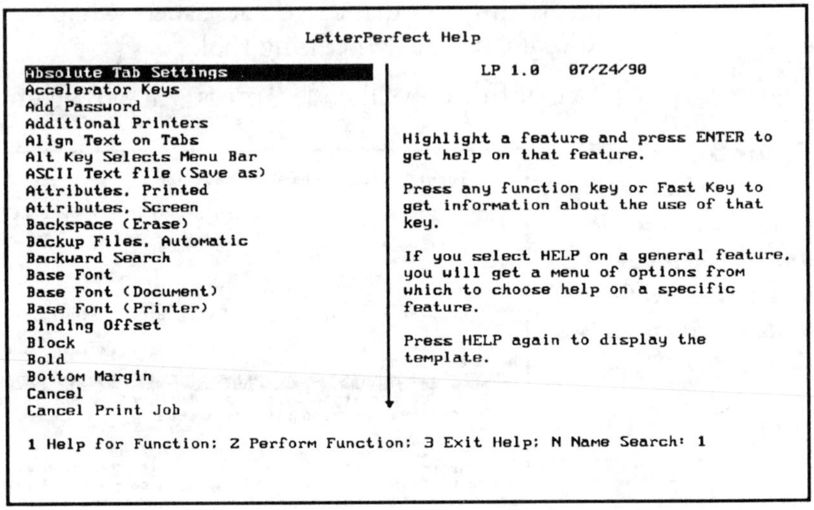

Figure 5.2 Help index screen.

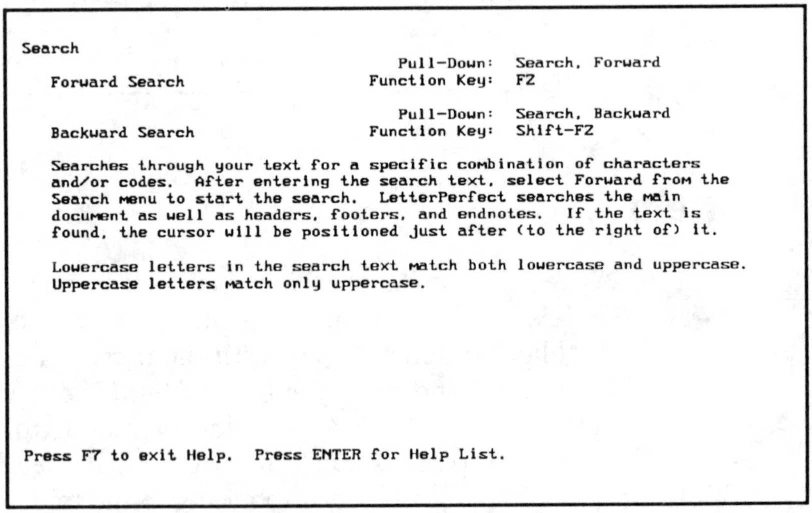

Figure 5.3 Help screen for Search function.

LetterPerfect's help system is also context-sensitive. That means whenever you press the Help key, LetterPerfect will provide you with help with the function you're using. For example, if you initiate the Search function and then press F3, LetterPerfect will display the screen shown in Figure 5.3. Press F7, (Esc), or (Spacebar) to exit from the Help screen.

To exit the help program altogether, press F7, (Esc), or (Spacebar).

F4 Key

Functions	Executed by	Usage
1. Move (R)	(Ctrl-F4)	Every day
2. Block (B)	(Alt-F4)	Every day
3. Indent (L/R) (G)	(Shift-F4)	Every day
4. Indent (Bl)	(F4) alone	Every day

Move

The Move feature can save you a great deal of time when you're moving and deleting sentences, paragraphs, and pages. When you select Move, you are offered four options:

`Move 1 Sentence  2 Paragraph  3 Block; Retrieve: 4 Block: 0`

The first two specify how much text you want to manipulate. The third allows you to move, copy, or delete a block, and the fourth retrieves a previously cut block of text.

Sentence

LetterPerfect defines a sentence as continuous text up to the next terminal punctuation mark (period, exclamation mark, or question mark), plus the space following the mark. When you select it, LetterPerfect will display the following menu:

`1 Move  2 Copy  3 Delete`

Option 1 allows you to move a sentence to another location quickly—simply move the cursor to the new location and press (Enter). Option 2 allows you to copy a sentence to another location without altering the original sentence. Option 3 deletes a sentence.

Paragraph

LetterPerfect defines a paragraph as continuous text up to the next hard return. You can move, copy, or delete a paragraph in the same way as you can a sentence (see preceding menu).

Block

The block option works as follows. When you select Block, LetterPerfect will display the message:

```
Position to top corner of text; press Enter
```

in the lower left-hand corner of the screen. This means you should indicate the start of the block of text that you wish to move. After you press (Enter), LetterPerfect will then display a second message in the lower left hand corner of the screen:

```
Position to bottom corner of text; press Enter
```

Move the appropriate cursor key in the desired direction. LetterPerfect will highlight the text that will be included in the block. When you release the cursor key, the block will be highlighted. Press (Enter) to tell LetterPerfect that the block has been defined. LetterPerfect will then display the following menu:

```
1 Move; 2 Copy; 3 Delete: 0
```

Move

If you select Move, the block will disappear (actually it will be stored in a temporary buffer). LetterPerfect will then display the message:

```
Move cursor; Press Enter to retrieve
```

Place the cursor where you would like the block to appear and press (Enter). The block will be copied from the temporary buffer into your document.

Copy

The copy function is the same as the Move function, with one difference. Instead of cutting the block from location A and retrieving it into location B, it leaves the block in location A and duplicates it in location B. The mechanics are the same as those used to move a sentence.

Delete

This deletes the block you've defined. You can undelete with the F1 key, as explained above, or with the last option on the Move menu.

Retrieve: Block

As mentioned above, with the Move and Copy functions, the block to be moved or copied is stored in a temporary buffer. When you press (Enter), it is placed back in the text. In fact, it is *not* removed from memory until you move or cut another block. You can retrieve it again by using the Retrieve: Block option. This is helpful when you want to copy the same sentence multiple times without having to repeat the copy procedure. Remember, the block stays intact in memory until you replace it with another one.

Block

When you select the Block option, the words "Block on" will flash in the lower left-hand corner of the screen. As you move any cursor key, you will highlight text to be included in the block. When you have finished defining the block, you can then apply any one of a number of functions to it. For example, you could block a whole paragraph and then press the bold key (F6—see below). The entire block will be bolded. You can also highlight a block and underline, italicize, or center the text. You can also delete, spell-check or print a block.

Once a block is defined, you can also press (Ctrl-F4), which will display the Move/Copy/Delete menu described above under the Move menu.

Another way to highlight a block is to use the mouse. Place the rectangular cursor at the beginning of the block. Press and hold the left button as you "drag" the mouse through your text. When you release the button, the block will be defined, and the words "Block on" will still be flashing. You can now use a function key to select the desired feature.

To redefine the last block that you have edited or formatted, select the Block function from the menu, then press (Ctrl-Home) twice.

Indent (L/R)

This function creates an equal indent from the left and right margins. The left margin is indented to wherever the next tab has been set, and the right margin is automatically moved in toward the left by an equal amount. Text is indented until you press (Enter), which issues a hard return. Indent is useful for quotations and other text that needs to be set off from the rest of the text and centered. If you insert an indent command in front of an existing paragraph, all text up to the next hard return will be indented.

Indent

The Indent function causes the text to left align at the next tab and remain there until you press (Enter), which inserts a hard return. If you edit the text or insert additional text in an indented paragraph, LetterPerfect automatically rewraps the text so that it conforms to the indented margin. This feature is extremely useful for creating indented paragraphs without having to reset the left margin. Again, if you insert the indent command in front of an existing paragraph, the text will be indented up to the next hard (carriage) return.

F5 Key

Functions	Executed by	Usage
1. Text Out (R)	(Ctrl-F5)	Depends on personal needs
2. Not Used	(Alt-F5)	
3. Date/Outline (G)	(Shift-F5)	Depends on personal needs
4. List Files (Bl)	(F5) alone	Every day

Text Out

When you press (Ctrl-F5), the following menu is displayed:

1 DOS **T**ext; **2** **P**assword; **3** Save **G**eneric: 0

DOS Text refers to various ways of saving a file in ASCII format, so that programs other than LetterPerfect can read it. When you save in ASCII format, you lose all the LetterPerfect formatting, such as bold, underline, tabs, etc.

When you select this option, LetterPerfect displays the prompt:

`Document to be saved (DOS Text):`

Enter the name of the file, and it will be saved in DOS format.

Password allows you to "encrypt" a document so that no one can view, retrieve, or print it without entering the correct password. When you select the password option, you will be presented with the following menu:

`Password 1 A``dd/Change;` **`2 R`**`emove:` **`0`**

Add/Change appends a password to the current document, or changes the password in a current document. The password becomes part of the document, although no one can see it. When you select this option, LetterPerfect prompts you to:

`Enter Password:`

For security purposes, your keystrokes are not echoed back to the screen, so be careful. As a caution, LetterPerfect asks you to re-enter the password to confirm your choice. If the password is different from your original input, LetterPerfect displays:

`ERROR: incorrect password`

and asks you to begin again and enter the password. The password is then added to the document on screen. You must still save it to a file on disk before password protection becomes effective.

when you go to retrieve a file with a password (see below, List Files and the F10 key), LetterPerfect will prompt you to:

`Enter Password:`

If you enter the wrong password, it displays the message:

`ERROR: File is locked`

and you have to start the retrieval process again.

CAUTION!! If you forget a password, there is no way to gain access to the file. Use passwords that mean something to you.

Remove is the only way you can get a password out of a document's file structure. To select Remove, however, you must have access to the file; you can't use the option unless the file has been "unlocked" and is on the screen. Again, you must resave the unlocked file to disk, overwriting the locked version, to deactivate the password.

Save Generic stores your file without LetterPerfect codes while maintaining the format. For instance, centered text remains centered, but with spaces inserted instead of LetterPerfect's centering codes. This arrangement may be useful if you are transferring LetterPerfect files to another word processing program.

Date/Outline

When you press (Shift-F5), you are presented with the following menu:

`1. Date Text; 2 Date Code; 3 Outline on; 4 Outline Off; 0`

Date Text inserts the current date. If your system clock (which remembers the date) is correct, or if you don't have a clock but you entered today's date correctly when you started your computer, the correct date appears at the cursor. Note that the Date Text option is a one-shot affair; once the date is in place, it will not change. If you need always to show the current date, select the next option, Date Code.

Date Code puts a code in the text, calling for the current system date so that the date in the document will be updated as the system date changes. If you have a to-do list, for example, you might want it always to display the current date. Or, you might want to include the date code in a standard memo format. When you retrieve the memo format and enter the text of the memo, it automatically prints with the current date. This "dynamic" approach contrasts with the static one used in the previous option.

Outline On activates the outliner.

Outline Off deactivates the outliner.

List Files

This option invokes LetterPerfect's file manager, and is a very convenient way to retrieve, delete, rename, print, view, or copy a file. When you select List Files, LetterPerfect first displays the current directory in the lower left-hand corner of the screen. You can change the directory either temporarily, by editing the directory name, or for the duration of the session, by pressing the (=) key, typing in a new directory name, and pressing (Enter).

When you press (Enter) after the directory name, the file manager is displayed (see Figure 5.4). Use the cursor keys to move the highlighted bar over the file you wish to act upon. Then select an option. The various options of the file manager are discussed at length in Chapter 13.

Figure 5.4 LetterPerfect File Manager

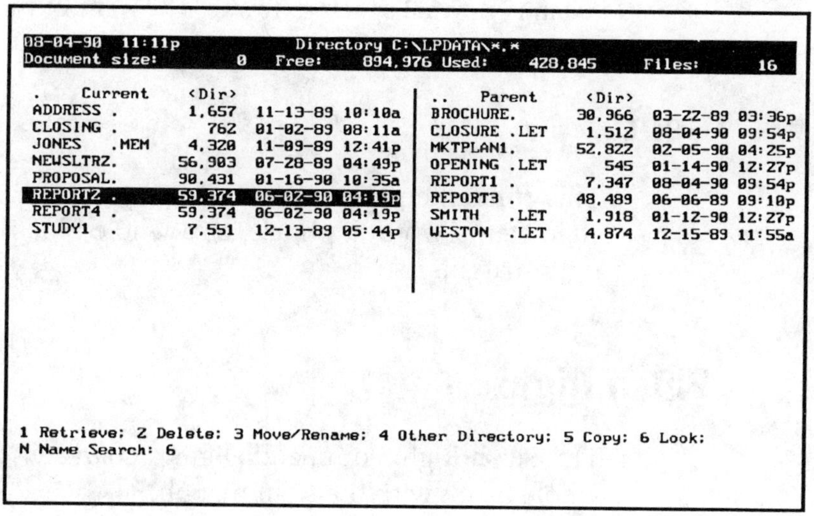

F6 Key

Functions	Executed by	Usage
1. Tab Align (R)	(Ctrl-F6)	Depends on personal style
2. Flush Right (B)	(Alt-F6)	Depends on personal style
3. Center (G)	(Shift-F6)	Every day
4. Bold (Bl)	(F6) alone	Universal

Tab Align

This feature is used to align decimal points, commas, or other characters. It is useful when you are typing columns of numbers that you wish to align by decimal point, rather than align by left or right edges. When you select Tab Align, you insert a Hard Decimal Tab code into the document. Everything you typed will be moved to the left of the tab. When you insert a character, such as a period or comma, normal spacing (toward the right of the screen) will resume.

Center

This fundamental function allows you to center text instantly (a character, a word, a phrase, or a whole block) between the left and right margins.

Flush Right

The Flush Right command aligns a character, a word, a phrase, or a whole block with the right margin.

Bold

Bold can act upon a character, a word, a phrase, or a whole block of text. When you press (F6), all characters are bolded until you press (F6) again.

F7 Key

Functions	Executed by	Usage
1. Endnote (R)	(Ctrl-F7)	Depends on personal style
2. not used (B)	(Alt-F7)	
3. Print (G)	(Shift-F7)	Every day
4. Exit (Bl)	(F7) alone	Every day

Endnote

LetterPerfect allows you to create endnotes in your documents. The automated endnote numbering system is explained in Chapter 7.

Print

LetterPerfect gives you excellent control over the printing process. When you invoke the Print function, the main print menu is displayed, providing options for printing the full document or the page of the document in which the cursor is currently positioned. Several other options are also available, and are discussed at length in Chapter 12.

Exit

The Exit function is the *only* "legal" way to exit LetterPerfect. If you are working on a document and press (F7), LetterPerfect displays the following message in the lower left-hand corner:

```
Save document: (Y/N) Yes
```

If you want to save the document you're working on, press (Enter). If you've never saved the document before, LetterPerfect prompts you for the document name:

```
Document to be saved:
```

Type the name you wish to assign the file. You may use a maximum of eight characters or numbers in the main name, plus three alphanumeric characters in the extension, which is separated from the main name by a period. When you press (Enter), LetterPerfect will ask you if you want to exit the program. If you say No, then you may create a new document. In other words, Exit really means that you can save with the option of either quitting LetterPerfect or starting with a blank screen. Save using the F10 key, however, only lets you save and continue working on whatever document is currently displayed on the screen.

F8 Key

Functions	Executed by	Usage
1. Font (R)	(Ctrl-F8)	Depends on hardware
2. Language (B)	(Alt-F8)	Rarely
3. Format (G)	(Shift-F8)	Every day
4. Underline (Bl)	(F8) alone	Every day

Font

The Font option allows you to change the type fonts of words, headlines, characters, or any other text. Your ability to choose fonts is entirely dependent on your printer. See Chapter 9 for a detailed explanation about changing fonts.

Language

See your LetterPerfect manual for details

Format

This option displays LetterPerfect's main formatting menu, which allows you to control many features, such as justification, line spacing, margins, page numbering, etc. Each of these options is described in Chapter 7.

Underline

Like Bold, Underline can act upon a character, a word, a phrase, or a whole block of text. When you press (F8), all characters typed will be underlined until you press (F8) again.

F9 Key

Functions	Executed by	Usage
1. Merge t (R)	(Ctrl-F9)	Depends on needs
2. Graphics (B)	(Alt-F9)	Depends on needs
3. Merge Codes (G)	(Shift-F9)	Depends on needs
4. End Field (Bl)	(F9) alone	Depends on needs

Merge

The Merge features are used to combine two documents on the screen or as output created by the printer. For example, you can merge a letter with a list of names and addresses to create a "personalized" letter (you know, the kind you get in junk mail that appear to be individually typed with your name—see Chapter 14).

Graphics

LetterPerfect 1.0 has unique graphics capabilities that enable it to incorporate graphic elements from other programs and to "flow" text around those elements. See Chapter 11 for a discussion of how to use these graphics features.

Merge Codes

This feature, as explained in Chapter 14, displays a box with the codes used in setting up a mail merge.

End Field

This function is used to indicate the end of a special "secondary" merge file. This is explained in Chapter 14.

F10 Key

Functions	Executed by	Usage
1. Macro Define (R)	(Ctrl-F10)	Depends on needs
2. Macro (G)	(Shift-F10)	Depends on needs
3. Retrieve (B)	(Alt-F10)	Every day
4. Save (Bl)	(Ctrl-F10)	Every day

Macro Define

Macros are special files that execute a series of keystrokes. To create macros, you must use the Shell program (see Chapter 14).

Macro

If you've created any macros with the Shell function, this key will enable you to execute them.

Retrieve

The Retrieve function allows you to load a file into the current document. If you know the name of the file, Retrieve is a convenient way to load a file; if you don't remember the exact name, you're better off using the List Files option (F5). You can also use Retrieve to combine two files on the screen, or to bring in "boilerplate" paragraphs at a desired location in a document.

Save

This function allows you to save the current document to disk, so you can continue editing. When you press the (F10) key, if a filename is not yet assigned to the document, LetterPerfect prompts you in the lower-left corner of the screen with:

```
Document to be saved:
```

Enter the filename (up to eight characters in the main body of the file name, and three characters in the extension—which is separated from the main name by a period— then press (Enter) to save the file to disk. If you have saved the file before, LetterPerfect prompts you with the previously assigned file name in the form:

```
Document to be saved: [followed by previously
assigned filename]
```

Press (Enter) to save the document with its current name. If you wish to save it under a different filename, edit the current name, or type a new one, followed by (Enter). Unlike the Exit function, the Save function does not ask if you would like to leave LetterPerfect; rather, it leaves you in the current document.

F11 Key

(Available only on the Enhanced AT and PS/2 type keyboards).

Functions	Executed by	Usage
1. Reveal Codes (Bl)	(F11)	Every day

Reveal Codes

This is functionally equivalent to pressing (Alt-F3). The advantage here is that if you have an enhanced keyboard, you can initiate this function with a single keystroke.

F12 Key

(Available only on the Enhanced AT and PS/2 type keyboards.)

Functions	Executed by	Usage
1. Block (Bl)	(F12)	Every day

Block

As with the preceding, this is functionally equivalent to pressing (Alt-F4). Again, the advantage is that if you have an enhanced keyboard, you can initiate this function with a single keystroke.

Fast Keys

A third way to access LetterPerfect is to use the Fast Keys. These carry out the same functions as the menus and function keys, by are sometimes easier to remember. To use the fast keys, press and hold the (Ctrl) key, then press the specified letter. The fast keys are as follows:

Ctrl-a	Paste Block
Ctrl-b	Bold
Ctrl-c	Center
Ctrl-d	Date Text
Ctrl-e	Endnote Create
Ctrl-f	Base Font
Ctrl-g	Graphics Create
Ctrl-i	Italics
Ctrl-k	Copy
Ctrl-m	Move (Cut)

Ctrl-n	Normal Text
Ctrl-p	Preview (View Document)
Ctrl-r	Reveal Codes
Ctrl-s	Spell
Ctrl-t	Thesaurus
Ctrl-u	Underline
Ctrl-v	Characters

At this point, you've been shown every conceivable way to deploy LetterPerfect's arsenal of features and functions. In the next chapter, you'll find out how to customize the program to your personal needs and tastes.

Chapter 6

Personalizing LetterPerfect: Using the Setup Options

Highlights

- The screen
- The backup functions
- Units of Measure
- Document file location
- Initial Codes
- Menu bar activator
- Menu bar control
- F1 function
- Retrieved document format

Your Choice

LetterPerfect allows you to control a number of important functions concerning the appearance of the program, as well as certain defaults or "startup" options. Your choices are made via the Setup function, which can be accessed by pressing (Shift-F1) or F,T from the pull down menu. However you select the Setup function, LetterPerfect will display the screen shown in Figure 6.1.

Figure 6.1
LetterPerfect setup menu.

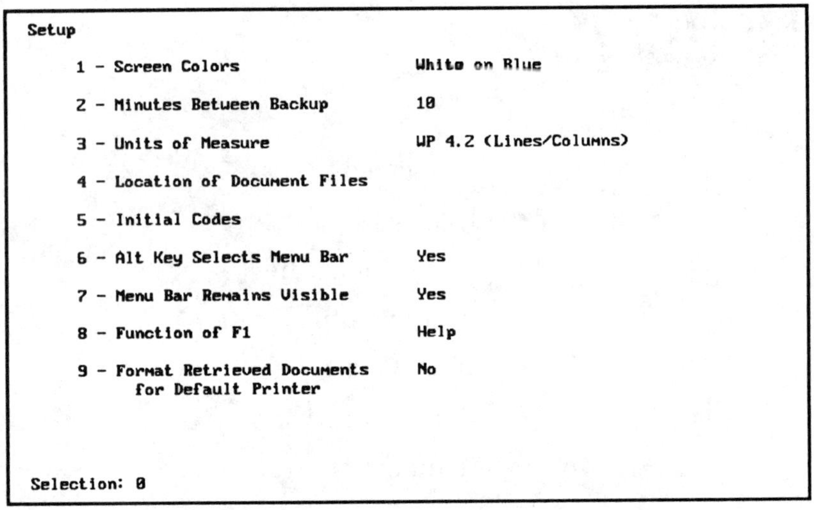

```
Setup

     1 - Screen Colors                 White on Blue

     2 - Minutes Between Backup        10

     3 - Units of Measure              WP 4.2 (Lines/Columns)

     4 - Location of Document Files

     5 - Initial Codes

     6 - Alt Key Selects Menu Bar      Yes

     7 - Menu Bar Remains Visible      Yes

     8 - Function of F1                Help

     9 - Format Retrieved Documents    No
           for Default Printer


Selection: 0
```

Each setup option is described below.

Screen Colors

When you select this option, LetterPerfect displays a screen with the choices shown in Figure 6.2. As you can see, there are two color choices, with white on blue being the default. Options 3 and 4 are for Liquid Crystal Displays (LCD) used on portables. The no intensity option is for models that do not have an intensity control. The plasma display option is for portables with gas plasma screen. The monochrome options is for computers with no color capabilities.

Figure 6.2 Screen color selector.

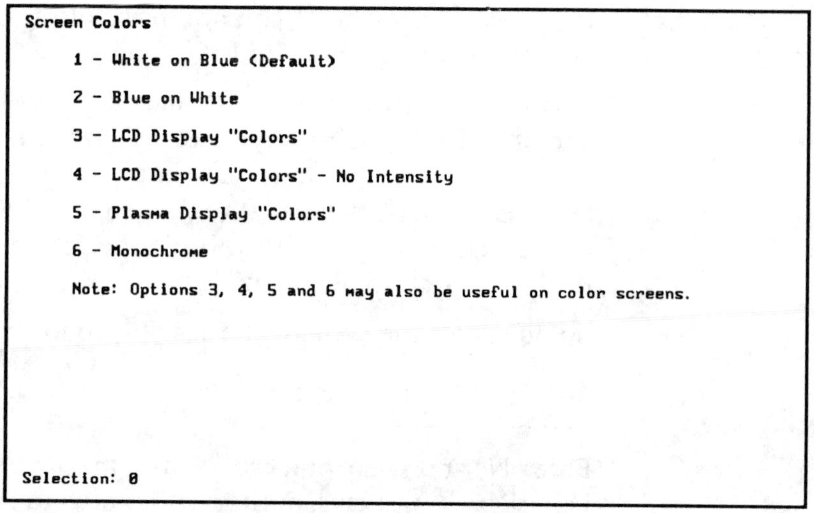

Hint: Experiment. Try the various options with your monitor and choose the one that looks the best. On a VGA color monitor, for example, options 3 and 5 present interesting alternatives (the no intensity LCD option is not readable). Mononchrome works well too.

When you make your selection, the Setup screen will be redisplayed.

Minutes Between Backup

LetterPerfect 1.0 can automatically back up your files as you go along, so that in the event of a hardware problem or power outage you won't lose any data. The default value is 10 minutes. The choice of a backup interval is up to you. You should make the time interval as short as you can tolerate—the backup process causes the system to pause while the backup is being made, and if you have a sluggish hard disk, you might find the process annoying. If you set the backup for once every 30 minutes, though, you're defeating the purpose of the protective mechanism—30 minutes worth of document is a lot to recreate from memory. (The author uses a three minute intervals and finds it satisfactory with an IBM Model 70. Even speedy writers can't generate all that much text in three minutes.) If your computer has a very slow hard disk, or you're using floppies, then backing up every couple of minutes may be too disruptive. Experiment. If you are insistent on turning off the backup altogether, set the value for 0.

It is important to understand that this is only *a temporary backup*, and it is only useful if you terminate the LetterPerfect session abnormally due to a power blackout or accidental crash. When you leave LetterPerfect normally, the backup file, called LP{LP}.BK1, will be *automatically deleted*. If you do terminate the session abnormally, the backup file, named LP{LP}.BK1, will be saved.

If you restart the system after leaving abnormally, the system asks:

```
Are other copies of LetterPerfect currently
running (Y/N)
```

Enter N, and then proceed. When the first timed backup occurs, LetterPerfect displays, at the bottom of your screen:

`Old Backup File Exists` **`1. R`**`ename;` **`2. D`**`elete`

You can either select to rename it at this time or delete the old backup (in which case you'll lose the backup file). If you rename it, you must use a unique name; LetterPerfect will inform you that it can't rename the file if one with the same name already exists.

If you do want to restore the contents in the backup file, retrieve it just as you would any file (it will reside in the same directory as your LetterPerfect program files), then give it a new name and place it in whatever directory it belongs.

Finally, note that the backup option does not provide any protection against failure to save your changes, or accidentally saving a bad copy of a document over a good original.

Hint: Save your work frequently as you go along. Develop an "F10" reflex, so you're updating your work every five minutes or so. Also, during long sessions on a computer with a hard disk, copy the files you are working on to a floppy at least once every 30 to 45 minutes. Even a hard disk can crash and leave you in the lurch with nothing to show for your time.

Units of Measure

LetterPerfect gives you five options for the units of measure on your status line and format menus.

Inches

This is the default, and for many people, it makes the most sense. The advantage is that you can pick up a ruler and decide where you want something to fall on a page. Most Americans think in terms of inches anyway, so when the Ln indicator says 3", you have a pretty good idea that the line is almost a third of the way down the page. The same holds with margins—it's easy to envision a letter with a one-inch margin on either side.

Centimeters

Use this if you are used to metric measures.

Points

A point is 1/72 of an inch. Typesetters and printers usually think in terms of this unit of measure. Not recommended for everyday use.

1200ths of an inch

This is used when you need hairsplitting precision. Definitely not recommended for everyday use.

WP 4.2 units

This is a holdover from the early days of WordPerfect, when measurements where made in terms of characters. Horizontal measurements refer to columns, and vertical measurements refer to lines. The measurements will depend on the font you are using. Unless you happen to find this approach appealing, you're better off with inches.

Location of Document Files

In the installation chapters, you learned how to start LetterPerfect from a separate data directory. You can also specify a data directory here, so that LetterPerfect will always know where to look for files after it loads. You can have many directories, too, and switch to them during word processing sessions by using option 4 of the List Files function (F,L or F5). If you fill in a location for your document files, make sure you specify the full path—drive and directory, as in C:\WORD.

Initial Codes

The initial codes feature allows you to set up any of the common formatting codes as you would in a regular editing session. The difference is that the codes that you enter here are used as the default codes for every new document you create. For example, if you always want to set the left margin to 1.5 inches and the top to 2 inches, set them up here. Thereafter, those margins are the defaults for each document you start.

When you select the Initial Code option from the menu, LetterPerfect will display the Reveal Codes screen (see Figure 6.3). Then invoke any of the following functions by means of the menu or the function keys:

Base font

Center Page

Justification (the program defaults to left justified)

Language

Left and Right Margins

Line Spacing

Page Number Position

Suppress (see Chapter 7, formatting)

Tab sets

Top and Bottom Margins

Various figure options

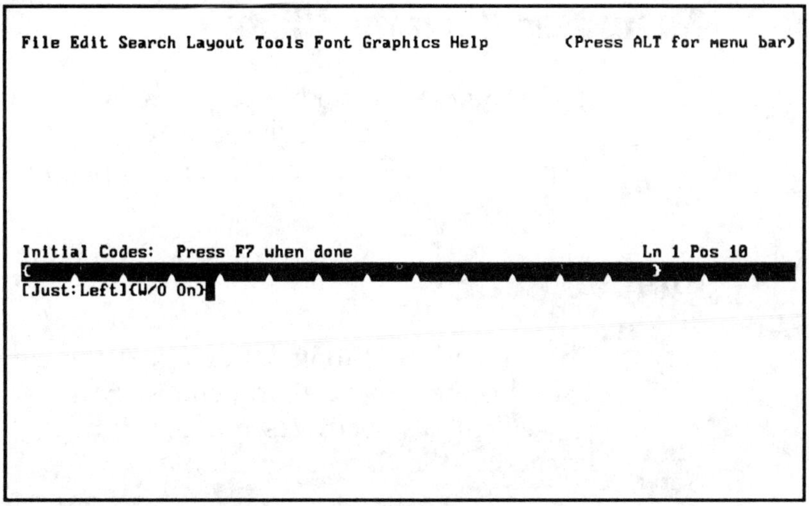

Figure 6.3 Initial codes input screen.

When you have finished adding codes, press F7 to return to the Setup screen.

(**Note:** The initial code default is left justification, widow and orphan protect, as shown in Figure 6.3. "Widows" are defined as the last line of a paragraph that prints out at the top of the next page. "Orphans" are the first lines of paragraphs that appear on the last line of a page. The widow/orphan protect feature prevents either from happening. It's hardwired into LetterPerfect, so you can't turn it off. Justification can be altered through the format menu, and you can insert a different type of justification code as an initial code—see Chapter 7, Formatting).

Alt Key Selects Menu Bar

If you don't want to be able to access the menu bar, enter No for this option. Even if you select No, and you also select No for the following option, you will be able to activate the menu bar by moving the mouse cursor to the top of the screen and pressing the right button.

Menu Bar Remains Visible

If you want the menu bar to be displayed at the top of the screen at all times, leave the default set to Yes. If you only want the menu bar displayed when you press Alt or the right mouse button, enter No.

Function of F1

The F1 key can either be assigned the cancel or help function. Cancel is the default. If you choose F1 to be the help function, the F3 key still also activates the help function. In that case, the ESC key adopts the Cancel function.

Format Retrieved Documents for Default Printer

When you save a document with LetterPerfect, it embeds certain information in an invisible "header." Part of that information concerns the type of printer that you selected when creating the document. If another user gives you a file that was formatted for a different printer, LetterPerfect will have two choices, depending upon what you indicated in this setup option.

Yes

LetterPerfect will reformat the document for your printer. If the document contains many fonts or attributes that your printer does not support, the output may not look the same as the output from the other user's printer.

No

LetterPerfect will try to match up the printer used to create the document with one on your list. If the printer is not on your list, LetterPerfect will warn you and then reformat the document for the printer that you have currently selected.

The LetterPerfect printer concept is discussed more fully in Chapter 9, which covers font usage and selection.

Section III

Document Processing

Chapter 7

Creating Documents With LetterPerfect

Highlights

- The Format menu
- Justification
- Line spacing
- Top/bottom margins
- Left/right margins
- Tabs
- Headers/footers
- Page numbering
- Paper size/type
- Center page (top/bottom)
- Document initial codes/base font

Onward

If you've been reading this book sequentially, you've built up a base of knowledge about how to navigate within LetterPerfect and how to use the function keys. If you're just tuning in and have no prior experience with LetterPerfect, you might want to quickly review Chapters 3 through 5.

In this chapter, you'll learn how to format documents; that is, how to set up the basic attributes that determine how a printed page will look. As you read along, you should be sure to input text and manipulate it according to the step-by-step instructions.

In addition to formatting, the chapter covers the use of endnotes (somewhat out of place here, but related to creating documents, and similar to headers and footers, which are included with the format menu). The endnote feature allows you to place one or more numbered notes at the end of your text. The numbers appear as superscripts in your document.

The Format Menu

LetterPerfect allows you to alter a number of different aspects of your document. When you select the Format option, (L,F) or (Shift-F8), LetterPerfect displays the Format menu, which lists all of the program's formatting commands (see Figure 7.1).

Figure 7.1 Format menu options.

```
Format

     1 - Justification                        Left

     2 - Line Spacing                         1.12

     3 - Top/Bottom Margins                   1"        1"

     4 - Left/Right Margins                   1"        1"

     5 - Tabs                                 Rel: -1", every 0.5"

     6 - Header/Footer

     7 - Page Numbering                       No page numbering

     8 - Paper Size                           8.5" x 11"
               Type                           Standard

     9 - Center Page (top to bottom)          No

     I - Document Initial Codes/Base Font     Courier 10cpi

Selection: 0
```

IMPORTANT: In order for several of the options to work, they must be executed while the cursor is at the very top of the document, and positioned before text or formatting codes such as bold, underline, etc. If you have done anything to a document before entering the desired formatting codes, the best way to ensure proper placement at the top is to press:

(Home) + (Home) + (Home) + (Up Cursor)

This combination places the cursor at the very beginning of the document, ahead of all existing codes.

Justification

When you select number 1 from the Format options menu shown in Figure 7.1, LetterPerfect displays four options:

```
1 Left; 2 Center; 3 Right; 4 Full: 0
```

Here's what each one means (see Figure 7.2 for a comparison of each option).

Figure 7.2 From top to bottom: left, right, center, and full justification.

Where a calculator on the ENIAC is equipped with 18,000 vacuum tubes and weighs 30 tons, computers in the future may have only 1000 vacuum tubes and perhpas weigh only 1 1/2 tons. (Popular Mechanics, March 1949, p 258.)

Where a calculator on the ENIAC is equipped with 18,000 vacuum tubes and weighs 30 tons, computers in the future may have only 1000 vacuum tubes and perhpas weigh only 1 1/2 tons. (Popular Mechanics, March 1949, p 258.)

Where a calculator on the ENIAC is equipped with 18,000 vacuum tubes and weighs 30 tons, computers in the future may have only 1000 vacuum tubes and perhpas weigh only 1 1/2 tons. (Popular Mechanics, March 1949, p 258.)

Where a calculator on the ENIAC is equipped with 18,000 vacuum tubes and weighs 30 tons, computers in the future may have only 1000 vacuum tubes and perhpas weigh only 1 1/2 tons. (Popular Mechanics, March 1949, p 258.)

Left

The text is aligned with the left margin only. (In designer lingo, this alignment is referred to as "ragged right" or "rag right".)

Center

The text is centered between the left and right margins.

Right

Text is aligned with the right margin, leaving a ragged left margin (this alignment is not widely used for common word processing tasks).

Full

Text is aligned with both the left and right margin (this alignment is sometimes called "justified" in designer terms). Justified text has a more formal, typeset look. Books (like this one) are typically set in justified type, although "rag" right is perfectly acceptable for many types of publications.

Fully justified text poses several problems. First, depending on the line length, you may find wide spaces or "rivers" between words. Very short lines may look especially bad. The problem is accentuated with "monospaced" type fonts, those in which the spacing for each letter is the same. Most type fonts on today's printer's are monospaced, unless they're specifically designated as "proportional," meaning that the spacing of letters is proportional to their width. With a monospaced font, a "l" and an "m" occupy the same amount of space; with a proportional font, a "l" takes up less space than an "m" (see Figure 7.3). Proportional fonts are far better suited to justified text, and if you don't have access to any, you should probably stick to an unjustified right margin (see Figure 7.4).

Figure 7.3 Monospaced font (Courier, 10 Pitch), versus proportional font (Times Roman 10 pitch).

```
The phonograph...is not of any commerical value.
--Thomas A. Edison.
```

The phonograph...is not of any commerical value.
--Thomas A. Edison

Figure 7.4 Monospaced paragraph (top) versus proportionally-spaced paragraph (bottom). Notice the extra-wide spacing in the monospaced paragraph. In contrast, the proportionally-spaced paragraph is much more evenly and tightly spaced.

```
Where a calculator on the ENIAC is equipped with
18,000 vacuum tubes and weighs 30 tons, computers in
the future may have only 1000 vacuum tubes and perhpas
weigh only 1 1/2 tons.

(Popular Mechanics, March 1949, p 258.)
```

Where a calculator on the ENIAC is equipped with 18,000 vacuum tubes and weighs 30 tons, computers in the future may have only 1000 vacuum tubes and perhpas weigh only 1 1/2 tons.

(Popular Mechanics, March 1949, p 258.)

A second problem with full justification is that it tends to create more hyphenation. When a paragraph contains multiple hyphenations, the hyphens can create a visual effect called a "ladder," which is considered poor graphic form.

Finally, if you ever plan to import one of your documents into a desktop publishing program for fancy production, justification may cause all sorts of problems.

Line Spacing

Use this option to control the amount of spacing between lines. The default setting is 1, for single spacing. Enter 1.5 for one-and-a-half spacing, 2 for double spacing, etc. You can enter fractions, too, and LetterPerfect will convert them to the decimal equivalent. For example, 1 1/8 will be converted to 1.12.

Note that only text *after* a line spacing setting reflects the new value. If you change from single to double spacing at the beginning of line 10 of a document, only text from that point forward will be doublespaced; text on lines 1 through 9 will be single spaced (or whatever spacing setting had been previously selected). Thus, if you want an entire document's spacing to be double, triple, or some other value than single, make sure that you enter a value for Line Spacing while the cursor is on the top line, upper left-hand corner. If you have a two-line title or headline and want it to be single spaced, start the new spacing command underneath the title.

You can change spacing as many times as you like throughout the course of the document. A single-spaced, indented paragraph is often useful for offsetting quotes in a double-spaced document. To create one, position the cursor beneath the last double-spaced line before the quote, enter a value of 1 for Line Spacing, then press L,N or (Shift-F4) to indent the paragraph. When you finish the quote, press (Enter) to break the indent and enter a value of 2 for the Line Spacing.

Experiment with the Line Spacing option a bit. You'll soon find it's one of the most frequently used options in your tool kit of LetterPerfect functions.

Top/Bottom Margins

Use this option to control how much space appears above and below the text. The first value refers to the top setting, the second to the bottom margin (see Figure 7.1). Note that the Top/Bottom Margin option sets the amount of space above and below the text for the rest of the document, unless you change the setting on a subsequent page.

Left/Right Margins

The left value refers to the left margin, and the right value controls the right margin. These margins settings, as with Line Spacing, only effect text beneath the changed setting. If you change the margins midway down a page, the new settings will not be reflected in the text on the top part of the page. Also, as with Line Spacing, you can change margins as many times as you want in a document—margin settings will remain in effect until new margin values are added.

To change the margins for an entire document, make sure that the cursor is in the upper left-hand corner of the top line of the first page. Remember, only text *after* a margin setting will have the desired placement on the page. Try setting a few different margins before going on to the next topic.

Tabs

When you select this option, LetterPerfect displays the tab ruler at the bottom of the document screen (see Figure 7.5). The tab ruler is a key to formatting LetterPerfect documents. The default setting is one left-aligned tab every half inch (different units of measure will have different tab set values—see Chapter 6).

Figure 7.5 Tab ruler.

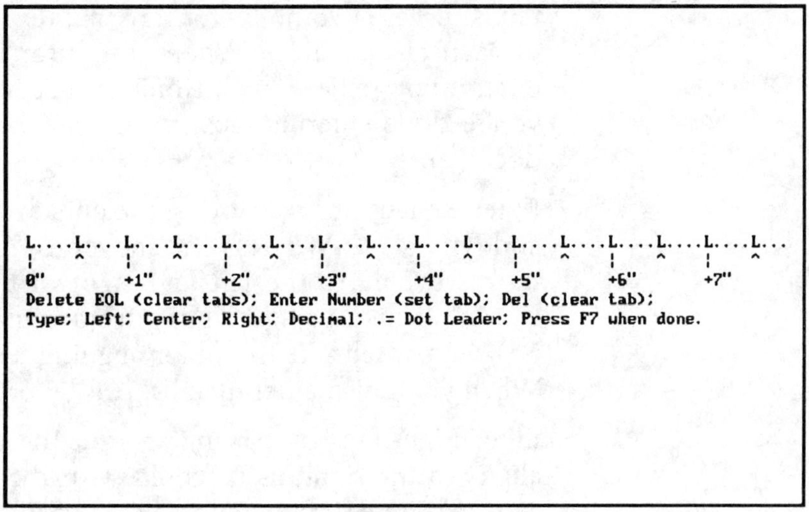

As you can see from Figure 7.5, each tab is marked with an "L" above the ruler. In addition to left-aligned tabs, LetterPerfect supports center, right-aligned, and decimal-aligned tabs, with or without dot leaders, or you can combine any or all of these into a single tab ruler. The tab settings can be altered as follows:

Delete all tabs from the cursor position to the end of the line by pressing (Ctrl-End). You can use the (Ctrl-End) function from any point along the ruler.

Delete individual tabs by moving the cursor to a specific tab, then pressing the (Del) key.

Select Type of tab. When you type T, LetterPerfect gives you the option of Absolute or Relative tabs. Absolute tabs are measured from the left edge of the paper, and remain at the same position regardless of changes in the margin. In contrast, relative tabs change as the left margin changes. This maintains a uniform distance between the tab and the margin. The type of tab is indicated on the main format menu screen as Absol or Rel.

Enter Left tabs by moving the cursor to each tab position you want to create and typing L, or by typing the number for the tab position (e.g., 2.3). The numbers will appear underneath the tab ruler on the right side as you type them. When you press (Enter), a left tab is placed at the desired position. A left tab is the most common form of tab; text is pushed to the right of each tab position. When you enter L's, you're really just customizing the conventional effect of the tab key. When you're done entering tabs, press (F7) twice to return to your document.

Enter Center tabs by moving the cursor to the desired position and typing a C. Whereas text moves to the right of a Left tab, it moves evenly to the left and right of a center tab. In other words, it's like using LetterPerfect's centering function (Shift-F6). Center tabs are useful for aligning text in lists and reports. When you finish entering tabs, exit by pressing (F7) twice.

Enter Right tabs by placing an R at the desired tab stop. Text aligns to the right, as it would with the Flush Right function (Alt-F6). Press (F7) two times when you've entered all your tabs.

Enter Decimal tabs by typing D at the desired tab stops. A decimal tab aligns text to the left of a decimal point. This is useful for aligning columns of numbers. As with all tab sets, press (F7) twice to return to your document.

Enter Dot Leaders by pressing the period (.) key at any tab setting (Left, Center, Right, or Decimal). The tab set position will be highlighted. To create a line of dot leaders, highlight a series of tabs. Then press (F7) two times to return to the document.

Each time you press (Tab) while creating a document, a dot leader is placed between the tab stops. This is useful for creating telephone lists, price lists, and other lists in which separate columns of data are made easier to read with leaders (see Figure 7.6).

Figure 7.6 Sample of dot leaders.

```
Product                                                    Price
________________________________________________________________

Computers

Model 100. . . . . . . . . . . . . . . . . . . . . . . . .$1,250
Model 200. . . . . . . . . . . . . . . . . . . . . . . . .$1,850
Model 300. . . . . . . . . . . . . . . . . . . . . . . . .$2,250
Model 400. . . . . . . . . . . . . . . . . . . . . . . . .$2,750
Model 500. . . . . . . . . . . . . . . . . . . . . . . . .$3,250
Model 600. . . . . . . . . . . . . . . . . . . . . . . . .$4,450
```

IMPORTANT: Only text *after* a tab setting will be affected by changes you've made to the tab ruler. Also, make sure that you make your tab changes at the beginning of a line; otherwise, you may not get the expected results. If you insert a new tab setting into a document, all subsequent text with tabs will be affected until you restore the original tab setting.

Header/Footer

A header is a line of type that appears at the top of a page; a footer is a line of type on the bottom of a page (see Figure 7.7).

Figure 7.7 Sample header and footer line.

Getting Started with LetterPerfect 08/06/90

INTRODUCTION

AN OLD TRUISM REVISITED

Two thousand years ago, the ancient Chinese philosopher, Lao Tzu, wrote the memorable phrase, "Reversal is the movement of the Way." Far more than mystical gibberish, this phrase simply says, "When anything reaches its maximal state, any further change will be in the opposite direction. For instance, the peak of daylight means that the next moment will represent an inevitable movement towards darkness. Similarly, the greatest moment of darkness heralds a steady movement towards the light of dawn."

The same applies to software. The trend in just about every genre has been increasing complexity and size. Take word processing--many packages started off as simple programs occupying a single disk. Today's monsters, with their advanced features and desktop publishing capabilities, now gobble up as much as four or five <u>megabytes</u> of precious hard disk space (that's 11 to 14 low-density 5 1/4 disks!). Manuals, too, have ballooned in size, with some tomes weighing in at 1,000 pages or more. How much more can our bookshelves stand?

The good news is that "reversal of the Way" seems to be in the winds, at least in terms of word processing software, as evidenced by WordPerfect Corp.'s simplified program, LetterPerfect. If you're the kind of person who needs to type memos, letters, basic reports, etc, and has no need to create

Introduction 1 Rev: A

A header or footer might contain the title of a manuscript, chapter name, and/or its author, the date, a draft number, or anything else that is appropriate. Headers and footers have been combined in this section, because they are identical in use, except for their placement on the page.

When you select the Header option, LetterPerfect prompts you with:

`1 Header; 2 Footer; 3 Suppress: 0`

The third option is used to suppress the printing of a header or footer on the current page (the page that is on the screen).

For the purposes of this discussion, only the Header option will be described—the mechanics of creating a footer are identical.

When you select the Header option, LetterPerfect displays three options:

`1 Discontinue; 2 Create; 3 Edit: 0`

Discontinue

Whereas the Suppress option will prevent the printing of a header or footer on the current page, the Discontinue option prevents the printing of a header or footer for the rest of the document.

Create

When you select this option, LetterPerfect will display a blank screen. Type your header or footer just as you would for any document, using any of the formatting or font features. You can use many of LetterPerfect's formatting functions. For example:

> **Center** L,C or (Shift-F6) centers the text of the header or footer.
>
> **Flush Right** L,L or (Alt-F6) aligns the header or footer text with the right margin.
>
> **Bold** O,B or (F6) bolds text.
>
> **Underline** O,U or (F8) underlines text.
>
> **Date** T,T or (Shift-F5) + 1 can be used to insert today's date. T,C or (Shift-F5) + 2 can be used to insert a date code so that the header or footer always displays the current date.

In addition, you can enter a unique page numbering code, ^B (Ctrl-B). Whenever LetterPerfect encounters ^B, it increments the page number. While LetterPerfect provides standard page-numbering options (see below), the ^B command allows you to customize the placement of the page number—wherever ^B appears, the page number appears. To insert a ^B in your header, use the menu (O,C) or (Ctrl-V) to activiate the Character function. When you issue the menu or keyboard command, LetterPerfect will display the word Key = in the bottom corner. Hold the Ctrl key and press the "B" key. ^B will then appear in your header or footer.

You can also add other text around a ^B. For example, if you want to link the chapter or section number of a report with the page number, you might include:

1-^B

in your header or footer line. This labels pages 1-1, 1-2, 1-3, etc. For the next section, you can change the header to include:

2-^B

so that pages are numbered 2-1, 2-2, 2-3, etc.

Alternately, you could use a colon (:) instead of a dash, or spell out Page, as in:

1:^B or

Page ^B

The former produces pages numbered 1:1, 1:2, 1:3, etc, while the latter prints pages numbered Page 1, Page 2, Page 3, and so on.

When you finish creating the text for your header or footer, press (F7) to return to your document.

HINT: Keep your headers and footers as short as possible; otherwise they become less effective. Also, if they consist of too many lines, you might have to increase your top and bottom margins to keep header/footer and body text from running together.

Edit

If you want to edit a footer or header later on, place your cursor at the top of the document, then select the Edit function. Change the copy as you like, then press (F7) to exit to Format options menu.

Bear in mind that like most of the formatting options, all headers and footers should be created when the cursor is at the top of the document, before your text; otherwise they may not print where you expect them. Also, headers and footers cannot be seen on the screen, except for print preview F,P + 3, or (Shift-F7) + 3.

Finally, if you create a header or footer that appears in, say, the left hand corner of the page, and then select a page numbering position in the same location, the header or footer will overprint the page number. If you want to have a page number appear in the same area that the header or footer would, leave an extra line above your header or below your footer.

Try creating a header or footer of your own before you go on to the next section.

Page Numbering

In order to print a page number, you must enter a page number position. When you select option 7 from the Format menu, LetterPerfect displays a number of page number positions, as shown in Figure 7.8.

Figure 7.8 Page numbering options.

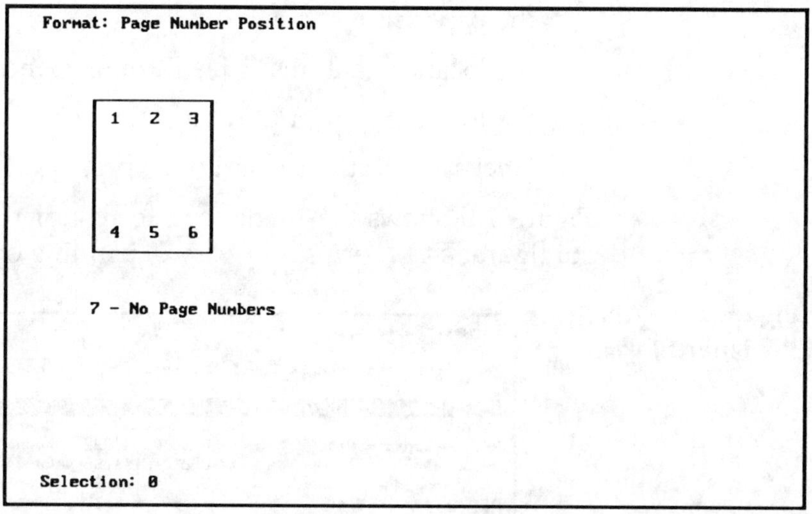

Enter the number corresponding to the desired page number position, and the display will return to the Format menu. All pages will print with the page number in the selected position until you issue a new page-number command.

Like many of the formatting options, a page numbering setting placed directly *after* a code such as Bold will produce a bold page number. The easiest way to avoid such problems is to ensure that the page number command appears at the very top of the page or document by pressing the (Home) key three times followed by the (Up Cursor) before using Page Numbering function.

Paper Size/Type

The Paper Size option allows LetterPerfect to determine correctly the number of lines to be placed on a page. When you select the option, you will be presented with a screen that contains all the predefined forms for your printer. A form is a specification that tells your printer certain key attributes about the paper you intend to feed it. A form designates:

the type (envelope, labels, etc.)

the orientation (whether it feeds vertically or horizontally, referred to as "portrait" and "landscape," respectively, in technical jargon)

the paper size

the location (automatic feed versus manual insertion)

the font type (print portrait or landscape)

label specifications (for label types)

Figure 7.9 shows the predefined forms for the HP LaserJet III (the configuration of forms may vary depending on your printer).

Figure 7.9
Predefined forms.

Format: Paper Size/Type

Paper type and Orientation	Paper Size	Location	Font Type	Labels
1 X 1 Labels - Wide	4" x 1"	Continuous	Portrait	1 x 1
3 X 10 Labels	8.5" x 11"	Continuous	Portrait	3 x 10
A4 Envelopes - Wide	8.58" x 4.33"	Manual	Landscape	
A4 Labels	8.27" x 11.69"	Continuous	Portrait	2 x 7
A4 Standard	8.27" x 11.69"	Continuous	Portrait	
A4 Standard - Wide	11.69" x 8.27"	Continuous	Landscape	
Envelope - Wide	9.5" x 4"	Manual	Landscape	
Half Sheet	5.5" x 8.5"	Manual	Portrait	
Half Sheet - Wide	8.5" x 5.5"	Manual	Landscape	
Standard	8.22" x 12"	Continuous	Portrait	
Standard	8.5" x 11"	Continuous	Portrait	
Standard	8.5" x 14"	Continuous	Portrait	
Standard - Wide	11" x 8.5"	Continuous	Landscape	
Standard - Wide	14" x 8.5"	Continuous	Landscape	
[ALL OTHERS]	Width ≤ 8.5"	Manual		

1 Select; 2 Edit; N Name Search: 1

The predefined forms should cover almost all word processing needs. If you do have a specialized task, you might want to modify a form by using the Edit feature. This allows you to change the paper location (manual, continuous, or, if you have a sheet feeder, the paper bin number—see the LetterPerfect manual for more details). In addition, Edit allows you to indicate whether or not LetterPerfect should prompt you to load the paper (unnecessary if the paper is loaded into a tray and always there), or to adjust the printed area of the form (in terms of vertical and horizontal position—again, see your manual for details).

To select a form, highlight it by moving the cursor or the mouse. When you press (Enter) or quickly press the left button two times in succession, the form will be selected, and the Format menu will be redisplayed. Note that the selected form will also be indicated on the Format menu following option 8. Figure 7.10 shows the Format menu after selecting an envelope form.

Figure 7.10 Format menu with envelope selected.

```
Format

     1 - Justification                        Left

     2 - Line Spacing                         1

     3 - Top/Bottom Margins                   1"        1"

     4 - Left/Right Margins                   1"        1"

     5 - Tabs                                 Rel; -1", every 0.5"

     6 - Header/Footer

     7 - Page Numbering                       No page numbering

     8 - Paper Size                           9.5" x 4"
                 Type                         Envelope

     9 - Center Page (top to bottom)          No

     I - Document Initial Codes/Base Font     Courier 10cpi

Selection: 0
```

Center Page (top to bottom)

As its name implies, this option centers texts vertically on a page. It is useful for centering letters, creating title pages, and creating tables.

Note: To make sure that you center all text vertically, press:

(Home) + (Home) + (Up Cursor)

before selecting the Center Page option. LetterPerfect defaults to No for this option; when you select option 1 of the Page format option menu, Center Page automatically changes to Yes. Selecting Yes, however, centers only the current page. At the next page, the Center Page option is again turned off again. In other words, you have to select Center Page for each page in your document.

Document Initial Codes/Base Font

The Initial Font option allows you to override the initial font you assigned during the printer installation—for the current document. It is quite similar to selecting a different base font from the font menu, O,F or (Ctrl-F8). You should use the initial font option when you want to make a change throughout a document. When you select the Initial Codes suboption, LetterPerfect will display the same Reveal Codes screen that was used to establish initial codes during setup. The Base Font option displays a list of the fonts your printer is capable of using—see Chapter 9 for details.

Endnotes

Endnotes are like footnotes, except that they are compiled at the end of a document. They can be used to explain text, cite sources, etc.

Figure 7.11 Endnote sample.

[X] bytes available on disk

To make additional space available, you have two options: 1) eliminate obsolete files from your disk or transfer them to floppies to clear up the space; or 2) only install the program files. By skipping the utility, help, speller, and shell files). By eliminating "drivers"[1] for hardware that you don't use, graphic samples, and the learning files, you can reduce the hard disk requirements to about 800K.

3. <u>Printer</u>

Before you can print with LetterPerfect, you must indicate what printer you're using[2] even if you do not have one connected to your computer at this time. You can always change your printer selection later.

* * *

1. Drivers are special files that enable your computer to properly use printers and other devices. LetterPerfect supplies drivers custom designed to take advanatge of all your printer's capabilities.

2. LetterPerfect supports more than 600 printers.

Creating an Endnote

Select:

L,R or (Ctrl-F7)

LetterPerfect will display the screen shown in Figure 7.11. The endnote number appears in the upper left hand corner, beginning with one. Type the note, using any of LetterPerfect's formatting features, then press (F7) to return to your document.

Figure 7.12 Endnote screen.

1.

Endnote: Press F7 when done Pg 1 Ln 1" POS 1.2"

The corresponding endnote number will also appear in your text. The next time you select the Endnote Create function, LetterPerfect will assign it number 2, and so on. If you delete an endnote (to do so, simply put your cursor under the number and press the delete key), LetterPerfect will ask if you want to:

```
Delete [Endnote:X]? No Yes
```

Where X is the number over your cursor. If you delete a number, LetterPerfect will automatically renumber the endnotes. Also, if you create a new endnote before note number 1, LetterPerfect will automatically designate the new note as number 1, and increase all subsequent note numbers by a value of one.

Editing an Endnote

Select

L,E of (Ctrl-F7) + 2

LetterPerfect will ask you for the number you wish to edit (the lowest numbered note to the right of the cursor). If you wish to edit a different endnote, type in the number and press (Enter). The endnote in question will then be displayed. Edit it and press (F7) to conclude the editing operation and return to your document.

Putting It All Together

At this point, you know quite a bit about LetterPerfect—how to navigate in it, how to use the menu system, function keys, fast keys, and how to format pages. If you experimented with the various features as you read along, you might have even created a document or two. If not, now is a good time to do so. Try the following exercise, in which you will create a letter or a memo. The memo is particularly important, for in creating it you'll review many of the features and commands you've learned so far. It's worth putting a little bit of time into creating your memo, because you can use it again in Chapter 8, when you learn how to edit a document.

Type a letter

1. Place the cursor where you want the date. If you're using a block format, the date will be flush with the left margin. Press:

   T,T or (Shift-F5) + 1

   and the date will appear.

   Alternately, if you want the date two-thirds of the way across the page or so, use the (Spacebar) key to move the cursor to the desired location. Press:

   T,T or (Shift-F5) + 1

   and the date will be displayed at the cursor location.
2. Press (Enter) as many times as necessary to place the addressee at the desired location. Then type in his or her name, title, company, city, state, and ZIP code. Press (Enter) twice.
3. Type in "Dear so-and-so," and press (Enter) twice.
4. Enter the body of the letter. If you indent paragraphs, use the tab key. If you intend to leave them in block form, just type. To separate paragraphs with an extra space, press (Enter) at the end of the paragraph.
5. Finish the letter with an appropriate closure.
6. Print your letter by turning on your printer, and pressing:

   F,P + 1 or (Shift-F7) + 1

   (make sure your printer is on line first).
7. If you wish, you can save the letter by pressing:

   F,X or (F7) + Y + [file name] + N

Type a memo

This exercise is most effective if you can type at least two pages of memo text. You might actually want to get an old memo and use it for copy. Better yet, compose a memo that you actually need to submit. That way, the exercise will yield a document that is immediately useful.

Memo formats tend to be idiosyncratic, but the following is commonly in use today. You can modify it as you see fit.

1. Set the page numbers to the bottom of every page by entering:

   L,F + 7 + 5 + (F7) or (Shift-F8) + 7 + 5 + (F7)

2. Create a footer by entering:

   L,F + 6 + 2 + 2 or (Shift-F8) + 6 + 2 + 2

   Then enter a couple of words describing the subject of the memo in the footer text. Next, move the cursor flush right by pressing:

   L,L or (Alt-F6)

   and enter today's date by pressing:

   T,T or (Shift-F5) + 1

   Finally, return to the document by pressing:

   (F7) + (F7)

   The footer will contain the subject matter on the left, and the date on the right. The page number will appear in the middle, because you selected "bottom middle" placement earlier in step 1.

3. Enter the tab ruler screen and delete existing tabs. Press:

   L,F + 5 + (Ctrl-End) or (Shift-F8) + 5 + (Ctrl-End)

   If you set your Units of Measure to inches during set up (or didn't change the LetterPerfect defaults, which are already set to inches), type:

   0.6 + (Enter)

   This will place a tab at 0.6 inches (assuming you've set your units of measure to inches). Return to your document by pressing (F7) twice.

4. Enter the heading:

   L,C O,B MEMORANDUM O,B (Enter) (Enter) or (Shift-F6) (F6) MEMORANDUM (F6)

(Enter) + (Enter)

Here's what you just did:

L,C or (Shift-F6) instructed LetterPerfect to center subsequent text. When you pressed (Enter), you turned off the centering code.

O,B or (F6) key told LetterPerfect to bold all following characters. The second time you issued the command from the menu or keyboard, you instructed LetterPerfect to turn off the bold code, so all subsequent characters would appear in the normal font.

5. Change the line spacing to double space by entering:

   L,F + 2 + 2 + (Enter) + (F7) or (Shift-F8) + 2 + 2 + (Enter) + (F7)

6. Start bold by pressing:

   O,B or (F6)

   then type:

   To:

   Turn off bold by pressing:

   O,B or (F6)

   Now press:

   (Tab)

   and type in the recipient's name + (Enter).

7. Turn on bold again by pressing:

   O,B or (F6)

   then type:

   From:

   and toggle bold off by pressing:

   O,B or (F6)

   Press:

   (Tab)

   Type in your name or some other sender's name + (Enter).

8. Press:

   O,B or (F6)

   then type:

   Date:

   and press:

   O,B or (F6)

   again to put the word "Date" in bold and press:

   (Tab)

   Press:

   T,T or (Shift-F5) + 1

   to insert today's date.

9. Press:

   O,B or (F6)

   then type:

   Re:

   Press:

   O,B or (F6)

   Press:

   (Tab)

   Type in the contents of the memo + (Enter).

10. Hold the dash key so that you create a line of dashes up to position 7.2 inches (if you haven't changed the default margins of Left = 1 inch, Right = 1 inch). This will separate the ID part of the memo. Press the (Enter) key twice to space down to the body of the text.

11. Turn single spacing back on by entering:

    L,F + 2 + 1 + (Enter) + (F7) or (Shift-F8) + 2 + 1 + (Enter) + (F7)

12. Type the body of your memo. While doing so, try the following: indent a paragraph by an equal amount left and right by pressing (Shift-F4). Indent a couple of paragraphs from the left by using the (F4) key. Remember, the words will continue to

indent as part of the same paragraph until you hit the (Enter) key. When you are ready to return to the full margin, press (Enter).

13. Print the memo by entering:

    F,P + 1 or (Shift-F7) + 1

    (make sure your printer is on line first).

14. Save the file (you'll need it for Chapter 9) by entering:

    F,X or (F7) + Y + [file name] + N

Congratulations! At this point, you've used many of the basic features that you'll need for everyday word processing. The next chapter explores LetterPerfect's powerful editing features. Naturally, you don't have to wait until you finish a document to edit it. In fact, most people learn to format, compose, and edit a document as they go along, so that the distinction between document creation and editing begins to blur and fade away. Document formatting/creation and editing have been separated into individual chapters here for the sake of instruction—it's a bit much to take it all in at once. Once you begin using the program, you'll find yourself using a variety of tools, ranging from initial formatting options to cut and paste features.

If you want to take a break and absorb the material in this chapter, this is a good time to do so. Otherwise, continue reading and experimenting—the more time you spend experimenting with LetterPerfect 1.0 and using it to create actual documents, the more quickly you'll become a Letter Perfectionist.

Chapter 8

Editing Tools

Highlights

- Editing text
- Block functions
- Deleting/cutting and pasting, inserting text
- Search rules and functions
- Search and replace text
- Search and replace codes
- Using reveal codes

Your Editing Tool Kit

There are many ways to edit a document, some of which you've already encountered earlier, such as with Reveal Codes and the Block functions. In this chapter, we revisit those and other features and explore how to use them to alter your text. The chapter is divided into two basic sections: editing text, and editing formats/appearances. The former refers to word, sentence, and paragraph changes; the latter concerns modifying various format settings.

Editing Text

The real power of a word processor is the ability to juggle words, sentences, paragraphs, and pages easily and instantly without resorting to scissors and tape, correction tape, or correction fluid.

This involves six basic actions: deleting text; electronically cutting and pasting text; copying text; inserting text; searching for text; and searching for and replacing text. This section explains how to use each action in editing a document.

As with other materials in this book, you'll learn the fastest if you experiment with these actions yourself. If you created a memo in Chapter 7, retrieve it with the following command sequence:

F,R + Name you gave to the file + (Enter)

or

(Shift-F10) + Name You Gave to the File + (Enter)

(If you haven't created a memo, you're best off returning to Chapter 7 and doing so before proceeding—it's worth the effort.) As you read through this chapter, try modifying your text with the features described. Since you'll need your memo for various experiments, *don't* resave the memo under the same name after you've made modifications. That way you can call up the original version again and again, keeping it intact. If, during the course of your experimentation, your memo gets changed too much to be of use, press:

F,X or (F7) + N + N

which will clear the screen. Then recall the original memo, as you did above.

Block Functions

Deleting Text

You already know how to delete text with the (Del) key and the backspace key. The block function is a much more efficient way to delete large chunks of text. (Some techniques for using the Block function were described in the chapters on using the menu system and function keys. Since Block is so important, the basic functions are recapped below, along with some additional information.) Place the cursor at the beginning of the words to be deleted. Press E,B or (Alt-F4) (or use the mouse by pointing to the first character of the block, pressing and holding the left button, then "dragging" the mouse down to the last character in the block and releasing the left button). However you do it, the block will appear highlighted. Note that you can block "backwards" too, from the last character to the first character.

As you "paint" (highlight) the block, the words "Block on" flash on and off in the lower left hand corner of the screen. Once you've included all desired characters within the block, press the (Del) key. LetterPerfect prompts you with:

```
Delete Block? (Y/N) No
```

If you enter a Y, the block is removed from the document. If you didn't really want to delete the block, you can undo it by pressing the (F1) key. When you press the (F1) key, the block reappears, highlighted. Select 1 for Restore to bring the block back into the document. (LetterPerfect stores your last three deletions; if you've deleted text after deleting the block, you may have to select 2 Previous Deletion.)

An alternative way of deleting a block of text is to save it to disk before you delete it from the document. To do so, press F,S or (F10) after the block is painted. The flashing "block on" will be replaced by the words:

```
Block Name:
```

Enter the name you wish to assign the block and press (Enter). The block will be saved in a separate file under the name you entered.

After the saving function is complete, the block will be turned off automatically. If you want to highlight the same block and delete it, press E,B or (Alt-F4) to turn on the block function, then press (Ctrl-Home) twice followed by the (Del) key.

Cutting and Pasting Text

Electronic cutting and pasting is one of the most powerful word processing tools at your disposal. Try this. Pick a sentence or paragraph that you want to move to another location of the document. Move the cursor to the first character, and turn on the block function by pressing E,B or (Alt-F4). Move the cursor to the end of the text you want to cut and paste (this highlights the block) and press:

E,B or (Ctrl-F4) + 1

The block then disappears from your document. (Actually, it hasn't been deleted—it's stored in memory.) The screen displays:

```
Move cursor; press Enter to retrieve
```

Move the cursor to the exact location where you want the block of text placed and press (Enter). Voila! The text reappears in its new location.

You can use this mechanism to cut and paste as little or as much text as you like. It's generally faster to retype a word or two, rather than cut and paste them into their new location, but the choice is yours.

Copying Text

Sometimes you might want to repeat a headline, a sentence, or a paragraph. For example, you might have a cautionary statement, a disclaimer, or some other text that gets repeated later in the text.

Instead of retyping it, you can block off the text, as above, but instead of pressing:

E,B or (Ctrl-F4) + 1

which cuts the block, press:

E,C (Ctrl-F4) + 2

which leaves the original block in place. A copy of the block is tucked away in memory, to be inserted into the document when you place your cursor at the desired location and press (Enter).

Try copying a paragraph from the top of your memo to the bottom. As you can see, it's a lot easier than retyping the material.

Inserting Text

Cutting and pasting is one way of inserting text into a particular location in a document. Another way is to retrieve previously saved paragraphs. There are two ways to do this.

1. Press F,R or (Shift-F10), type the name of the file containing the text, and press (Enter).
2. Press F,L or (F5), which lists all your files; use the cursor to highlight the file you want to insert, then press 1.

LetterPerfect will warn you that you're about to retrieve the file into a document on screen—which is nice if you happen to be working on a document and don't want an extraneous one dropped into the middle of it. But since you intend to retrieve the file into an existing document, indicate Y when LetterPerfect displays:

```
Retrieve into current document? No (Yes)
```

Either way, the file is placed in your document at the location of the cursor. The first method may be trickier, since it requires you to remember the filename. It also doesn't ask you to confirm the fact that you're about to insert text into the current document. This can be dangerous; if you enter the wrong filename, you might wind up injecting a 75 page document into your two page memo, in which case you'll have to block off the entire invading document and press the (Del) key.

The second method has several advantages. First, you get a list of all files, in case you forgot the exact filename. Second, you can view any file without retrieving it, by selecting option 6—no mistaking your two-paragraph long file for your 75-page-long file (the number of bytes, also shown on the List Files screen, is a dead giveaway as to which is which).

As with many aspects of LetterPerfect, the choice of which method you use is a matter of personal preference. However you retrieve the text, the technique is very useful for bringing in previously created "boilerplate" material. For instance, let's say you have a standard paragraph, a disclaimer, that appears in all your contracts. The first time you create the contract, block off the disclaimer by typing E,B, (Alt-F4), or use the mouse, and then activate the save function—F,S or (F10). LetterPerfect prompts you in the lower left-hand corner of the screen to enter a block name. You might call it "DISCLAIM." (Keep file names as short as possible to still be meaningful.) Then, the next time you type a contract, when you reach the point where the disclaimer should be placed, insert "DISCLAIM," using either of the two methods described above.

Try it yourself with your own memo. Pick a paragraph, save it as a block, then retrieve it into another location. As you can see, inserting previously saved work is a highly efficient way to get your typing done.

Search for Text

You will often find it helpful to search for a particular word or phrase during your editing. If you've proofread from hard copy and have some specific changes, it is sometimes faster to search for the specific word or phrase than to use the (PgDn) key and cursor keys to find the text in question.

Let's say that, upon reflection, you decide to change the sentence reading, "In short, we find your product to be ill-conceived, cheaply produced, and totally unfit for the marketplace." In your hard copy, the sentence appeared on page 53, but you've deleted a number of paragraphs, so it will be tricky to find it with the GoTo command, S,G or (Ctrl-Home) + page #.

The solution? Search for key words in the sentence. The following procedure gives you step-by-step instructions for carrying out such a search.

Conducting a Search

You can initiate a search from the menu (S,F) or the function keys (F2). While in general using the menu versus the function keys is a matter of personal preference, in this case the author strongly recommends that you use the function key—as you'll see below, when you're looking for many instances of a word or phrase in a document, it is much more efficient to press (F2) than to press Alt to call up the menu, F for forward, and S for Search. To begin the search, press S,F or (F2), forward Search. When LetterPerfect displays:

```
-> Srch:
```

enter the words you want to find. You don't need to enter the whole sentence, just enough so LetterPerfect can make a match with your text. Besides, if you entered the whole sentence, you might make a typographical mistake, and LetterPerfect, in trying to make an exact match, would report:

```
* Not Found *
```

The goal, then, is to find the shortest possible chunk of the sentence that is specific enough for LetterPerfect to report a match. If you just type "In," LetterPerfect stops at the first instance (of which there are probably plenty), and you will have to repeat the search until you find the sentence. "In short" is better (unless you abuse the phrase). The word "ill-conceived" is also a good candidate, because it probably occurs only once in the document. From a standpoint of efficiency, "In short" would take you right to the beginning of the sentence, while "ill-conceived" would take you to the middle.

Whatever method you choose, enter the search criteria words *without* pressing (Enter). If you press (Enter), you add a hard return [HRt] code to your search criteria, which may cause LetterPerfect to come up empty-handed. Instead, press (S,F) (F2) or (Esc), and the search begins. The cursor stops at the first instance it considers a match. If it is not, press S,F or (F2) twice to continue. If LetterPerfect can't find a match, or any additional matches beyond the last one found, it indicates:

```
* Not Found *
```

Searching Rules

Two rules must be followed if Search is going to yield anything useful.

1. If you want to find a complete word, it must be separated by spaces. For example, if you are looking for "any," LetterPerfect will stop at "many," "anyway," and "zany." You must therefore enter a space, using the (Spacebar) before and after "any" to make it a discrete, searchable word.
2. LetterPerfect is somewhat "case-sensitive," meaning that it distinguishes between lower- and uppercase letters under certain circumstances. If you search for the word "horse," it stops at "Horse," even though you entered a lowercase "h." On the other hand, if you enter "Horse" for your search, LetterPerfect stops only for "Horse" with a capital "H."

Changing the Direction of the Search

You can search forward (from the current cursor location to the bottom of the document) by pressing (F2), or backwards (from the current cursor location to the top of the document) by pressing S,B or (Shift-F2). You can also reverse the search by using the menu. Sometimes LetterPerfect might report "* Not Found *" even when a match exists, because you are searching in the wrong direction. In other words, you are beyond the text you were seeking, and continue searching away from it.

One solution is to press (Home) + (Home) + (Up Cursor) before beginning a forward search (this takes you to the top of the document), or if you are near the end of the document, (Home) + (Home) + (Down Cursor) before starting a backwards search. In part, it's a matter of judgment; if you are reasonably sure you're near the text being sought, there may not be any need to go all the way back to the beginning or end of a long document. Take a chance that you're pointed in the right direction. The worst that can happen is that you'll have to repeat the search.

Finally, a shortcut for changing directions is to press the (Up Cursor) or (Down Cursor) keys after pressing the (F2) key. This changes the search to the opposite direction, starting with the current location of the cursor. Try it yourself. Press (F2), then alternate pressing the (Up Cursor) and (Down Cursor) keys. Notice how the arrow in front of the word "Srch:," which indicates the direction of the search, changes from right (forward Search) to left (backwards Search) and vice versa.

Repositioning the Cursor After a Search

It is often helpful to reposition the cursor to your original location after completing a search.

The express method is to press (Ctrl-Home) twice.

Your Turn

Now that you know the basics of searching, press (Home) + (Home) + (Up Cursor) and try a forward search with your memo. Check out the differences in searching for lower- and uppercase text.

Searching for and Replacing Text

Next to cutting and pasting, searching and replacing is one of most important advantages that a word processor has over conventional typewriters. Imagine what it would have been like in the olden days if you had been asked to write a major speech for the president of your company. At the last minute, the cranky old executive tells you to change all instances of "the company" to "the firm." And to provide clean copy, of course. Panic! Administer 5cc of correction fluid. Today, with the Replace function, relief is just a few keystrokes away.

Like Search, LetterPerfect's Replace function finds all words or phrases that match your search criteria. But it goes one step further and replaces the text with a word or phrase of your choice. This isn't to say that Replace is better than or eliminates the need for the Search function; both have their places in your editorial tool kit. When you want to hone-in on a word, Search is easier and quicker to use.

Using the Replace Function

To carry out a "global search and replace" operation—that is, replace every occurrence of a word or phrase in a text—carry out the following procedure:

1. Press (Home) + (Home) + (Home) + (Up Cursor) to place the cursor at the top of the document. As in the forward and backward Search feature described above, LetterPerfect can't locate all occurrences of a word or phrase if the cursor is already beyond the point in the document where the word or phrase resides. By starting at the top, you can't miss anything.
2. Press:

   S,R or (Alt-F2)

   LetterPerfect prompts you with:

   `w/Confirm (Y/N) No`

   If you press (Enter) to accept the default, No, LetterPerfect charges through your document, replacing every occurrence of the search criteria text (see step 3) with the specified replacement text (step 4). If you press Y for Yes, LetterPerfect stops at each occurrence it finds and ask if you want to replace the text or not. If you enter Y, your text is substituted and LetterPerfect continues looking through the document for the next occurrence.

   While it is certainly faster to search and replace without confirming each choice, it's also much more dangerous. First, let's say you made a mistake. Instead of telling LetterPerfect to find the word "any," with a space before the "a" and a space after the "y," you just told it to search for the word "any" with no leading or trailing spaces. Then let's say you instructed LetterPerfect to replace "any" with "all." As explained above in the section on Search, without spaces in front and in back of "any," LetterPerfect would consider "many," anyway," and "zany" to be matches. As a result, when it replaced "any" with "all," your document would acquire the word "mall," and the nonsense words "allway" and "zall."

   Another reason to confirm the Replace operation is that there are times when you might only want to selectively substitute text. For example, you might want to leave some occurrences of the search text as is, for stylistic variation. Or, you might have a word that is used in two different senses. Let's say you're writing a computer manual, and you start off designating the carriage return key "(Return)." Later, you decide to refer to the carriage return key as the "(Enter)" key. There are plenty of contexts in which "return" means "to go back to," rather than the carriage return key, such as "to return to the document screen press..." If you indiscriminately replace all occurrences of "Return" with "Enter," your sentence will be rendered into gibberish: "to enter to the document screen press..." Therefore, when there is a possibility that the wrong text might be changed, select Confirm.

3. Once you've answered the Confirm question, the lower side of the screen prompts you with:

   ```
   -> Srch:
   ```

   as it did with the Search feature. You can change the direction of the search by pressing the up and the down arrows. An arrow pointing right means search and replace forward through the document from the current cursor position, while an arrow pointing left means search backwards through a document from the current cursor position.

   Enter the word or phrase that you wish to replace. All of the rules for upper-and lowercase described for Search apply to the Replace function as well. Do NOT press (Enter) after you make your entry—that includes a hard return code as part of the search. Instead, press S,R or (F2) or (Esc). LetterPerfect then prompts you with:

   ```
   Replace with:
   ```

   Enter the text, again *without* pressing (Enter), for that will insert a carriage return when the word or phrase is substituted for the word or phrase being sought. Press S,R (F2) or (Esc) to start the search.

Canceling a Search and Replace Operation

If you discover that you made a mistake and want to cancel the operation, press (F1). When you initiate the search again by pressing S,R or (Alt-F2), your last entry for the search part of the operation is displayed. You can modify it or accept it by pressing S,F or (F2) or (Esc). The replace selection, however, will be blank, and you must reenter it.

Searching and Replacing in a Block

If you know that the text you want replaced is located in only a small chunk of text, don't bother searching through the whole document. Rather, block off the text as described above with the E,B or (Alt-F4) keys, then conduct a search and replace operation. The mechanics for the search and replace are the same as for a regular "global" search and replace. When the cursor reaches the end of the block, the block turns off.

Returning to the Original Cursor Location

When LetterPerfect finishes a search and replace operation, the cursor remains at the last occurrence of the searched word. To return to wherever the cursor was before you began the operation, press (Ctrl-Home) twice.

Your Turn

The Replace function is one of LetterPerfect's most powerful editing features. Call up your memo and experiment with it. See if you can sharpen your sense of how the program decides whether any text in the document matches your search criteria.

Now you should have a good idea of how to use LetterPerfect's basic tools for editing text. As you begin to use them one by one, you'll develop a natural sense of how and when each tool should be used. The next set of editing tools enable you to modify the format and appearance of individual characters, words, or the document as a whole.

Editing Formats and Appearances

Changing Formats and Appearances from the Document Screen

In the first section, you saw how to use the Block functions to accomplish various tasks. In this section, you'll learn how to change the overall appearance of an entire block with one or two keystrokes. After you block off the selected text, whether it consists of one word, a sentence, a paragraph, a page, or 100 pages, you can use any of the following functions. Remember, to block off text, move the cursor to the beginning of the selected text, press (Alt-F4), then move the cursors. The block will be highlighted, and the words "Block on" will flash in the lower left-hand corner of the screen.

Center

Press L,C or (Shift-F6) and each line of the block will be centered. LetterPerfect asks you to confirm that you want to center the block before doing so. When LetterPerfect centers a block, it inserts a hidden [Cntr] code before each line (see Reveal Codes, below).

Flush Rt

Press L,L or (Alt-F6) and the block is right aligned. LetterPerfect asks you to confirm before executing the command. (Note: The block may not come out perfectly right aligned, since spaces at the end of lines will be moved to the right margin, and spaces count as characters. You can quickly edit a right-aligned block by deleting these spaces.)

When LetterPerfect right aligns a block of text, it places a hidden [Flsh Rgt] code in front of each line. The significance of the coding will become clear after you read the section below on Reveal Codes.

Bold

Press O,B or (F6) and the entire block is bolded (code [Bold] in front of the text and [bold] at the end).

Underline

Press O,U or (F8) and every character within the block is underlined (code [Und] in front of the text and und at the end).

Your Turn

The best way to absorb all the information you've just read is to try it with your memo file. Retrieve it, using the method explained above. Try modifying the appearance of several paragraphs of the memo using the various block functions described above. Then read the next section, which reveals the meaning of the hidden codes.

Behind-the-Scenes Editing

Using Reveal Codes to Undo Formats

The most basic way to undo a format command is to switch from the document editing screen to Reveal Codes. As described earlier, whenever you issue a formatting command, LetterPerfect creates a code or pair of codes that send the proper commands to the monitor and the printer. These codes are invisible while you create or edit a document, but can be seen in the Reveal Codes mode.

For example, if you press O,B or (F6) to turn on bold, type the word "Subject," and then press O,B or (F6) again to turn off bold, you simply see the word "Subject" in bold. When you press E,R or (Alt-F3), though, LetterPerfect displays a starting and ending code, as shown in Figure 8.1. (You can toggle between document mode and Reveal Codes mode by repeatedly pressing E,R or (Alt-F3). Try it yourself.)

Figure 8.1 Starting and ending codes.

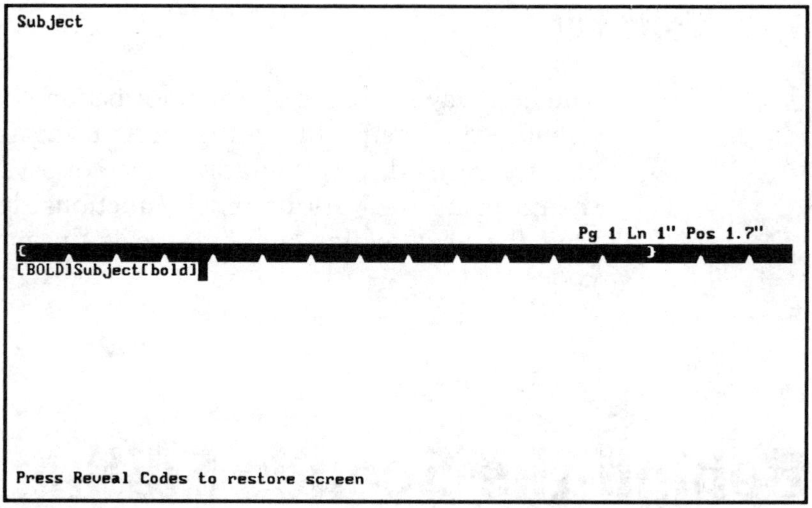

The top part of the screen shows the word "Subject" as it appears on your screen, and the bottom part shows the codes themselves. The pair of codes, [BOLD] and [bold], which surround the word "Subject," tell LetterPerfect to turn bold on beginning with the "S" and turn it off after the "t." Other formatting codes also appear as pairs, such as Underline, which places [UND] before text and [und] at the end of text. The majority of codes, however, appear as single codes, such as:

[Pg Num Pos] for Page Number Position

[L/R Margin:] for Left and Right Margin

[HRt] for Hard Page

(See Appendix C for a complete listing of all codes used in LetterPerfect.)

When you begin to add multiple formatting features, the Reveal Codes screen can get to be quite a mess, as demonstrated by the screen in Figure 8.2. (Dashes appear between brackets as [-].)

Figure 8.2 Complex Reveal Codes screen.

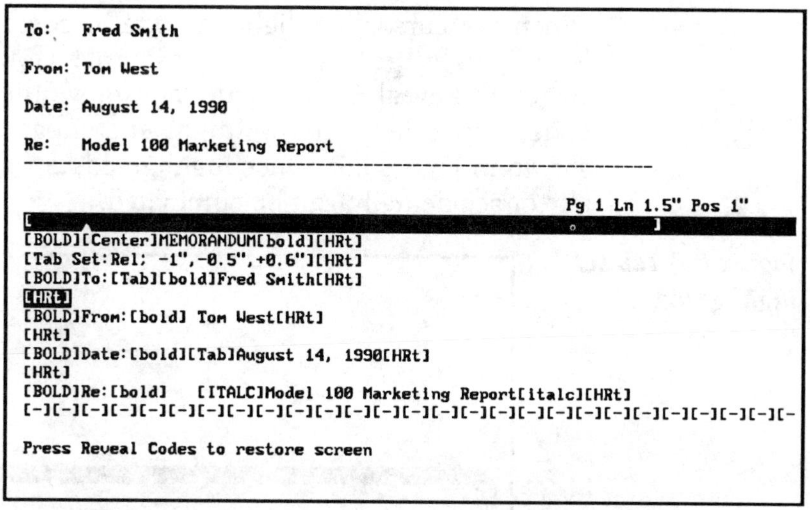

Why bother working with a screen that resembles a Rorschach blot on the bottom part when you can see the same thing "clean," in regular document mode, as shown in the top part of Figure 8.2?

The answer is that the Reveal Codes command is often the best way to eliminate an unwanted code. For example, if the word Subject is still on your screen in bold, switch into Reveal Codes mode by pressing E,R (Alt-F3). The cursor appears as a block, highlighting each letter or code as you move the cursor keys. Slide the cursor over the [BOLD] or the [bold] code, then press the (Del) key. You'll notice the word "Subject" immediately switches from bold to regular intensity on the screen. It also prints in regular weight rather than in bold. Paired codes can thus be turned off by eliminating either code surrounding the text. With nonpaired codes, all you have to do is highlight the code by moving the cursor keys, then press (Del).

The alternative is to try and position the cursor near the code while in regular document viewing mode and remove it with the (Del) key. If you hit the code, LetterPerfect prompts you with:

```
Delete [X]? (Y/N) No
```

where X is a the code name. Unfortunately, finding the exact location of the code can be like looking for a needle in a hay stack, and you are likely to delete numerous other characters as well. Eliminating codes in Reveal Codes is much more precise, because you can see exactly what you're editing out.

When the cursor highlights a code, it covers all text between the left and right brackets, [ ]. For example, if you enter a tab set, then switch to Reveal Codes mode, and move the cursor to the Tab Set code, notice how the highlight encompasses the entire code, as shown in Figure 8.3. Once highlighted, *any* code, placed intentionally or accidentally, can be eliminated.

Figure 8.3 Tab set highlighted

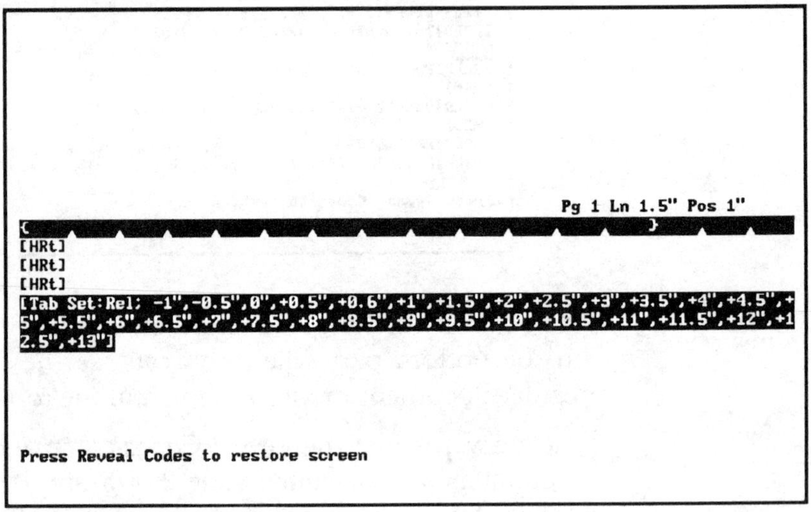

Moving Through a Document in Reveal Codes Mode

You can scroll through an entire document in Reveal Codes mode, using the cursor keys, PgUp and PgDn, screen up and screen down keys. As you do so, the document, without codes, appears on the top part of the screen as it would in normal viewing mode. It is generally less confusing, however, to traverse large numbers of pages in regular document mode and go to the approximate spot where you believe the code is located, and then switch into Reveal Codes mode.

One nice feature of Reveal Codes is that you can also edit out or add text without returning to the regular document mode. As you add characters in Reveal Codes, the text changes in the top portion of the screen, and the Status Line indicator shows all the vital statistics regarding the current cursor location. When you switch back into regular document mode, the new text appears as if you had typed it under "normal" circumstances.

Correcting Problems with Reveal Codes

Switching into Reveal Codes mode can allow you to correct certain pesky problems. For example, what if:

A large section of text is unexpectedly underlined.
The (F8) key was accidentally pressed at some point, or you forgot to toggle underline off at the end of an intentionally underlined section. Move the cursor to the place where the unwanted underline first appeared, switch into Reveal Codes mode, look for a "rogue" [UND] code and delete it. Or, move to the place where an intentional underline should be turned off. Press (F8) + (Del), and an [und] command, which turns off underline, will be inserted at the desired location.

A page with no text, but a page number, appears between two "normal" pages.
You have an unwanted hard page command [HPg] sitting in your document. Move your cursor to the page in question, which will be displayed as a double-dashed line instead of the regular dotted line for soft or "regular" pages [SPg]. Move the cursor to the line immediately above the double dashes and you'll find the [HPg] command. Zap it with the (Del) key, and the blank page disappears.

The margins or indents have suddenly changed, creating inconsistent pages.
Move the cursor to the problem area, switch into Reveal Codes, and delete the offending margin or tab command.

Using Search and Search and Replace to Find Codes

Searching for Codes

Earlier you learned how to use the Search function and the Replace function to locate specific text, and to substitute text. You can do the same thing with hidden codes. Instead of entering words or phrases when prompted for the search criteria, call up the function you wish to find. LetterPerfect then knows what code you are seeking. For example, let's say that have a stray line-spacing command somewhere in your document. You can locate it by using the search command. Here's how:

1. Move the cursor to the top of the document by pressing: (Home) + (Home) + (Home) + (Up Cursor)
2. Use S,R or (F2) to activate the search.
3. Press L,F or (Shift-F8). LetterPerfect displays an abbreviated format menu, shown in Figure 8.4.

Figure 8.4
Abbreviated format menu.

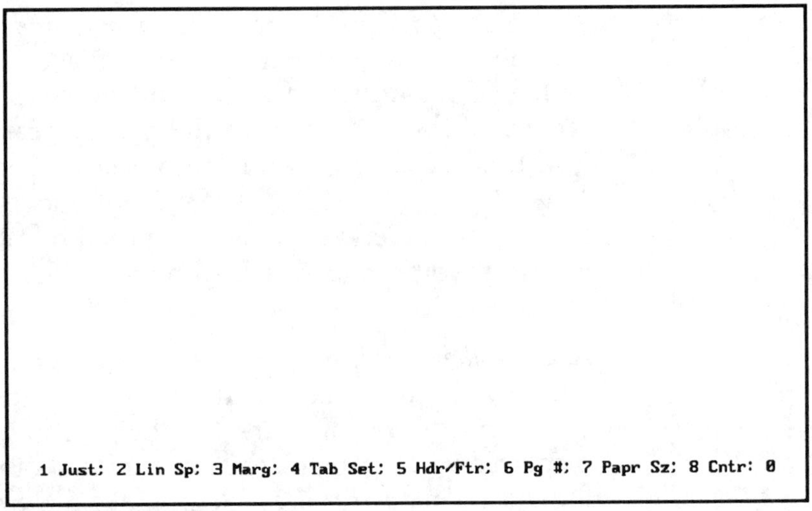

4. Select 2 and the code [Ln Spacing] appears after the

   `-> Srch:`

   prompt.

5. Press S,F or (F2) or (Esc). When LetterPerfect finds the code, the cursor stops to the right of it. You can then delete the code with the (Backspace) key.

Seek and Destroy

The method just described takes you to the first occurrence of a code, after which it's up to you to do something about it. An alternative way to knock out an undesirable code is to use the search and replace function as a "seek-and-destroy" mechanism. Here's what to do to knock out a margin code:

1. Move the cursor to the top of the document by pressing: (Home) + (Home) + (Home) + (Up Cursor)
2. Press S,R or (Alt-F2) to activate the Replace operation.
3. Select Y for Confirm.
4. Press L, F or (Ctrl-F8). LetterPerfect displays the format options shown in Figure 8.4, above.

   Select 3. LetterPerfect will prompt you to indicate Left/Right

Margins or Top/Bottom Margins. Select 1 for Left/Right Margins and [L/R Mar] will appear after the:

```
-> Srch:
```

prompt.

5. When the Replace with: prompt appears on the screen, press L,R or (F2) or the (Esc) key, which instructs LetterPerfect to replace the margin code with...a blank.
6. When LetterPerfect finds the first code, it asks you if you want it replaced. If you respond Y, it replaces the code with "nothing," which is tantamount to deleting it. It then goes on to find any other occurrences of the code. It is advisable to use the confirm option when doing seek-and-destroy missions against unwanted codes, because you might have some codes that you don't want deleted, especially in the very top portion of the first page of the document.

Again, you might be wondering why you'd ever want to bother with Search to find a hidden code, when you can eliminate it with Replace. The answer is that if you're not careful, you can potentially make things worse with Replace. If Replace is analogous to "seek and destroy," then think of Search as a reconnaissance operation that lets you snoop around the hidden codes and then decide whether to attack them.

Altering Paired Codes with Replace

In addition to locating and zapping codes, you can use Replace to find instances of text with a paired code (bold or underline) and change them. For example, if you have underlined the word "Fact" throughout a document, and want to make it bold instead, use the following procedure:

1. Move the cursor to the top of the document by pressing: (Home) + (Home) + (Home) + (Up Cursor)
2. Press S,R or (Alt-F2) to activate the Replace operation.
3. Select N for "No Confirm." (If there are likely to be multiple replacements, and no danger of an unwanted alteration, it's safe—and much faster—to search and replace without confirmation.)

4. At the —> Srch: prompt press and type:

   O,U + Fact + O,U

   or

   (F8) + Fact + (F8)

   Your prompt will look like:

   `—> Srch: [UND]Fact[und]`

5. Press S,F or (F2) or (Esc). When the Replace with: prompt appears on the screen, press and enter:

   O,B + Fact + O,B

   (F6) + Fact + (F6)

   Your prompt will look like:

   `Replace with: [BOLD]Fact[bold]`

6. Press S,F or (F2) or the (Esc) key. When LetterPerfect finds each instance of "Fact," it replaces it with Fact. Since you selected No Confirm, LetterPerfect passes through and alters all occurrences in the document.

The same thing could have been done if you wanted to change "Fact" (no underline) to "Fact" (underline) or "Fact" (bold + underline). All you have to do is put in the appropriate codes when you structure the search.

Your Turn

Look into your memo and see what LetterPerfect has created behind the scenes. Try deleting some of the codes manually, and some using the Replace function. If you've read *Getting Started with LetterPerfect* sequentially, you've been exposed to all of the key functions you need to create documents, from simple letters to sophisticated newsletters. The next chapter teaches you how to change fonts.

Chapter 9

Changing Fonts

Highlights

- Base font concept
- Selecting a base font
- Changing the base font for existing text
- Changing the base font for new text
- The effect of changing printers

Overview

One way to jazz up the look of your documents is to bold text or use different type fonts. A font is a group of characters related by certain characteristics, such as style (Courier, Times, Universe); weight (bold, regular); and size (10, 12, or 16 points). Figure 9.1 shows a variety of type fonts.

Figure 9.1 Font samples (generated with a LaserJet III).

This is 10 point Prestige Elite

This is 12 point Courier

This is 12 point Courier italic

This is 14 point CG Times

This is 14 point CG Times italic

This is 16 point Universe

This is 16 point Universe italic

Some printers have many built-in fonts, and allow you access to still more fonts with a plug-in font cartridge or fonts that reside on disk, called "soft fonts." The HP LaserJet Series II and LaserJet III, for example, allow you to use two plug-in cartridges at a time, and to download whatever soft fonts you have installed on your computer.

The key to using the full potential of LetterPerfect 1.0's font selection and printing capabilities is to understand a few of the fundamental ideas on which it is based. The information LetterPerfect needs about each font is transferred from the Printer disk to your computer during the installation procedure and contains the physical dimensions of each character in the selected fonts.

Each printer has a default font that is used until you specify another. LetterPerfect calls the default font for the selected printer its "Base Font," which defines a family of type styles. In other words, you can describe all the variations of bold, italics, underline, etc. in terms of their relation to the to the Base Font. For example, if you select a Times font as a Base Font, when you instruct LetterPerfect to italicize a particular word, it inserts the command to use the italics version of Times. If your printer is capable of printing italics, it does so. If not, it finds the nearest substitute. If no substitutes for italics are available, it may underline the word instead.

In addition to offering variations on the Base Font capabilities, LetterPerfect can reformat documents instantly if the Base Font is changed. Suppose you had set up a document with the Base Font of Courier 10, and you used several variations of it, such as bold and italics. Now you decide that you want to print the document in Times 12-point proportional type. With many word processors, you would have to go back and reset each of the font changes to correspond to the new font and its variations. With LetterPerfect 1.0, however, all you need to do is position the cursor at the beginning of the document and reset the Base Font to Times Roman 12 point. Since all the variations are defined relative to the Base Font, they are all changed to variations of Times Roman 12 point. Furthermore, LetterPerfect will repaginate the entire document to accomodate the spacing requirements of the new proportional font, without any effort on your part.

Selecting Your Base Font

As you can see from the above discussion, a great deal depends on the Base Font you select. When you first open a document, the Base Font is assumed to be the Initial Font for the currently selected printer (see Appendix A for more information on Initial Fonts). Suppose that you are using a HP LaserJet III, which has 15 built-in fonts. How do you tell LetterPerfect that you don't want to accept the Initial Font (Courier 10) as your Base Font, but want to use Helvetica instead? It's quite simple. Move the cursor to the very beginning of the document by entering:

(Home)+ (Home) + (Home) + (Up Cursor)

Then open the Base Font list by pressing:

O,F + 4 or (Ctrl-F8) + 4

You will be shown all the fonts for the currently selected printer (see Figure 9.2).

Figure 9.2 Base fonts, LaserJet III.

```
Base Font

   CG Times (Scalable)
   CG Times Bold (Scalable)
   CG Times Bold Italic (Scalable)
   CG Times Italic (Scalable)
 * Courier 10cpi
   Courier 10cpi (Bold)
   Courier 10cpi (Italic)
   Courier 12cpi
   Courier 12cpi (Bold)
   Courier 12cpi (Italic)
   Line Printer 16.67cpi
   Univers (Scalable)
   Univers Bold (Scalable)
   Univers Bold Italic (Scalable)
   Univers Italic (Scalable)

1 Select; N Name search: 1
```

The currently selected Base Font will be marked with an asterisk. To change to another Base Font, use the (Up Cursor) and (Down Cursor) to highlight the desired font—say CG Times, for example—and press 1 to select it. You can confirm that the new Base Font command has been inserted into your document by shifting into Reveal Codes by pressing E,R or (Alt-F3).

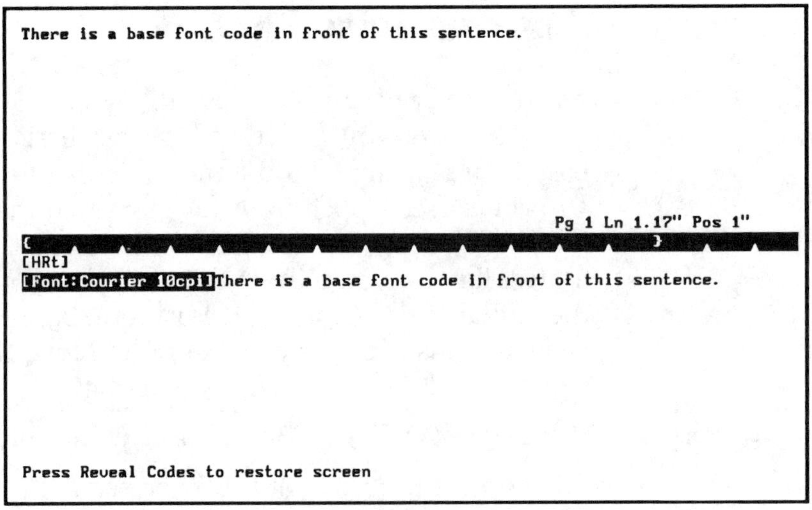

Figure 9.3 Base font code.

Note: The LaserJet III contains a number of built-in "scalable" fonts, and can also use scalable font cartridges. This term means that you can "scale" the font to any size. When you select a font with the word "scalable" in parentheses, you will be asked to indicate a point size. Enter the desired value, and the LaserJet III will create the font. This technology, by the way, makes the LaserJet III a superb adjunct to LetterPerfect.

Variations on the Base Font

Once you select a Base Font, you can make several variations on it. Press:

O or (Ctrl-F8)

You will be presented with a pull-down menu or horizontal screen menu with the following attributes:

1 Bold; **2 U**nderline; **3 N**ormal; **4** Base Font; **5 I**talic **6** Su**p**rscpt: **7 S**ubscpt: **0**

To select a particular variation, enter the options desired. For example, to select Bold or Italics, select the appropriate menu item.

As you can see, the Base Font concept provides considerable flexibility for defining the fonts in a document. If you consider the possible combinations of styles and your ability to change the Base

Font within a given document, you'll see how easy it is to create the most complex documents.

Changing the Base Font for Existing Text

To select a variation of the Base Font for existing text, place the cursor on the first letter of the text to be changed. Then:

1. Press E,B or (Alt-F4) to start the Block command.
2. Highlight the text to be changed.
3. Press O or (Ctrl-F8) to bring up the font menu.
4. Select Italic.

Changing Fonts for New Text

When you are changing fonts for new text, you have two choices: you can either select a new Base Font or you can describe the new font as a variation on the existing Base Font. If the current Base Font is the best choice, leave it as selected. To do this, simply position the cursor in the location you wish to insert the new text using the new type font and press O or (Ctrl-F8). Select the desired attribute. You can then begin entering the new text, and it will print in the variation selected.

If you shift into Reveal Codes by pressing E,R or (Alt-F3), you can see the new text located between the code to turn on the variation and the code to turn it off again. You can continue to insert text between these two codes, and it will continue to be printed in the selected variation.

To terminate the variation, either select the Normal option from the font menu, or use the cursor key to move the cursor to the right of the character on which the variation ended. After this, any further text entered prints in the font selected before the variation was started (usually the Base Font unless you have other variations also in use).

The concept of base fonts and font variations can be somewhat confusing. The best way to sort out the options is to try your own variations. Once you get the hang of it, you'll have a remarkable capability at your fingertips.

Chapter 10

Fine Tuning Your Document

The Last Step

Once you've edited your document, you can put the finishing-touches on it by running it through the electronic Thesaurus and Speller. In practice, if you use the Thesaurus at all, you'll probably bring it up "on the fly," to find synonyms as you write. But it's also helpful after the fact, when you proofread a document and discover that you need to find a better word, or that you've used a particular word 10 times per page and need some stylistic relief.

Using the Speller is a slightly different story. While you might occasionally use it to check words as you go along, most of your spell-checking will probably be postponed until you are ready to print. After all, while you're still juggling words in a document, you're likely to introduce typos and other errors along the way, so why waste your time spell-checking before you have finished your work?

This chapter is divided into two major sections, one for the Thesaurus, and one for the Speller. Unlike the Speller, which is easy to use, the mechanics of the Thesaurus are anything but obvious. To help you learn both features, you should call up your memo, if you've created one, so you can see how the various options actually work—they're slick!

Finding The Right Word: The Thesaurus

A thesaurus contains lists of synonyms, words whose meanings are identical, and antonyms, words that are opposite. LetterPerfect's Thesaurus provides thousands of synonyms and antonyms for words in your text. The clever thing about the electronic Thesaurus is that you don't have to tell it what word you're looking for—LetterPerfect picks up whatever word is at your cursor and instantly displays lists of words with like and opposite meanings. You can also look up words, as you would with a conventional thesaurus.

If you have a hard disk, make sure you've installed the Thesaurus file, WP{WP}US.THS, located on the disk labeled "Thesaurus," before proceeding. The Thesaurus file consumes a hefty 170,000 bytes, so if hard disk space is at a premium, it's a prime candidate for deletion if you don't think you'll use it. If you don't have the Thesaurus on your system at this time, stop and install it. Refer to Chapters 1 and 2 for instructions.

Using the Thesaurus

The procedure for using the Thesaurus or the Speller is different for floppy and hard disk computers. The following sections cover both types of machines.

Dual-Drive Floppy System

To invoke the Thesaurus with a floppy-based system, use the following steps:

1. Save your file to your data disk.
2. Remove your data disk from your B drive.
3. Insert your Thesaurus disk into your B drive.
4. Move the cursor to the word for which you want to find a synonym.
5. Press T,T or (Alt-F1). LetterPerfect displays a list of synonyms. If none are found, it indicates:

   `Word Not Found,`

   and gives you an opportunity to enter another word. This is explained below. To exit the Thesaurus at any time, select "0" from the Thesaurus menu, or press cancel, (F1) or exit, (F7).
6. Remove your Thesaurus disk and reinsert your data disk.

Hard Disk System

To invoke the Thesaurus on a hard disk system, all you have to do is move the cursor to the word for which you want to find a synonym, and press T,T or (Alt-F1). The Thesaurus displays a list of potential synonyms. If none is found, it indicates:

```
Word Not Found
```

and gives you an opportunity to enter another word. See below for what to do next. To exit the Thesaurus at any time, select "0" from the Thesaurus menu, or press cancel, (F1) or exit, (F7).

The Thesaurus Screen

The Thesaurus screen consists of three columns, as shown in Figure 10.1. The screen displays three types of entries, with the following hierarchy: Headwords; Subgroups; and Reference Words.

Headwords

are major entries in the Thesaurus, and appear in bold. They are organized by whatever part of speech they represent. The part of speech appears in parentheses: (a) for adjectives, (n) for nouns, and (v) for verbs. Antonyms are marked with (ant).

Subgroups

are related groups of synonyms (such as "archaic" and "obsolete" in one group, and "primal" and "primitive" in another subgroup).

Reference

words are synonyms that can also be Headwords. Reference words are distinguished from nonreference words by the bullet that precedes them.

Figure 10.1
Thesaurus screen.

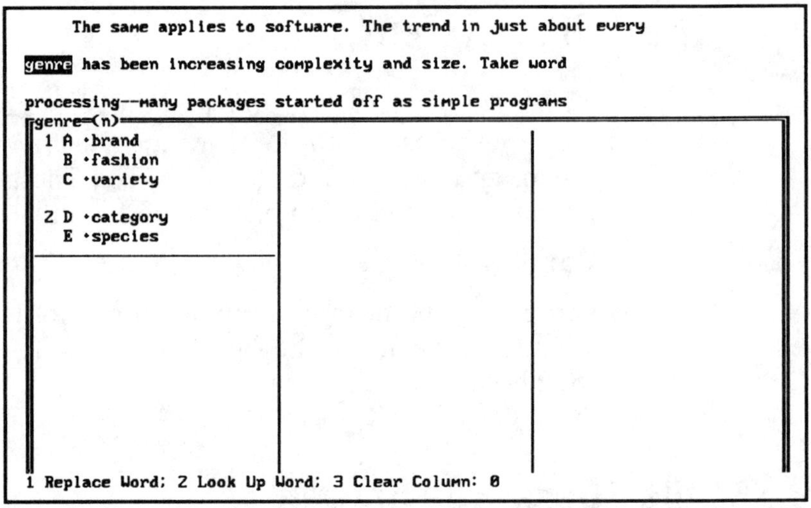

In point of fact, you can forget about all of the above terms-they are only presented here in case you wish to consult the LetterPerfect manual. More important than knowing the nomenclature is understanding the mechanics of the Thesaurus.

You can use the Thesaurus in two ways: to find a word to use in your document as you're composing, or to swap an existing word for its synonym. Both uses are described below.

"Free Form" Brainstorming with the Thesaurus

Let's say you're writing a sentence and stop for a moment to find another word for "contaminate"; you have one on the tip of your tongue, but you just can't remember it. Rather than waiting until 3 AM, when the word jolts you from a sound sleep, move the cursor now to a blank line at the bottom of the document and press T,T or (Alt-F1) to call up the Thesaurus. LetterPerfect prompts you for a word in the lower left-hand corner of the screen (see Figure 10.2). Enter "contaminate," and a list of synonyms will be displayed, including the elusive word "pollute," for which you were searching all along (see Figure 10.3).

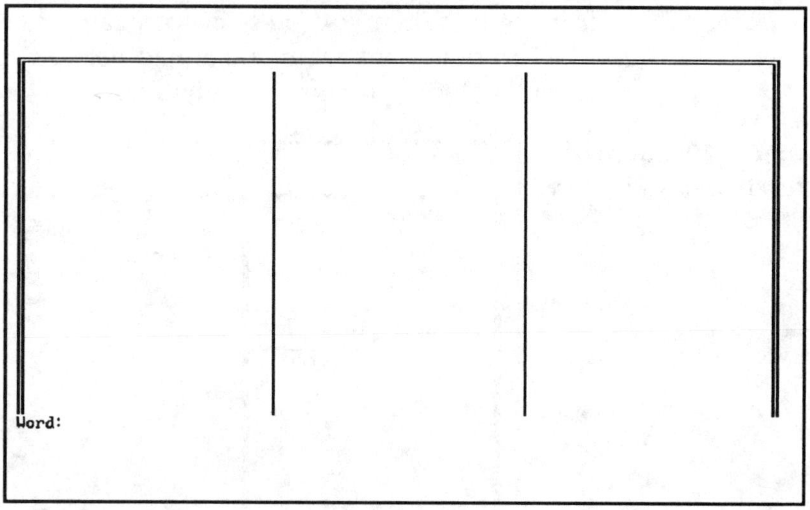

Figure 10.2 Enter a word to be checked.

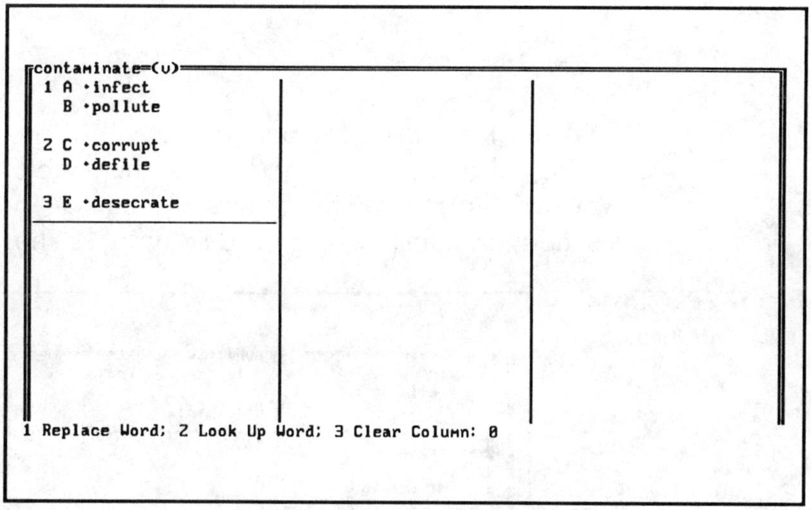

Figure 10.3 Results of word search.

Select option 1, Replace Word, and LetterPerfect prompts you to:

`Press the letter for word`

That means press the letter corresponding to the desired word on the screen, "B," in this case, and it will be inserted into the document at the cursor location.

So far, no problem. But here's where things get a bit complicated. Let's say that you weren't satisfied with the first set of synonyms. You can find additional synonyms for any word that has a bullet in front of it. When you press B, for example, corresponding to "pollute," in our example, an expanded list of synonyms appears in the second column, as shown in Figure 10.4.

Figure 10.4 Second level synonyms.

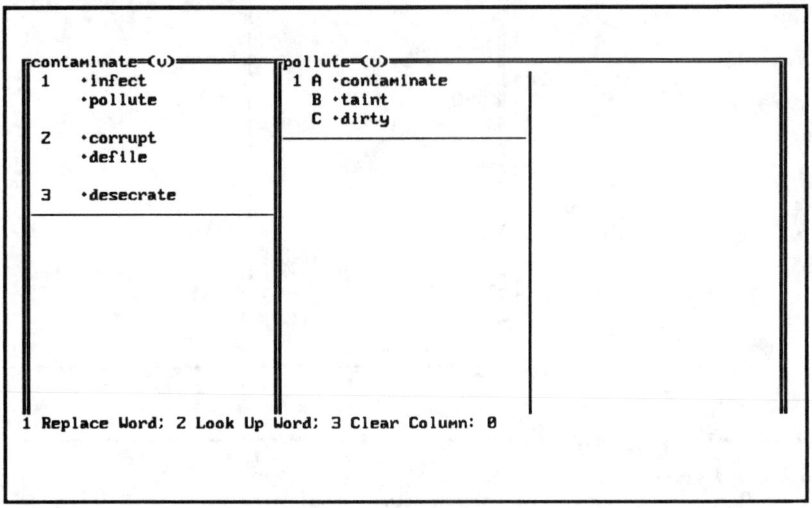

Within the entries for pollute, several of the entries, including "B. taint," also have bullets in front of them. To expand them, press any of their corresponding letters. When you press "B," for taint, the synonyms appear in the third column, as shown in Figure 10.5.

Figure 10.5 Third level synonyms.

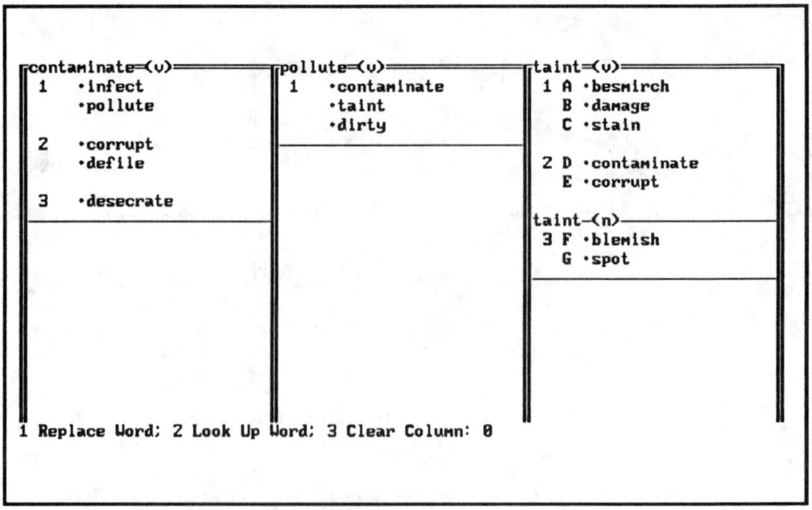

If you want to expand any bulleted entries in the third column, press their corresponding letter and the expanded list will replace the current entries in the third column. If you want to expand the new entries in the third column, they will be replaced by the next set of entries, and so on.

If you are duplicating the "contaminate" exercise, you'll probably notice that the alphabet letters only appear in the column in which new entries are displayed. For example, when you press B in the first column to expand "pollute," the letters jump to the second column, where the synonyms for "pollute" appear. The letter "B" then corresponds to "taint." When you expand "taint," the letters jump to the third column, to correspond to a new set of entries. (You can see this progression by comparing Figures 10.3 through 10.5.)

But what happens if the letters are in the third column, and you decide that the word your really want to use as a synonym is in the first column? The answer is, use your (Left Cursor) key to move the letters to the first column. When you move the (Left Cursor) and (Right Cursor) keys, the entire column of letters "peels" off and is transported from column to column. Once you select a word and move the letters to the right column, select Option 1, Replace Word, and select the appropriate letter. The word will be placed in your text at the cursor location.

Using the Thesaurus to Check Existing Text

When you call up the Thesaurus, it first checks whatever word is at the cursor. The cursor can be anywhere within the word to be checked. If the cursor is in a blank space, the Thesaurus will look up the word to the left of the cursor.

If LetterPerfect can't find any synonyms for the word on the screen, it informs you that the word was not found, then prompts you to enter a word. At this point, use the above procedure to operate the Thesaurus.

When LetterPerfect does find the highlighted word, it will display the first level of synonyms, as described above. You can call up the second and third level synonyms by entering the letter of the synonym you want to expand. When you have found the "perfect replacement," select Option 1, Replace Word, and enter the letter of the selected word, which will then be inserted into your text in place of the original word.

Looking Up Other Words

Perhaps you really don't want to use "contaminate" or any of its synonyms. Instead of exiting the Thesaurus, by selecting a synonym or pressing (F7), (F1), or "0," you can choose another word by selecting Option 3, Look Up Word. Once again, LetterPerfect prompts you in the lower left-hand corner of the screen for a new word. If the word is not in the Thesaurus, LetterPerfect responds with:

```
Word not found
```

and again prompts you for another word.

If the word is found, LetterPerfect places the synonyms in the next blank column. If all columns are filled with previous entries, it overwrites entries in the third column. If you expand the new entries while in the third column, they replace the old entries in the third column. This makes it difficult to follow the new entries, so the best thing to do is clean out the last two columns by moving the cursor to the second column, and selecting Option 3, Clear Column. The contents of the third column are cleared instantly.

First, however, the original contents of the third column slide over to the second column. If the synonyms for the word you are checking would normally fill two columns, the excess synonyms will appear in the third column. Now clean out the first column, using option #3. The contents of the second column slide over to the first. Any entries that couldn't fit in one column also "flow over" to the second and third columns.

If this seems confusing, be assured, it is. But once you try the Thesaurus a few times you'll be a pro at using it. You might it even find it a handy and useful writing tool.

Note that the Thesaurus maintains case, tense, and part of speech; that is, if it is replacing a word that has an initial uppercase letter, it will upper case the first letter of the synonym it inserts into the text. If it is replacing a verb, the Thesaurus will try to match tense (past, present, etc.). If it is replacing a noun or an adjective, the Thesaurus will try to match that part of speech.

Your Turn

If you've been reading the text without trying the above example, go back and try it yourself. There are some computing actions that can only be mastered by hands-on experience, and the Thesaurus is one of them.

Words On Tap: The Speller

LetterPerfect's spell-checker is a superb tool, and should always be used before sending off your documents for others to read.

Dual-Drive Floppy System

To start the Speller, use the following steps:

1. Save your file to your data disk.
2. Remove your data disk from your B drive.
3. Insert your Speller disk into your B drive.
4. Press T,S or (Ctrl-F2). The Speller menu appears, as described below.
5. Leave the Speller disk in your B drive during the spell-checking session.
6. When the spell-check is complete, replace the Speller disk with your data disk and *save the file*—whatever corrections you made must be saved in the new file.

To exit the Speller during a checking session, press (F1) at any time. You might have to press (F1) twice, depending on what the Speller is doing.

Hard Disk System

All you have to do is press T,S or (Ctrl-F2) to display the Speller menu under your document. Each option is explained below. When you finish the spell-checking, make sure you save your file to preserve the changes and corrections. To exit the Speller during a checking session, press (F1). You might have to press (F1) twice, depending on whether the Speller is waiting for input from the menu or checking a word.

Menu Options

When the spell-checker is invoked, it will check whatever document is on the screen. The speller menu is shown in Figure 10.6.

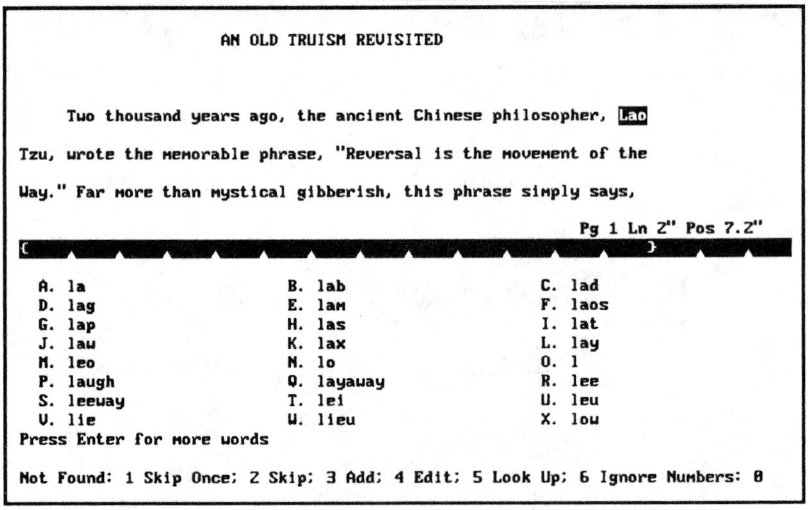

Figure 10.6 Speller main menu.

If the Speller does not recognize a word, because it is misspelled or simply not in the dictionary, it highlights the word and displays a list of options underneath a double-dashed line, as shown in Figure 10.7. If you see the word spelled correctly, press the letter to which it corresponds, and that word replaces the incorrectly spelled version in your document. As with the Thesaurus, the Speller maintains case. If the word "Occassional" [sic] has an initial uppercase letter in your document, when you insert the correctly spelled word, it appears with an initial uppercase letter also ("Occasional," correctly spelled out).

Figure 10.7 Highlighted word and options for unknown spelling.

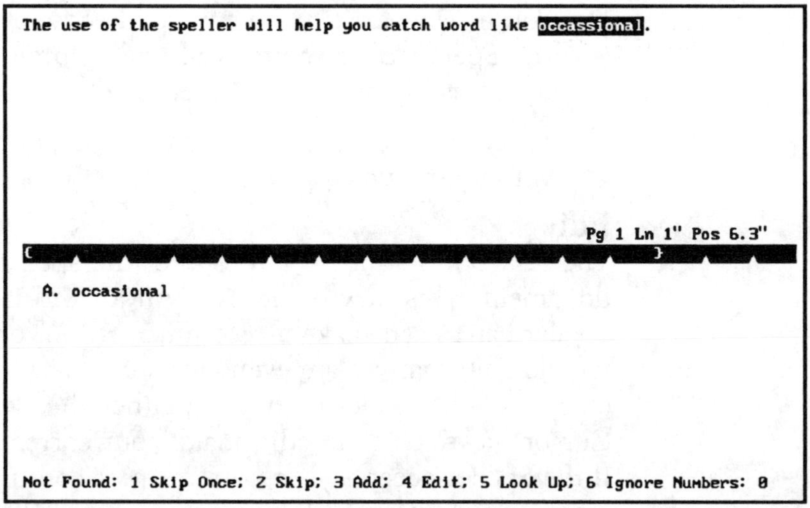

When a word isn't found, the Speller displays the message:

`Not Found:`

in the lower left-hand corner, and displays the following menu options:

Skip Once

This instructs the Speller to ignore this single occurrence of the word and continue.

Skip

This option tells the Speller to skip every occurrence of the word and continue with the spell-checking operation. This is a particularly useful option when it comes to names and technical words. If you instruct the Speller to skip all occurrences of the word, but it stops at one occurrence later on, you know that you've spelled the word differently from the first instance, which is why the Speller considers it a different word. You can then correct it or make it consistent by using the editing options below.

Add Word

There are several occasions on which you will want to add words to the Speller dictionary file.

1. You are certain that the word is spelled correctly

   (Good as the Speller is, you can't expect it to know everything, especially technical jargon peculiar to your field.)

2. You have a variation on a word already in the dictionary. While the Speller does pretty well with plurals and contractions, it does miss a few here and there.

3. You want to enter a proper name, title, or company name. Start with your own.

Edit

The Edit option allows you to alter the spelling of a word in your document. This may be necessary if a word is so jumbled that the Speller can't even make a recommendation, or none of the recommended alternatives are even close to what you want. You can also enter the edit mode by pressing either the (Right Cursor) or (Left Cursor) keys. Once in edit, make your correction, then press (F7). If the Speller accepts your correction, it continues. If it still considers the word misspelled, it presents a list of alternatives.

Hint 1: Sometimes it is faster to edit a word than to read through the list of alternatives, especially when the word is short and the list of alternatives is like a visual obstacle course. For instance, if you misspell "hyde" as "het," you are presented with two pages of options (see Figures 10.8-10.9). You have to read through more than 35 alternatives to find your word! Obviously, it's quicker just to pop into the edit mode and make the correction yourself.

Figure 10.8 First set of alternatives for "het."

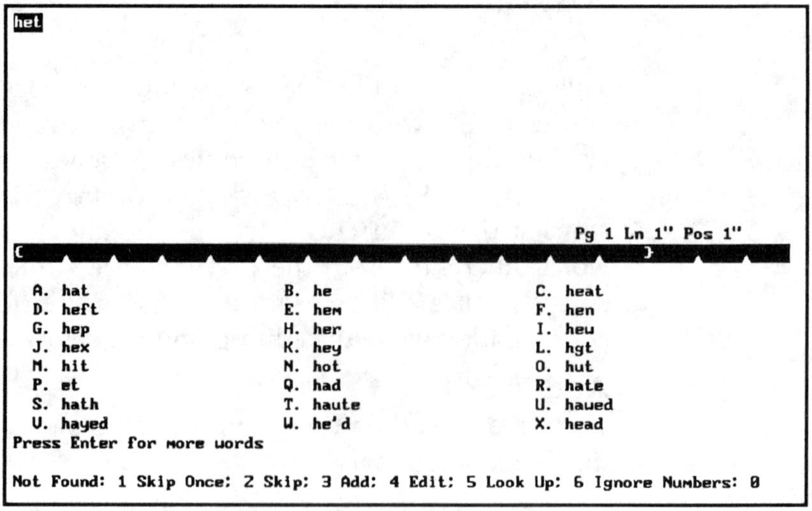

Figure 10.9 Second set of alternatives for "het."

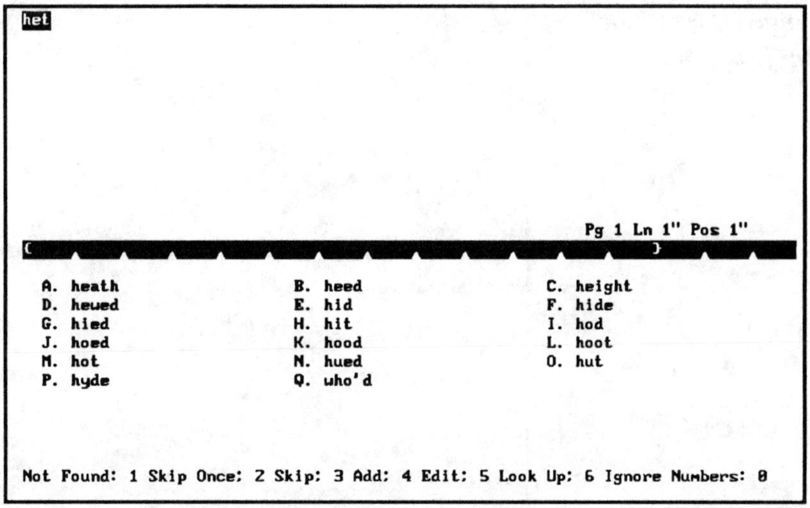

Hint 2: Even if you don't know the correct spelling of a word, you may be able to recognize that it has an impossible mix of consonants and vowels. With luck, you can find a word close enough to a form for which LetterPerfect can recommend alternatives. This "one-two punch" approach is often very effective.

Look Up

If you don't want to check any specific words, but would rather look one up, select this option. The Speller prompts you to enter the word or word pattern in the lower left-hand corner of the screen. If you think you know how to spell the word, enter it in its entirety. For example, let's say you want to check the spelling of the word "antediluvian." You enter it at the prompt, and LetterPerfect indicates that it's correct by displaying it, as in Figure 10.10. If you didn't spell it correctly, LetterPerfect displays the correct spelling beneath the double-dotted line. If LetterPerfect finds several possible matches, it shows all of them, allowing you to select the correct one by letter.

Figure 10.10 Look up function.

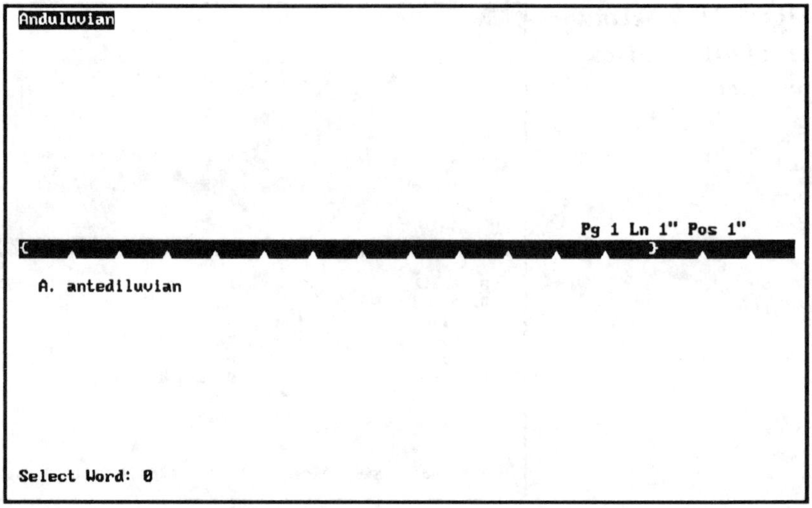

If you're not sure exactly how to spell a word, type in as much of the word as you think is correct, and insert "wildcard" characters for the parts you are unsure of. The "?" wildcard means "any single letter," while the "*" wildcard means any number of any characters.

The trick works like this: Let's say you aren't sure whether "antediluvian" is spelled with an "e" or an "i" after the "d." When prompted for the word or word pattern, enter:

anted?luvian + (Enter)

This instructs the Speller to look for the exact sequence of letters you've entered, and report any word that has any single letter in the position of the question mark. The only word fitting that description happens to be "antediluvian," so it displays the word on the screen, as shown in Figure 10.10. If the Speller can't find any matches, it prompts you for another word or word pattern.

What if you aren't sure about whether "antediluvian" is spelled with an "e" or an "i" after the "t," as well as an "e" or an "i" after the "d"? No problem—use two "?" wildcard characters when prompted for a word or word pattern:

ant?d?luvian

You get the same results.

You could also use the "*" wildcard character as well in the last instance, entering:

ant*

which instructs the Speller to look up all words with "ant," followed by any number of any characters.

Hint: In some cases, entering a "wildcard" is quicker, so it saves you time on the input. But as in the case of "het" and "hyde" above, the time savings may be negated by the time it takes to flip through the screens of alternatives.

Ignore Numbers

This feature allows you to skip words with numbers. Numbered words can greatly slow up your search. When you select this option, you tell the Speller not to bother with numbers for the rest of the checking session.

Double Word Options

In addition to the above options, the Speller offers one other set of options when it encounters a double word. As you can see from Figure 10.11, the Speller gives you four choices:

Figure 10.11 Double word detection system.

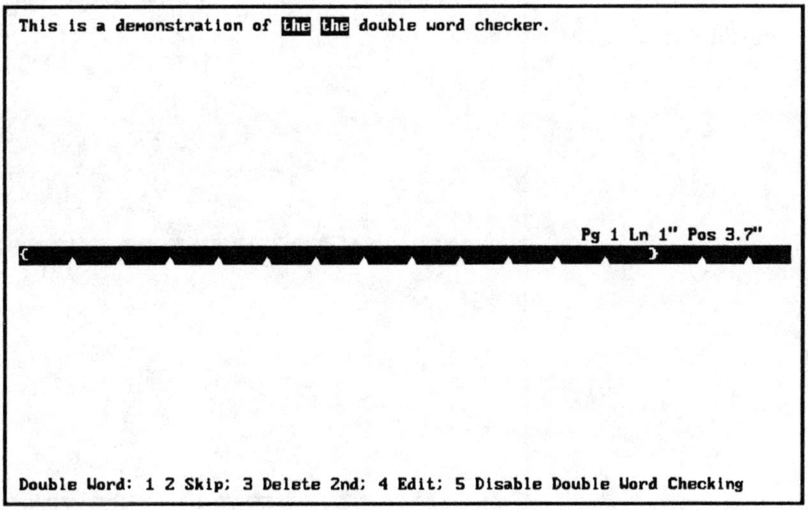

Skip

This option instructs the Speller to ignore the double word.

Delete 2nd
If the second word is a mistake and you want it removed, select this option.

Edit
This is the same editing feature as that described above. Use it to alter the second (or first) word.

Disable Double Word Checking
In some cases you will want to turn off double word checking for the rest of the document. For example, if you have columns of numbers, many of which are the same, the Speller stops incessantly and asks if you want to delete the second instance. In that case, you should probably turn off the double word checking function.

Irregular Case Option

A final feature of the Speller is also worth noting. When the speller detects two uppercase letters in a row (called "irregular case"), it flags them and gives you four options (see Figure 10.12).

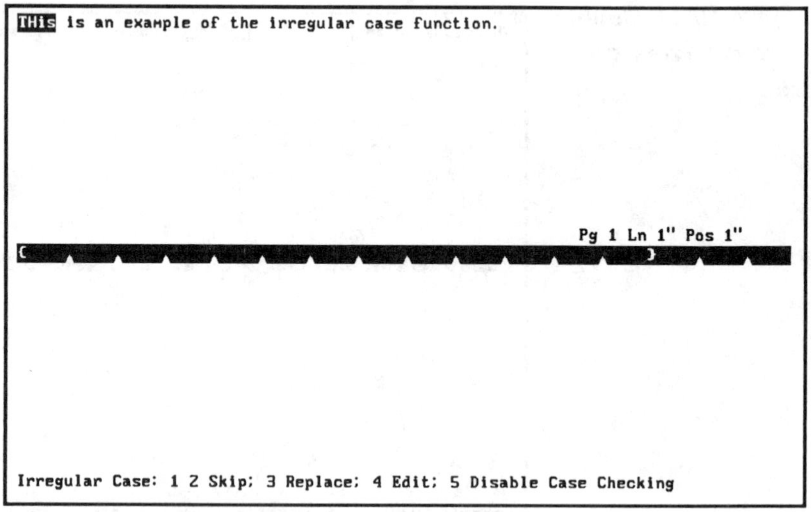

Figure 10.12 Irregular case options.

Skip
This option instructs the Speller to ignore irregular case.

Delete 2nd
Select this option to lowercase the second letter.

Edit

Use this to alter the second (or first) letter.

Disable Case Checking

In some cases you will want to turn off irregular case checking for the rest of the document. For example, you might have some unique technical words or trade names that do actually have an irregular case. Chances are, though, you'll probably want to leave this function on.

Final Caveat

The LetterPerfect Speller is a powerful tool, and you should spell check every document before printing it. The speller is so fast and easy, and you'll be surprised at what your own readings miss. But it's not foolproof. LetterPerfect checks the spelling of words, but not whether they are the correct or appropriate words. You must still proofread your work to ensure that you have entered the words you intended. For example, you may have intended to enter the word "bead" but accidentally typed "mead." When you spell check, the speller won't find your error, since mead is spelled correctly.

Worse, you can use the speller to insert correctly spelled, but embarrassingly incorrect, words into your document by pressing the wrong letter when selecting replacement words. The author illustrated this pitfall when he submitted a manuscript in final form to his editor without paying close attention to the spell checking process. The editor wanted to know if a "house orgy" was an original concept. No, it's just an illustration of the danger of misspelling house "organ" and letting the Speller make the fix.

Your Turn

If you haven't spell checked your memo, now's the time to do it, because you'll soon learn how to print it. The more you use the speller, the more you'll come to rely on it as an essential word processing tool.

Chapter 11

Adding Graphics

Highlights

- The graphics functions
- Graphics definition screen
- Filename
- Horizontal position
- Size
- Wrap text around box
- Border

LetterPerfect Graphics

LetterPerfect allows you to insert pre-defined graphic elements into your document, such as 1-2-3 graphs, images created in other programs or entered through a scanner, or "clip art" files supplied with the program. This chapter describes how to incorporate these graphics into your text.

Graphics Definition

The first step in placing a graphic image in your text is to call up the Graphics Definition screen (see Figure 11.1). This is done via the menu command G,C or the keyboard combination (Alt-F9).

Figure 11.1 Graphics definition screen.

```
Graphics Definition

     1 - Filename

     2 - Horizontal Position  Right

     3 - Size                 3.25" wide x 3.25" (high)

     4 - Wrap Text Around Box Yes

     5 - Border               Yes

         Note: Each time you specify a border option,
               a figure option code ([Fig Opt]) is inserted
               in your document.  This code affects all
               subsequent figures until LetterPerfect
               encounters another figure option code.




Selection: 0
```

Each option is described below:

Filename

Enter the name of the file. All files must be in WPG (Word Perfect Graphic format). The conversion technique is discussed later in the chapter. For now, we'll assume that you have some WPG files handy—namely, the graphic images that you installed during installation (if you didn't install the images, you might want to go back and do so now—seeing is believing when it comes to graphics).

If you don't know the exact name of the graphic file, press the (F5) key after selecting the Filename option. Highlight the desired graphic file with the cursor keys, then press 1 for Retrieve. The file will automatically be inserted into the space after Filename on your Graphics Definition screen.

Horizontal Position

Enter the left-right positioning of the chart. You have four choices:

`1 Left; 2 Right 3 Center; 4 Full:0`

Left

This aligns the left edge of the box surrounding the graphic image with the left margin.

Right

This option aligns the right edge of the graphics box with the right margin.

Center

To place the graphics box equidistant between the left and right margin, use this option.

Full

When you select this option, the graphics box will fill up the space between the left and right margins.

Size

When you select the Size option, LetterPerfect will display the following choices:

```
1 Set Width/Auto Height; 2 Set Height/Auto Width;
3 Set Both; 4 Auto Both
```

Set Width/Auto Height

In this case, you set the width, but LetterPerfect will automatically size the height (to keep it in proportion with the original graphic). LetterPerfect automatically sizes a graphic by applying the following rule: take one-half of the distance between the margins. With default margin settings of one inch, that leaves 6 1/2 inches of actual space, or a default width of 3 1/2 inches.

Set Height/Auto Width

This is the inverse of the preceding option: you set the height, and LetterPerfect will auto-size the width to keep the graphic in proportion.

Set Both

With this option, you're in control—watch your proportions!

Auto Both

LetterPerfect calculates the height and width based on the size and dimensions of the original graphic.

Wrap Text Around Box

This is a Yes/No option. If you select No, LetterPerfect will print text despite the presence of the image. If you type to the right of the image, the image will be pushed to the left—eventually, you could squeeze it off the bottom of the page. If you select No wrap, images will not "bump" to the next page. Also, graphics in which the type does not wrap are not visible on the regular document editing screen. Reveal codes, however, will show the code: Fig Box:1 Filename] (see Figure 11.2).

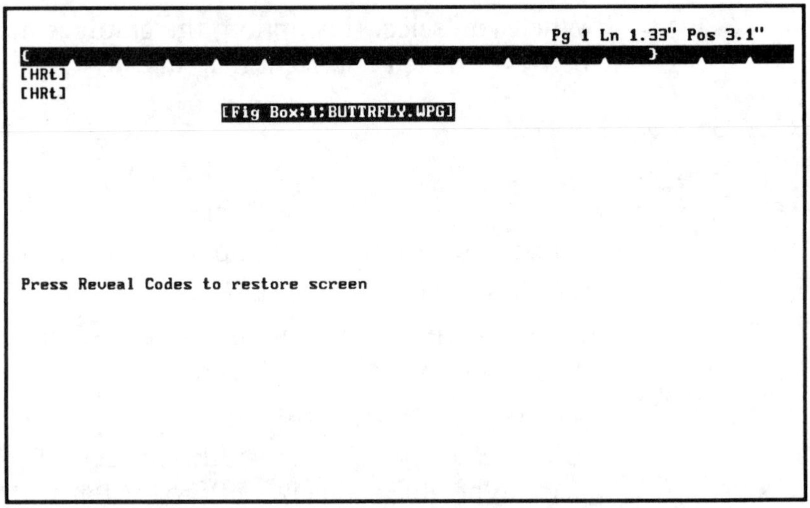

Figure 11.2 Reveal codes shows figure box.

If you select Yes for wrap, the box will be visible on the regular document screen (see figure 11.3).

Figure 11.3 Wrapped figure visible on editing screen.

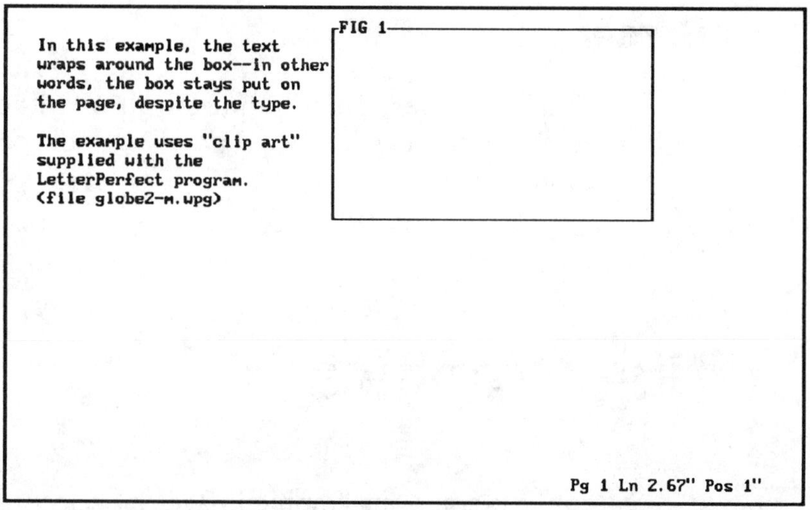

Finally, any graphics box can be seen with the View Documents mode F,P + 3 or (Shift-F7) + 3 (as long as you have a graphics monitor).

Figure 11.4 Graphic element in View Document mode.

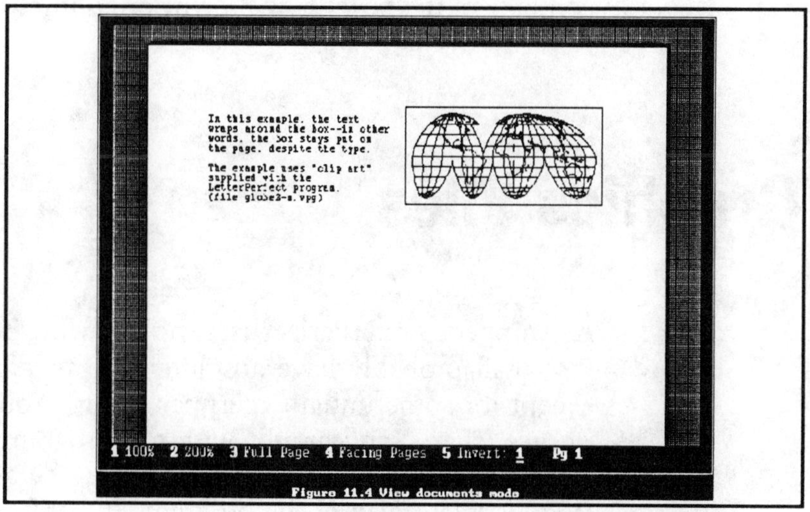

Border

Graphic images can be printed with or without a border. This is a Yes/No option. Hint: Most graphics look better with a border to contain them.

Editing Graphics

You can edit your graphic images by selecting G,E from the menu, or (Alt-F9) + 2 from the keyboard. LetterPerfect will prompt you for the number of the graphic you wish to edit. Editing is done via the Graphics Definition screen (same as in Figure 11.1). If you change the Filename, LetterPerfect will ask if you want to replace the contents of the current file with the new file. Enter Yes, and the contents of the new file will be inserted into the graphics box.

Graphics Files

As shipped, LetterPerfect is supplied with 30 pieces of "clip art." (You will probably have absolutely no use for most of the pieces, except for some initial experimentation). You can create your own images, charts, and graphs with the programs listed in Table 11.1. Then use the GRAPHCNV program (see below) to convert them to WPG format. Each of the programs in Table 11.1 will have its own routine for exporting files—consult the manuals supplied with the individual software packages, and look for an explanation about exporting to the file types listed in the right column of the table.

Table 11.1 WPG=compatible graphics programs

Program	Export File Type
Adobe Illustrator	EPS
Anvil-5000	HPGL
Arts & Letters	CGM
AutoCAD 9.0, 10.0	DXF,HPGL
AutoSketch 1.03	DXF, HPGL
Boeing Graph 4.0	IMG
CCS Designer	HPGL
ChartMaster 6.21	HPGL
Chemfile 11	HPGL
Chemtext	EPS
CIES (Compuscan)	TIFF
Designer 1.2 (Micrografx)	HPGL
Designer 2.0 (Micrografx)	EPS,CGM,PCX,TIFF
DFI Handy ScannerIMG,	TIFF
DiagramMaster 5.02	HPGL
Diagraph	HPGL
Dr. Halo II, IIID	HP
DrawPerfect	CGM,HPGL,WPG
Easyflow 4.4	HPGL
Energraphics 2.1	IMG,TIFF
Freelance Plus 2.0, 3.0	CGM
GEM Draw	GEM
GEM Paint 2.0IMG,	TIFF
GEM ScanIMG,	TIFF
Generic CAD	HPGL
GeniScan	TIFF
Graph-in-the-Box 2.0	HPGL

Table 11.1 Continued

Program	Export File Type
Graph Plus 1.3 (Micrografx)	HPGL,EPS,CGM,PCX,TIFF
Graphics Editor 200	HPGL
Graphwriter	CGM
Harvard Graphics 2.1	HPGL,CGM,EPS
HiJaaK	WPG
HOTSHOT Graphics 1.5	WPG
HP Scanning Gallery A.01	TIFF,PCX
IBM CADAM	HPGL
IBM CATIA	HPGL
IBM CBDS	HPGL
IBM GDDM	HPGL
IBM GPG	HPGL
Lotus 1-2-3 1A, 2.0	PIC
Lotus 1-2-3 3.0	PCX,CGM
Macintosh Paint 1.5	PNTG
Microsoft Chart	HPGL
Microsoft Excel	HPGL
Mirage	HPGL
Paradox 3.0	PIC
PC Paint Plus 1.5, 2.0	PPIC
PC Paintbrush	PCX
PicturePak	WPG,CGM,PCX
Pixie	CGM
Pizazz 1.01	PCX,TIFF
PlanPerfect 3.0, 5.0	CGM
PFS: First Publisher	PCX
Reflex 2.0	PIC

Table 11.1 Continued

Program	Export File Type
Quattro	PIC,EPS
SAS/Graph	HPGL
ScanMan	TIFF
Schema	HPGL
SignMaster 5.11	HPGL
SlideWrite Plus 2.1	HPGL,TIFF,PCX
SuperCalc 4	PIC
Symphony	PIC
Versacad	HPGL
VGA Paint	WPGL,TIFF,PCX
VP Graphics	HPGL
VP Planner	PIC
Windows Draw	HPGL
Windows Paint	MSP
Words & Figures	PIC

Converting Graphics

If you installed the utility files, you can convert exported files from any of the programs in Table 11.1 to WPG format. If you haven't installed the utility files, now's the time to do so. The particular file to use is called GRAPHCNV.EXE. To use it, switch to the directory in which you installed your program files, or the floppy that you labeled Utility Files. At the DOS prompt, type:

GRAPHCNV

The conversion program will display the message:

```
Enter name of file to convert:
```

Make sure that you list the full file and extension name, as in BUDGET.PIC. Next, the conversion program will prompt you to:

```
Enter name of output file:
```

You can specify any directory on your hard disk, or either floppy drive, as in B:BUDGET.WPG or C:\LPDATA\BUDGET. When you press (Enter), the conversion program will automatically convert the file to .WPG format.

Your Turn

Take a few minutes to create a graphic element with one of the supplied clip art files (extension .WPG). Experiment with sizing, placement, and wrap. You might even take the memo you created earlier and try inserting a graphic image. If you want to be even more adventuresome, take a Lotus 1-2-3 graph, convert it, and incorporate it into your memo as a graphic element.

At this point you know how to create and edit documents, and add a graphic element for a bit of flair. The next step is to print your work—which is what the next chapter is all about.

Section IV

Printing

Chapter 12

Printing Your Documents

Highlights

- Main printer menu
- Print full document
- Print multiple pages
- View document
- Initialize printer
- Controlling a print job
- Select Printer
- Binding offset
- Number of copies
- Graphics Quality
- Text Quality

From Screen to Paper

Having set up and formatted your document as described in earlier chapters, you are now ready to print. This chapter assumes you are using the basic printer installation described in Chapter 1. If you want to carry out a more complex printer installation, using multiple font cartridges, refer to Appendix A, which describes the installation of an HP LaserJet Series II or III.

Main Printer Menu

To start the print process, you must select the Main Print menu, shown in Figure 12.1, by selecting F,P or (Shift-F7).

Figure 12.1 Main print menu.

```
Print

     1 - Full Document
     2 - Multiple Pages
     3 - View Document
     4 - Initialize Printer


Options

     5 - Select Printer                HP LaserJet III
     6 - Binding Offset                0"
     7 - Number of Copies              1
     8 - Graphics Quality              Medium
     9 - Text Quality                  High






Selection: 0
```

This menu is divided into two sections. The first section, titled Print and containing options numbered 1 to 4, controls the primary printing functions. The second section, titled Options, is used to alter several of the print options. Each option is described below.

Print Menu Options (Top Portion)

Full Document

This print option initiates printing of the complete current document, regardless of the cursor position in the document. The print job is executed immediately, using the currently selected printer and the current settings shown in section 2 of the print menu.

Multiple Pages

This option prints the current page of the current document—the page on which the cursor is currently positioned, or a range of pages. When you select this option, the prompt:

```
Page(s),
```

will appear in the bottom left corner of the screen. You can print a single page, by entering, say 2, or a range of pages, such as 2,3 6-9, which will print pages 2 and 3, as well as 6,7,8, and 9. (You can enter up to 30 characters). If you type 6-, that tells LetterPerfect to print every page from 6 on. Conversely, -6 instructs LetterPerfect to print everything up to and including page 6. To print just odd pages, type "o" when prompted for the Page(s), or "e," for even numbered pages.

View Document

LetterPerfect 1.0 introduces a very sophisticated document preview feature. If you have a graphics monitor, you can view your document exactly as it will print in full graphics splendor. If you have specified fonts of different sizes or styles, they can be seen in the WYSIWYG (what-you-see-is-what-you-get) display (see Figure 12.2). Furthermore, if you have incorporated any graphic elements into you document, these will be properly positioned and displayed as well.

Figure 12.2 View documents screen—200%.

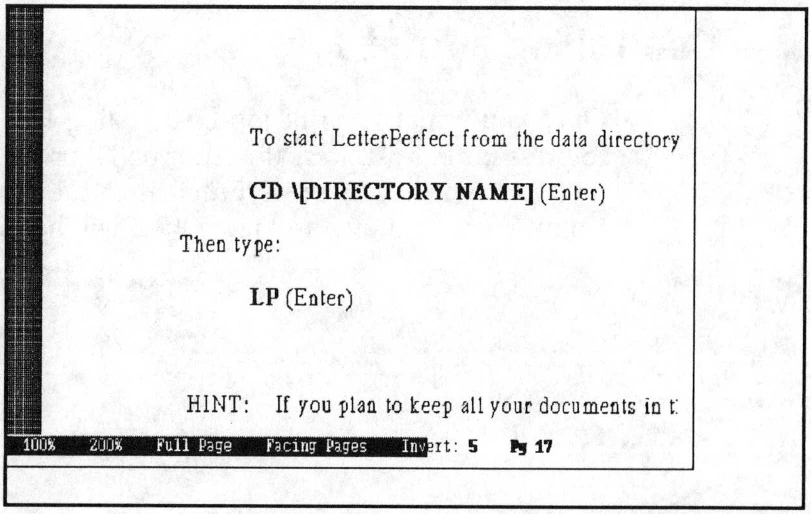

You can view the document at several different levels of magnification including:

1 100% 2 200% 3 Full Pages 4 Facing Pages

In addition, a fifth option, invert, allows you to invert the image, which will reverse the foreground and background.

In addition, you can use the (Page Up) and (Page Down) keys to view preceding and subsequent pages. In the higher magnifications, you can also use the cursor keys to move about the page.

Note: Font attributes (bold, italic, etc.) can be displayed by the View Document option only if the currently selected printer can print the designated attributes.

Initialize Printer

This option is used to control the downloading of soft fonts to your printer. If you marked soft fonts during the printer installation, you can download them by selecting this option (see Appendix A). In fact, you will need to initialize the printer before you can use the fonts, so you might as well get into the habit of selecting the initialization option each time you begin a word processing session. When you select this option, LetterPerfect will ask you whether or not you want to proceed with the Initialization. Answer Yes to begin downloading fonts.

Controlling a Print Job

Once you initiate a print job by selecting Full Document (no need to press Enter; just press the letter or 1), or Multiple Pages (printing will start when you press Enter after the last number) the Print Control Screen shown in Figure 12.3 will be displayed.

Figure 12.3 Print Control Screen.

```
Print: Control Printer


Port:        LPT 1                                  Page Number:  1
Status:      Printing                               Current Copy: 1 of 1
Message:     None
Paper:       Standard 8.5" x 11"
Location:    Continuous feed
Action:      None









1 Cancel Job; 2 Go (start printer); 3 Stop: 0
```

This screen shows you the status of the print job, what page is being printed, and actions to be taken (you may need to feed paper manually, for instance, or give the printer a "Go" to continue with the print job (see below). Three options are available:

1 Cancel Job; 2 Go (start printer); 3 Stop: 0

Cancel

Use the Cancel option to cancel the current print job. This option can only cancel that portion of the document not yet sent to the printer. If you have a short document or a large print buffer, you may not be able to cancel the job before the entire document is sent to the printer. In general, to cancel a print job, you must physically stop the printer by taking it off line first, canceling the print job, and then resetting the printer to clear its buffer.

Go (Start Printer)

Use the Go option to restart the printer after it has been stopped with the Stop option below or by a printer error or prompt. (Your LetterPerfect manual contains an extensive list of printer errors and solutions.) If you stop a print job, restart it using this option. If LetterPerfect detects a serious printer error (i.e., more serious than "out of paper"), it stops the print process, and you must select the Go option to restart it.

If you have selected manual feed for one of your forms during the printer installation process, LetterPerfect automatically alerts you to insert the desired form the first time the print process calls for it. Then you must select the Go option to restart the printer.

Stop

Use the Stop option to pause during the current print job. Select Go, described above, to restart the print job. Remember, Stop does not recall data already sent to the printer.

Option Menu (Lower Part of Print Menu)

Select Printer

As mentioned in Chapter 1 and discussed in detail in Appendix A, you can install several different printers or printer configurations. Once they are installed, you can select from among them by pressing S for the Select Printer option. The currently selected printer is marked with an asterisk, as shown in Figure 12.4.

Figure 12.4. Printer selection screen.

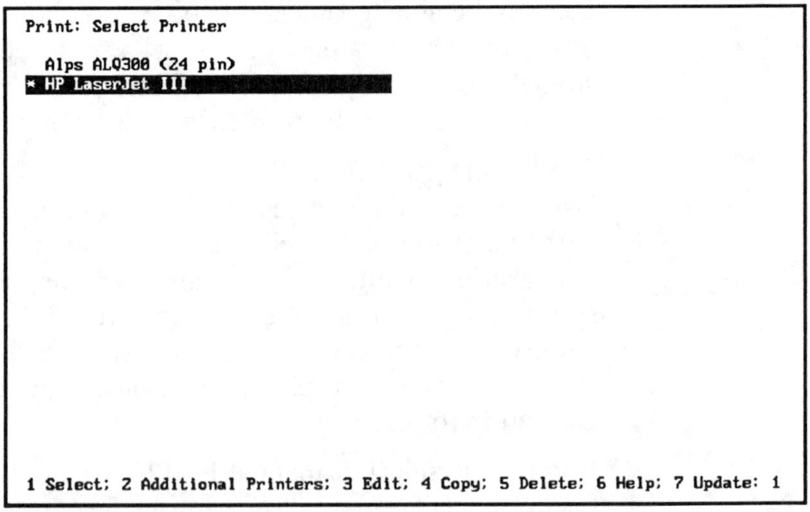

To select another printer, highlight its name and press S for Selection.

Additional Printers

If you want to add additional printer definitions, use this option. LetterPerfect will display other related printers in the .ALL file(s) copied during installation. You can copy other .ALL files to a floppy disk during installation and use them later with this option (see your LetterPerfect manual for details). When you don't see the desired printer, though, the easiest technique is to rerun the installation routine and use the install printer option.

Edit

This is used to refine a printer definition—Appendix A explains how to edit a LaserJet Series II or LaserJet III definition.

Copy

This feature is used to copy the definition for whatever printer is highlighted. Once you've cloned the printer definition, you can edit it with the previous option, thereby creating two separate printer selections. (See your manual for further details.)

Delete

This option deletes an installed printer from the print selection screen. To remove it from the program altogether, you must delete the associated file with a .PRS extension. (If you choose Additional printers, then List Printer Files, LetterPerfect displays a list of all definitions. Again, this gets fairly detailed, and you won't be using the function very often. Refer to the manual supplied with your program for more information.)

Help

This option displays a set of mini-help screens for each printer you've selected.

Update

WordPerfect Corporation occasionally revises its printer files. In the event that you purchase an updated printer disk, use this option to include the changes in your printer definitions.

Binding Width

When you are creating two-sided pages, you should shift the even numbered pages to the left and the odd numbered pages to the right to allow a fixed inside margin for binding the pages together or for punching holes for use in a three-ring binder. This width is added to the normal left and right margins, changing the line length, so your entire document may require reformatting if you change the binding width significantly.

Number of Copies

This option allows you to specify the number of copies of the document or page to be printed. If you are printing a multipage document, this prints out multiple *sets* of the document in collated order.

Graphics Quality

If your printer has variable print resolutions for graphics, you can control that feature through this option. Many of the earlier laser printers, for example, did not have enough memory to permit large 300 dot-per-inch (DPI) graphics, but they can print the same graphic at 150 DPI or 75 DPI. In addition, for draft documents, lower quality graphics will usually print more quickly. You can then print the final draft with the highest resolution available with your printer. The specific choices when you select this option are:

1 Do **N**ot Print; **2** **D**raft; **3** **M**edium **4** **H**igh

The first option forces LetterPerfect to print text and graphics separately. This is useful if your printer does not have enough memory to print simultaneous text and graphics.

Text Quality

Many printers, especially dot matrix printers, have different quality text printing capability. The lower resolution type is usually referred to as draft quality, while the higher quality type is referred to as near-letter quality. Draft quality printing is often two or three times faster than near-letter quality and is therefore desirable for early drafts of a document. The options are the same as those for Graphics Quality.

Printing a Block of Text

You can print a block of text at any time by placing the cursor at the beginning of the block, turning on the block feature by pressing E,B or (Alt-F4), highlighting the desired block with the cursor keys or mouse, and then selecting the print option by pressing F,P or (Shift-F7). You will be asked to confirm your choice, and the block will be printed on the currently selected printer, in accordance with the currently selected print options.

Note that wherever the block falls on the page on your screen, that's where it will be printed on the paper; if the line indicator on your status line shows that the block is six inches down the page, it will also be printed six inches down the page on paper.

Your Turn

Print your memo, or portions of it, using the functions described above. Experiment with each option until you are comfortable with the way it works.

Section V

File Maintenance

Chapter 13

Managing Your Files

Highlights

- The file manager
- Retrieve files
- Delete files
- Move/rename files
- Other directory
- Copy files
- Look at (view) files
- Mark files

Maintaining Your Files

In addition to creating and printing documents, file maintenance is an important aspect of word processing—or any computer application, for that matter. LetterPerfect includes a first-rate file manager that allows you to store, retrieve, delete, rename, and back up files easily. In addition, the file manager provides extremely useful features for viewing files without retrieving them. This chapter reviews all of the options, and describes their use.

Using the File Manager

To initiate the file manager, press F,L or (F5), list files. The lower left-hand corner of the screen will then display the name of the current directory. If that is the directory in which you wish to manage files, press (Enter), and the List Files screen will be displayed (see Figure 13.1). If you wish to change directories temporarily, edit the directory name shown on the screen, and press (Enter). The files for that directory will be displayed, but when you exit the List Files screen, the directory will be the same as before.

If you actually wish to make another directory the current directory, enter an equal sign (=) and LetterPerfect will prompt you for the name of the new directory. Enter the name, and press (Enter). The List Files screen will then be displayed, showing the files in the new directory.

Figure 13.1 File manager screen.

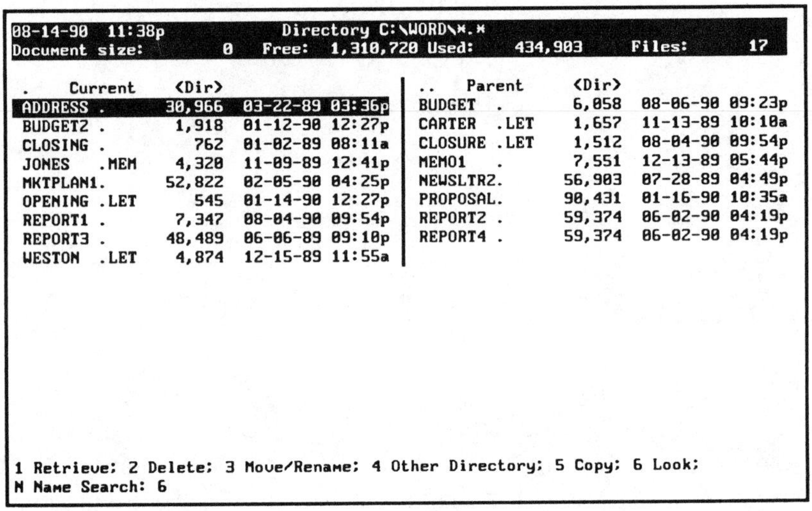

The top of the screen reveals key information about your system, including:

1. The current date.
2. The current time.
3. The name of the directory.
4. The size of the current document (i.e., the one on the screen).
5. The amount of space free on your hard disk or floppy (data) disk.
6. The total amount of bytes occupied by the files in the current directory.
7. The number of files in the current directory.

The individual files are shown with their main filenames and extensions. You can select a file for one of the file management options by moving the cursor and highlighting the name. The options are listed on the bottom of the screen.

List File Options

Retrieve

This option retrieves the highlighted file. If the retrieved file is the only document on the screen, it is considered the current document. If text already exists on the screen and you attempt to retrieve a file, LetterPerfect asks you to confirm by asking:

```
Retrieve into current document (Y/N) No
```

in the lower left-hand portion of the screen. This confirmation is included to prevent you from accidentally combining two files on screen. Of course, there are many times when you want to insert one file into another intentionally, such as when you have created a "boilerplate" and wish to retrieve it into your document, rather than retyping it each time you wish to use it (see Chapter 7 for more information about this technique).

Delete

The Delete option erases a file. Before doing so, LetterPerfect asks you to confirm your deletion, by asking:

```
Delete [highlighted file name] (Y/N) No
```

If you indicate yes, the file is erased by the DOS delete/erase command. (If you were too hasty, you can always undelete it using a third-party file recovery program.)

Move/Rename

This option allows you to rename files. When you highlight a file and select Option 3, LetterPerfect prompts you in the lower left-hand side of the screen with:

```
New Name: [directory\highlighted file name]
```

Edit the file name as you choose, and press (Enter). The file will be listed with its new name.

That's the "rename" part of this option. The "move" part comes in if you alter the directory in front of the filename. For example, if you want to move the file TC003.SAM from the directory named C:\SAMPLE to the directory named C:\WORD, you would simply edit the directory name, C:\SAMPLE and change it to C:\WORD or enter the new directory name by itself at the prompt. When you press (Enter), TC003.SAM will be transferred to C:\WORD and deleted from the C:\SAMPLE directory listing. In this regard, Move is a "move and delete" function.

Finally, you can rename a file and transfer it to another directory. Let's say that you want to transfer the file named C:\SAMPLE\TC003.SAM to the directory called C:\WORD, and rename it INTRO.SAM. At the new name prompt, edit both the directory and the file name so that they read:

New Name:C:\WORD\INTRO.SAM

When you press (Enter), TC00.SAM will be transferred to C:\WORD, and renamed INTRO.SAM.

Other Directory

Use this option to change the current directory. When you press 4, LetterPerfect prompts you for a new directory in the lower left-hand corner of the screen. Edit the current directory name, or enter a completely new one. When you press (Enter), the contents of the new directory will be displayed in the List Files screen.

If the directory you enter does not exist, LetterPerfect asks if you want to create it. Type Y to confirm, and N if you change your mind. (It's easy to make a mistake typing in the name of a directory. If LetterPerfect prompts you to create a new directory, and you know the directory you entered exists already, that's a sure sign you've made a typo. Enter N, and select Option 7 to start over again.)

Copy

This option lets you copy the highlighted file to another directory, or a floppy disk. It is extremely useful for backing up your work, especially if you're using a hard disk. Remember, no hard disk is infallible, and it pays to copy valuable files to floppies frequently...just in case. (Unfortunately, many people do not get into a regular backup routine until after disaster strikes and they must recreate their files. Why become a statistic? Use the Copy function on a regular basis. Remember, the LetterPerfect backup feature makes a copy only of the current file, and keeps it only until the machine is turned off. If your hard disk crashes, ALL your files may be lost.)

To use the Copy option, highlight the file to be copied and select Option 5. LetterPerfect prompts you with:

`Copy this file to:`

Enter the drive and the directory, as in C:\WORD, or the floppy drive name, as in B:. Press (Enter) to copy the file. If the file already exists in the other directory or on the floppy, LetterPerfect asks if you want to replace it. Respond with a Y if you do, which will probably be the case if you're updating a backup file.

Here is a useful variation. You can copy the file to another directory, but assign it a different name when it gets there. For instance, if you highlight the file called TC003.SAM, and want to copy it to the C:\WORD directory as TC003.REJ, at the Copy this file to: prompt you would type:

C:\WORD\TC003.REJ (Enter)

When the file is copied to C:\WORD, the contents will remain the same, but the name will be new. You can do the same thing when copying to a floppy disk:

B:\TC003.REJ (Enter)

Look

This feature lets you examine the contents of a file without actually retrieving it. You can also examine the contents of various directories. Look is extremely useful because it allows you to examine many different files quickly without waiting for LetterPerfect to load them.

Let's say you are working on a document and you need to check another file to see if you covered a certain topic. Press (F5), select the third file, and scroll through in Look mode. When you find what you're looking for, return to your document. Note, however, that you can't cut and paste from or to the file in Look mode—it is strictly for viewing. Here are some rules for using Look.

Viewing Files

When you highlight a file and select 6, the contents of the document appears in a special format, as shown in Figure 13.2. The directory, filename, and file size appear in the highlighted bar at the top of the screen, along with the last date and time that the file was revised. The document shows various formatting features, such as tabs, indents, bold, underline, etc., but it can only appear for viewing in single-line spacing.

Figure 13.2 File view mode.

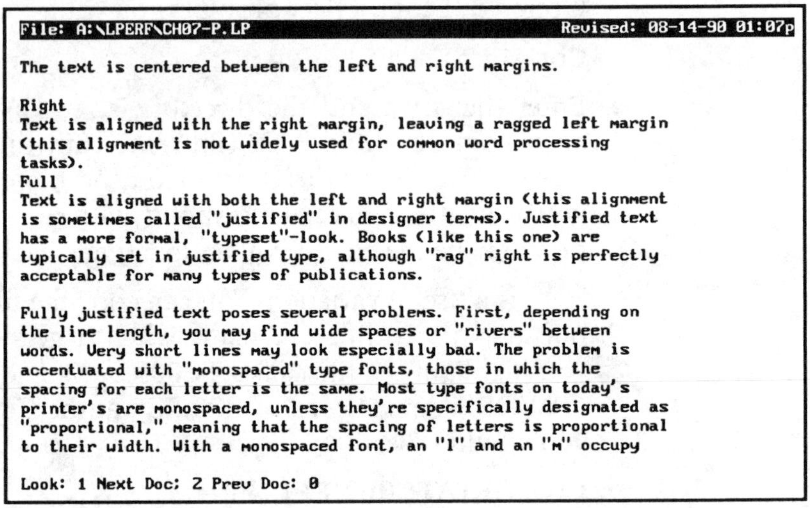

```
File: A:\LPERF\CH07-P.LP                          Revised: 08-14-90 01:07p

The text is centered between the left and right margins.

Right
Text is aligned with the right margin, leaving a ragged left margin
(this alignment is not widely used for common word processing
tasks).
Full
Text is aligned with both the left and right margin (this alignment
is sometimes called "justified" in designer terms). Justified text
has a more formal, "typeset"-look. Books (like this one) are
typically set in justified type, although "rag" right is perfectly
acceptable for many types of publications.

Fully justified text poses several problems. First, depending on
the line length, you may find wide spaces or "rivers" between
words. Very short lines may look especially bad. The problem is
accentuated with "monospaced" type fonts, those in which the
spacing for each letter is the same. Most type fonts on today's
printer's are monospaced, unless they're specifically designated as
"proportional," meaning that the spacing of letters is proportional
to their width. With a monospaced font, an "l" and an "m" occupy

Look: 1 Next Doc; 2 Prev Doc: 0
```

While viewing a document, there are certain restrictions:

1. You can move up or down through the document, but not left or right. Up or down movement is achieved by using the cursor keys, the (PgUp) and (PgDn) keys, and the screen up (+) and screen down (-) keys.
2. To scroll continuously from top to bottom without having to press any cursor movement keys, press S. To stop the forward scrolling, press S again.
3. You can use forward or backward Search, but not Replace or any other feature that alters the text. (The menu bar can also be activated—observe the bracketed options, which cannot be used in Look mode.) The Search function itself has a few wrinkles when used in Look mode. After pressing Search, enter the text as you normally would. But here, you *must* press (F2) to initiate the search.

   When a search is successful, LetterPerfect highlights the found text, but the cursor goes only to the line on which the text occurs. You cannot search for text that wraps from one line to another; when you try to enter a hard return, LetterPerfect will simply continue the search with whatever text you have already entered as the search criteria.

To continue searching for other occurrences of the text, press (F2) and repeat the operation. To continue scrolling through the text, press any of the scrolling keys described above. Do not press (F1), (Esc), or (F7)—you will return immediately to the List Files screen.

If the search is unsuccessful, LetterPerfect beeps. You can then proceed to scroll through the document or try another search.

Finally, you can search only for words, not codes. Remember, Look is strictly for viewing. If you try to alter text, LetterPerfect either does nothing, scrolls continuously, or returns you to the List Files screen.

4. To return voluntarily to the List Files screen, press (F1), (Enter), (Esc), or (F7). Then press (F7) to return to your document.

5. To view other files without returning to the file management screen, select an option from the bottom left corner menu (see Figure 13.2). Each time you press 1, LetterPerfect will display the next document in the file in Look mode. Pressing 2 moves backwards through the file manager (documents are organized alphabetically by filename in the file manager).

Viewing Directories

If you want to view the contents of a directory, highlight the words CURRENT <DIR>, which will always appear above the first file on the left side of the List File screen, and press (Enter). At the bottom of the screen, LetterPerfect displays the current directory name. Edit the name to the directory you wish to view, then press (Enter). The new directory will then be displayed. You can use Look to peer into any of the files.

If you are using a floppy disk system and are reviewing the directory of your data disks and trying to locate a particular file, you can use the CURRENT <DIR> to update the directory listing each time you swap data disks. When you press CURRENT <DIR> without changing the directoy name, LetterPerfect rereads the current directory and relists the files. If you have changed data disks, the new list of file names will be displayed.

Note that when you use Look to view the files of another directory, your current directory hasn't changed. In other words, if your current directory is called C:\SAMPLE, and you use Look to view the contents of C:\WORD, when you press (F1) or (F7), you return to your document, and the current directory is still C:\SAMPLE. The only way to change the current directory from within LetterPerfect is by pressing the (=) sign and entering a new directory after pressing (F5), as described above, or by selecting Option 4 from the file manager.

Finally, you can use the "?" and "*" wildcard characters when viewing the contents of a different directory. The "?" wildcard means any single character, while the "*" means any number of characters.

When you highlight the words "CURRENT <DIR>," the directory name in the lower left-hand corner of the screen lists the directory, followed by a backslash and *.*. The string "*.*" means any file name followed by any extension, i.e., all files. You can refine that portion to generate a more selective listing.

For example, let's say that in the directory C:\WORD, you want to view only the files with the extension "LET." In this case, when prompted for a directory, you would enter:

C:\WORD*.LET (Enter)

This means display files that have any main name, but only .LET as an extension. Refer back to Figure 13.1 for a directory with a full assortment of files. Figure 13.3 shows the results of viewing only the .LET files. As you can see, this technique makes it easier to identify like files.

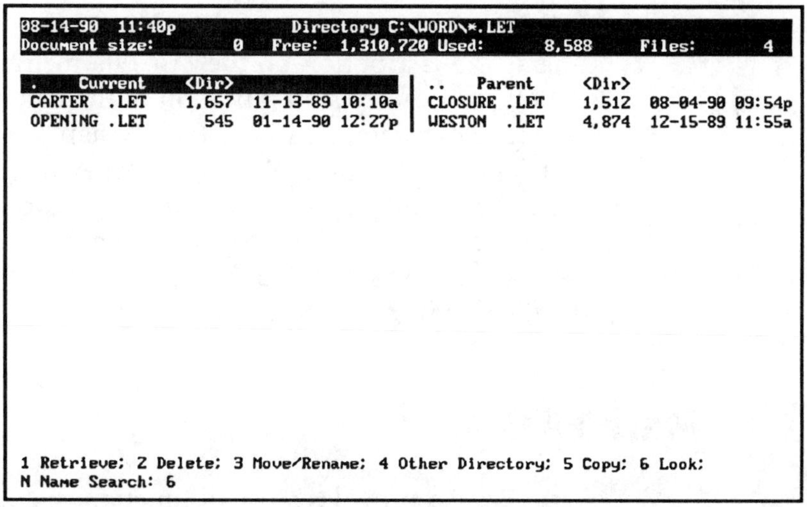

Figure 13.3 View of selected files with .LET extension.

Conversely, you might want to find files with the same main name, say "CHAP1," but with different extensions. In that case, you'd enter:

C:\WORD\CHAP1.* (Enter)

to specify the main name, and include any extension. To further refine your viewing, you might be interested in files with specific combinations of letters in the extension. Perhaps you want to find all files that have an extension consisting of "R" plus one letter or number. You would enter:

C:\WORD*.R? (Enter)

The "?" character tells the program to include any single character. Thus, R1, R2, and RA would be selected, but not REJ or R12. If you had used the "*" character, as in:

C:\WORD*.R* (Enter)

extensions with one or more character starting with the letter R will be displayed.

As you can see, between the two wildcard characters, you can be as broad or specific as you like, and can zero in on any file or set of files.

N Name Search

This is the last option on the List File menu. When you select this option, you can type in a portion of the name of the file to be highlighted. For example, if you type "Chap," the cursor moves to the first file with "C" in it. When you type "h" it moves to the first file with "Ch," and so on. If you have a short listing, it is definitely faster just to move the cursor and highlight the desired file. If you have a very long list, this may be a more efficient way to highlight the file you want to act upon.

Mark Files

LetterPerfect provides a useful function that lets you execute several of the File List functions upon a group of files by first marking the files and then calling the desired function. To mark a group of files, highlight each file to be included and press (Shift-8). This marks the highlighted files with an asterisk before the filename (see Figure 13.4).

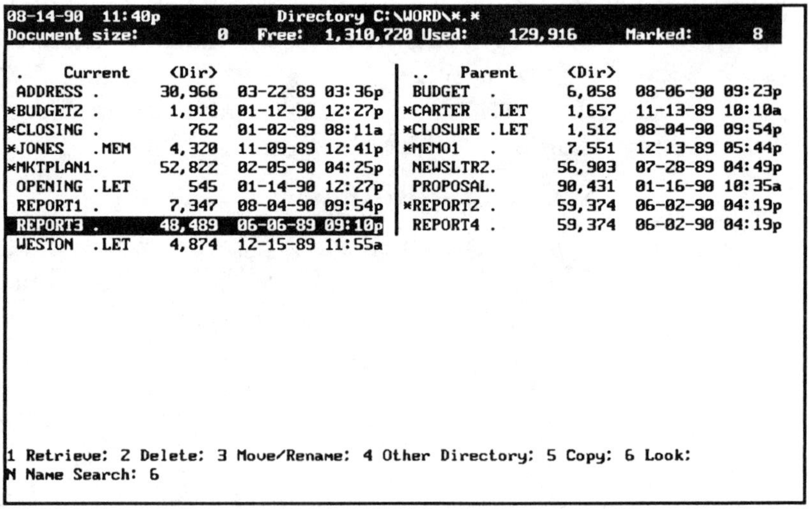

Figure 13.4 Marked files (asterisks on left of filename).

The following functions can then be used with the group of marked files:

Delete

When you select delete, LetterPerfect will ask you to confirm the mass deletion by asking:

```
Delete marked files (Y/N) No
```

If you say yes, they will all be deleted. If you say no, LetterPerfect asks if you want to delete the *single* file underneath the highlight. Answer Y or N.

CAUTION: This is a very powerful and potentially dangerous feature. If you are not paying strict attention when you use it, you could wipe out many hours or days worth of hard work!

Move/Rename

You can't rename a group of files, but you can move them to another directory or a floppy disk. Remember, once moved, they are deleted from the current directory and transferred to the new directory. LetterPerfect prompts you with:

```
Move marked files (Y/N) No
```

If you answer Y, it will prompt you with:

```
Move marked files to:
```

Enter the desired directory or the floppy drive. Make sure you include a colon after the drive letter.

If you enter N when asked if you want to Move marked files, LetterPerfect assumes that you want to rename or move the single file under the highlight.

Copy

As with the other options that work with a marked group of files, LetterPerfect asks if you want to:

```
Copy the marked files (Y/N) No
```

If you respond Y, it will prompts you with:

```
Copy all marked files to:
```

Enter the name of the directory or floppy drive. Make sure you include a colon after the drive name.

Your Turn

The List Files options are very powerful and very useful. Try using each of the options described above. When you begin using LetterPerfect on a regular basis, you'll pick and choose those that can make your daily word processing go most smoothly.

Section VI

Special Features

Chapter 14

Other LetterPerfect Features

Highlights

- Mail merge
- Outliner
- Shell
- Convert
- Graph converter

So far, everything you've read in this book has focused on the basic tools you need for routine word processing. In addition, LetterPerfect offers a wealth of other powerful features that you may or may not want to learn after you become more familiar with the basic word processing tools. The following discussion is meant to give you a brief taste of how several of the features work. If your appetite is whetted, and you feel like you can absorb yet more information, you can turn to the LetterPerfect reference manual and learn how to use these and other features by yourself. By now you've probably come to realize that trial and error is the best way to get a handle on any LetterPerfect feature (or for that matter, *any* software program, whether it's a word processor, a database, or a spreadsheet).

Mail Merge

The mail merge function allows you to combine the contents of a "primary file," say a letter, with the contents of a "secondary file," such as an address list. You can create either the primary or the secondary merge file first, depending on your needs. The primary file is coded so that each line of the address appears in the proper position. There are many types of merges, as explained in the LetterPerfect reference manual. Here's the most common one:

Primary File: A Letter

Type a letter, but leave out the specific addressee and the name following the "dear." Instead, insert merge codes, by using the following procedure:

1. Move the cursor to the first line of the addressee area.
2. Press T,E or (Shift-F9). LetterPerfect will display a window with the available merge codes (see Figure 14.1).

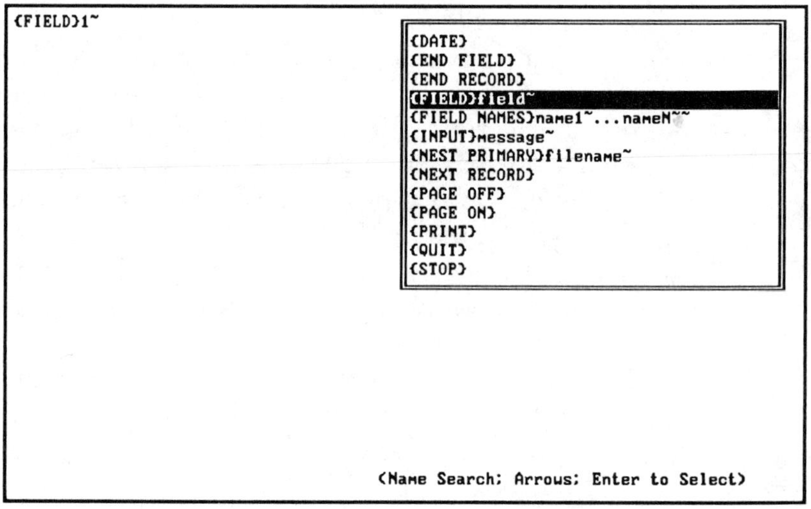

Figure 14.1 Merge code window.

3. Highlight the {FIELD}field~ option by using the cursor keys or the mouse.
4. When you press (Enter) or click quickly on the left-hand button, the prompt:

   `Enter Field:`

   appears on the bottom of the screen.
5. Type 1 and press (Enter). This tells LetterPerfect that during a merge, the first field of the addresses in the secondary file (generally a name) should be printed here (assuming that the secondary file is coded properly—see below).
6. Repeat this process for the address (you need only one field number even if the address is multi-line—see below, under secondary file).

7. Move the cursor to the space after the "Dear." Place another field, followed by a comma or colon or whatever punctuation mark you normally use in your correspondence. This will allow you to personalize the letters—if field 3 happens to correspond to the person's first name, or a special line in the secondary file with an appelation, such as "Mr. Smith," then the first name or the full name will appear in the merged letter, followed by the proper punctuation.

8. Type the body of the letter. While the text will be your own, the structure should look like the sample shown in Figure 14.2.

Figure 14.2. Primary file codes.

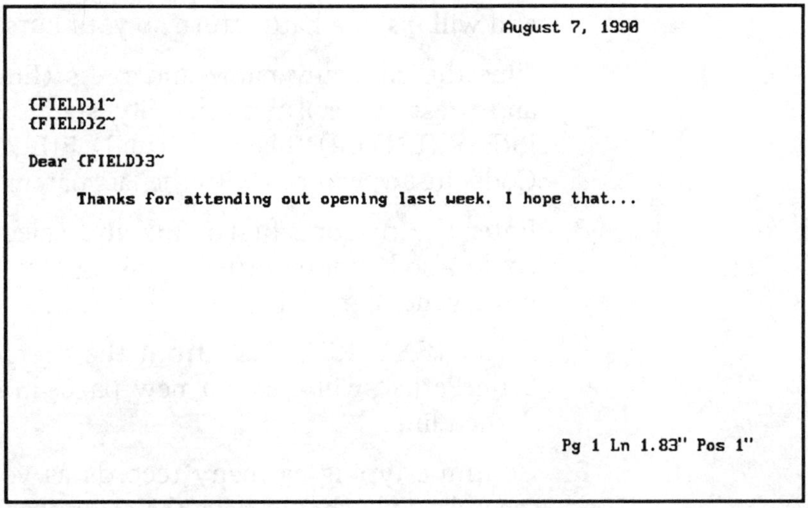

Note: You can insert the current date by using either the {DATE} merge code, or the built-in date function T,C or (Shift-F5) + 2.

9. Save the letter as you would any document.

Secondary File: Address List

The primary letter you just created will be merged with secondary files containing addresses. LetterPerfect will match the fields that you designated in the letter with the fields in the address file. In the following model, each address constitutes a "record." Within each record, the following structure will be used:

Name = Field 1

Company, Address, city, state, Zip Code = Field 2

First Name = Field 3

When you merge the address with the letter described above, the name field will appear first, followed by the address, city, state, and Zip. The appelation plus name will appear after the "Dear" (refer to Figure 14.2). To create the secondary file:

1. Type the name line (e.g. Mr. Joe Smith). DO NOT PRESS (ENTER)—instead, open the merge code window, T,E or (Shift-F9), highlight and select {END FIELD}. This will place the merge code after the last name (do not enter any spaces), and will insert a hard return so your cursor is on the next line.
2. Type the company name and press (Enter), type the address and press (Enter), type the city, state, and Zip but DO NOT PRESS (ENTER). Place an {END FIELD} code after the Zip Code, just as you did with the last name.
3. Enter the person's first name and select {END FIELD} (You could also be more formal by using Mr., Mrs., Ms., etc—this is just a generic model).
4. Select {END RECORD} from the merge code window, and LetterPerfect will create a new page, indicated by the double dashed line.
5. Continue typing as many records as you like. Your finished secondary file should have the same structure as that shown in Figure 14.3.

Figure 14.3 Secondary file structure.

```
Mr. Jeff Smith{END FIELD}
West Corp.
123 Main St
Eberly, MN 23212{END FIELD}
Jeff{END FIELD}
{END RECORD}
================================================================================
Ms. Cynthia Certa{END FIELD}
CompuCalc
P.O. Box 333
Weston, NJ 73234{END FIELD}
Cynthia{END FIELD}
{END RECORD}





Field: 1                                               Pg 2 Ln 1.83" Pos 1"
```

As you can see in Figure 14.3, each record (i.e., each address set) contains three fields. The first ends after the top line, the second encompasses the company and address lines, and the third includes the first name.

6. Save your secondary file as you would any other file.

Merging the Primary and Secondary Files

Once you create and save your primary and secondary files to disk, clear the screen, then press T,M or (Ctrl-F9). LetterPerfect prompts you with:

```
Primary file:
```

Type in the name and press (Enter). LetterPerfect then prompts you with:

```
Secondary file:
```

Type in the name and press (Enter).

LetterPerfect will pause and display the message, "Merging." When it finishes, you'll see individual letters on your screen, each separated by a hard page (see Figure 14.4). You can then print the merged file from your screen, or save the merged file and print it later.

Figure 14.4 Letters merged on the screen.

```
                                              August 7, 1990



Mr. Jeff Smith
West Corp.
123 Main St
Eberly. MN 23212

Dear Jeff,

     Thanks for attending out opening last week. I hope that...

==========================================================================


                                              August 7, 1990



Ms. Cynthia Certa
CompuCalc
P.O. Box 333
Weston, NJ 73234
                                                      Pg 2 Ln 1" Pos 1"
```

Alternately, you can insert the codes {PAGE OFF}{PRINT} beneath the last line of text in your primary merge file (see Figure 4.5)—this will instruct LetterPerfect to do the merging at the printer. Each letter will be printed individually, with each name and address in the secondary file inserted in order.

Figure 14.5 Primary merge file coded for print merge.

```
                                              August 7, 1990



{FIELD}1~
{FIELD}2~

Dear {FIELD}3~,

     Thanks for attending out opening last week. I hope that...




Sincerely,



Steve Bennett

{PAGE OFF}{PRINT}

                                                      Pg 1 Ln 3" Pos 1"
```

There are several other merge options available, but the ones just described cover the most basic merge situations. If you're interested in doing more complex merges, consult your LetterPerfect reference manual.

Outliner

Many people find it helpful to organize their thoughts into an outline before proceeding to write. LetterPerfect offers a built-in outliner to help you do this. While it does not offer the power of a full-featured, stand-alone outliner, or programs based around an outliner, such as Framework, it is a useful tool and easy to learn.

To create an outline:

1. Press T,O or (Shift-F5) + 3.
2. The word "Outline" appears in the lower left-hand corner to remind you that you are in outline mode.
3. Press (Enter), and the Roman numeral "I" will appear on the screen. Press (F4) indent, then enter your text.
4. When you press (Enter) again, Roman numeral "II" will appear. If you have a subsection for "I", press the (Tab) key, and the "II" will change to an "A". Type your text and press (Enter). On the next line, "B" will appear. If have a subpoint for "A," press the (Tab) key until "1." appears. Type your text and press (Enter), and "2." will appear on the next line. You can either type a head at the same level as "1.", or you can press tab to create yet another sublevel (you can create up to seven sublevels from the Roman numeral).

   LetterPerfect will remain at the current outline level until you move backwards, (i.e., to higher levels on the same line, from, "1." to "I," for example) by pressing L,M or (Shift-Tab). (You can also move the cursor to the left of the number or letter and press the Delete key—this will advance the line one level per deletion.)
5. When you're finished, press T,U or (Shift-F5) + 4 to turn the outliner off and return to normal text entry mode. Save the outline as you would any text.

   A sample outline is shown in Figure 14.6.

Figure 14.6 Sample outline.

```
I.CORPORATE GOALS
     A.Product Development
          1.Consumer electronics line
          2.Industrial division
               a. New control system
               b. Upgrade model 100
          3.Service Department
     B. Market Share
          1.Increase by 10% through promotions
          2.Lower pricing to match Carbex
     C. Customer Service Improvements
     D. Quality Program

II.DIVERSIFICATION
     A. Opportunities





Outline                                              Pg 1 Ln 3" Pos 1.8"
```

To convert an outline into text, conduct a search and replace on [Par Num: Auto] codes (which create the outline numbers). Replace the code with a blank, and the outline will be "static"—each entry can be edited as you would any other type of text.

Shell and Utility Files

During installation, you were prompted as to whether or not you wanted to install the Shell and Utility files (see Chapters 1 and 2). If you didn't install the utility files, reinstall the program. (You only have to say Yes when prompted for the Shell files and Utility files—say No to all others.)

Shell Files

LetterPerfect is shipped with a shell program that allows you to run many other programs from a central menu. Note that it is not a "multitasking" system that enables you to run different programs simultaneously. Rather, it swaps the programs in and out of memory, so that you can move from one to another easily. As you move from one program to another, the program swapped out of memory is "frozen" at whatever point you left. A "clipboard" feature of the shell program enables you to move information from compatible programs and move it to other programs.

A complete discussion of the Shell program is beyond the scope of this book, and your LetterPerfect package includes an excellent separate user's guide. Even if you don't plan on using Shell to manage a number of programs, you might want to use it as a means of going to DOS without leaving LetterPerfect. This is useful when you want to format a disk, for example.

To use the Shell program after you've installed it, switch to your LetterPerfect program directory. For example, if the directory containing your LetterPerfect files is C:\LP10, you would type:

```
CD\ LP10
```

Then type:

Shell

The screen shown in Figure 14.7 will be displayed.

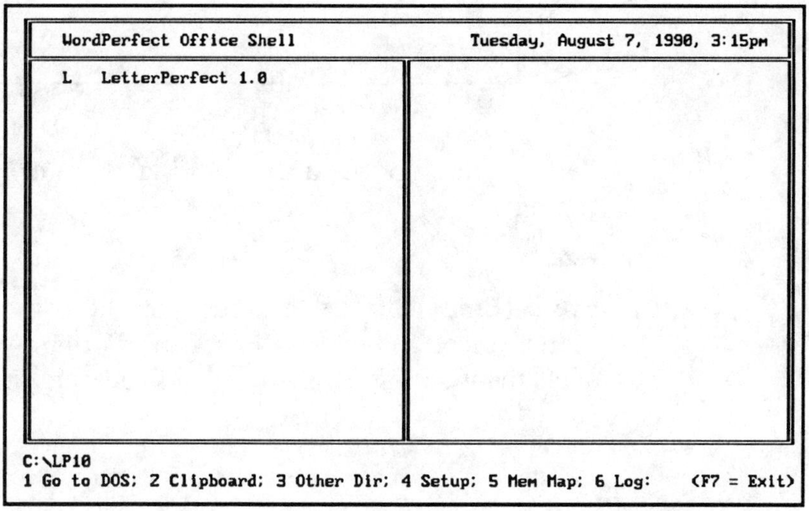

Figure 14.7 Shell screen.

LetterPerfect will appear as the only menu item (if you install other programs, they will appear on the menu, too).

Press (Enter) or "L" to select LetterPerfect, and LetterPerfect will load. To go to DOS without exiting LetterPerfect, you can select F,G or (Ctrl-F1). This will display the following options:

1. Go to Shell; Clipboard: **2 S**ave; **3 A**ppend; **4 R**etrieve: **0**

Select Go to Shell, and the screen shown in Figure 14.7 will again be displayed. Select 1, Go to Dos, from the bottom menu, and your screen will display the DOS prompt with the message shown in Figure 14.8.

Figure 14.8 DOS message when exit to prompt through Shell.

```
Enter the DOS command 'EXIT' (or Press F7) to return to the shell.


The IBM Personal Computer DOS
Version 3.30 (C)Copyright International Business Machines Corp 1981, 1987
             (C)Copyright Microsoft Corp 1981, 1986

(shell) C:\LP10>
```

You can now format a disk, and later return to the Shell Menu by typing:

```
exit
```

Press (Enter) or "L" to return to the same spot you left off in LetterPerfect. When you exit LetterPerfect, you will return to the shell menu. Press (F7) to unload the shell program and return to DOS.

Utility Files

The LetterPerfect utility files include a number of programs. The two of primary interest are CONVERT.EXE and GRAPHCNV.EXE. The former enables you to convert LetterPerfect files to a number of other word processing formats and vice versa. The latter is used to convert the files of supported graphics prorgams into Word Perfect Graphic format (see Chapter 11).

CONVERT.EXE

The conversion prorgam is run from DOS. At the DOS prompt, type:

CONVERT

The conversion utility will display a title screen that says "WordPerfect 5.1 Conversion Utility (see Figure 14.9). Don't worry, WordPerfect and LetterPerfect have the same structure (whenever you see "WordPerfect 5.1" in the conversion process, just think "LetterPerfect 1.0").

Figure 14.9* *Conversion title screen.

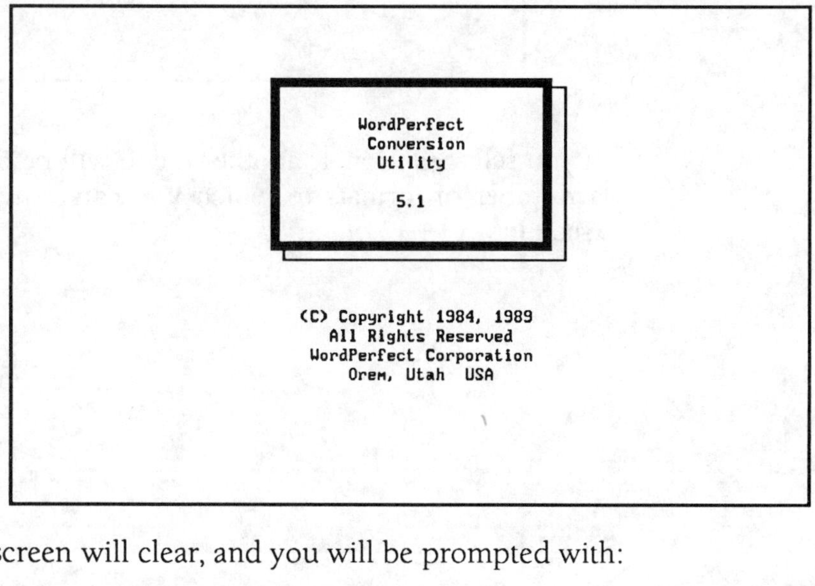

The screen will clear, and you will be prompted with:

```
Name of Input File?
```

Enter the full path if the file is not in the same directory or on the same disk as CONVERT.EXE, as in C:\WORD\MEMO1. The conversion program will then prompt you with:

`Name of Output File?`

Type in the desired name for the file after conversion—your original file is not altered.

The conversion routine will then display the menu shown in Figure 14.10. The first option is for converting LetterPerfect to another format. The remaining options are for converting from other formats into LetterPerfect.

***Figure 14.10* Conversion menu: from other programs to LetterPerfect.**

```
Name of Input File? c:\word\memo1
Name of Output File? c:\word\memo2


0 EXIT
1 WordPerfect to another format
2 Revisable-Form-Text (IBM DCA Format) to WordPerfect
3 Final-Form-Text (IBM DCA Format) to WordPerfect
4 Navy DIF Standard to WordPerfect
5 WordStar 3.3 to WordPerfect
6 MultiMate Advantage II to WordPerfect
7 Seven-Bit Transfer Format to WordPerfect
8 WordPerfect 4.2 to WordPerfect 5.1
9 Mail Merge to WordPerfect Secondary Merge
A Spreadsheet DIF to WordPerfect Secondary Merge
B Word 4.0 to WordPerfect
C DisplayWrite to WordPerfect

Enter number of Conversion desired
```

If you select Option 1, another menu will be displayed offering you a number of formats to which you can convert LetterPerfect files (see Figure 14.11).

Figure 14.11
Conversion menu: LetterPerfect to other programs.

```
Name of Input File? c:\word\memo1
Name of Output File? c:\word\memo2


0 EXIT
1 Revisable-Form-Text (IBM DCA Format)
2 Final-Form-Text (IBM DCA Format)
3 Navy DIF Standard
4 WordStar 3.3
5 MultiMate Advantage II
6 Seven-Bit Transfer Format
7 ASCII Text File
8 WordPerfect Secondary Merge to Spreadsheet DIF

Enter number of output file format desired
```

Whether you're going to or from LetterPerfect format, select the desired word processor. If the word processing format to which you want to convert isn't listed, you'll have to use a third-party program.

GRAPHCNV.EXE

This file converts files from supported graphics programs (see Chaptter 11) to WordPerfect Graphic format. To use it, switch to whatever directory you installed your program files in, or the floppy that you labeled Utility Files. At the DOS prompt, type:

GRAPHCNV

The conversion program will display the message:

```
Enter name of file to convert:
```

Make sure that you list the full file and extension name, as in REVENUE.PIC. Next, the conversion program will prompt you to:

```
Enter name of output file:
```

You can specify any directory on your hard disk, or either floppy drive, as in B:REVENUE.WPG or C:\LPDATA\REVENUE. When you press (Enter), the conversion program will automatically convert the file to .WPG format.

Appendix A

Installing the HP LaserJet Series II or LaserJet III

Overview

LetterPerfect can be customized for hundreds of printers, to take advantage of their special features. It does an exceptionally good job of this with laser printers in general, and the Hewlett-Packard LaserJet Series II or III in particular. This appendix provides detailed instructions for installing a LaserJet Series II or LaserJet III with a font cartridge and a soft font. The steps described apply to any printer; if you don't have font cartridges, simply skip that step of the installation procedure. This appendix assumes that you have a computer with a hard disk; consult the LetterPerfect manual for modifying the instructions if you have a floppy system. While you can use the LaserJet with a floppy-based system, as you begin to add soft fonts, you will find it extremely slow, as well as a disk juggling act.

Basic Concepts

Drivers

LetterPerfect uses a number of *drivers*, software files that enable the software to communicate with the printer. The drivers are contained on the Printer disk. During the installation procedure, you have the opportunity to select your printer from the printer list. You can change or add additional printers at any time. For the purpose of this appendix, it is assumed that you selected an HP LaserJet Series II or LaserJet III.

Customizing Your LaserJet Printer Definition

Selecting a Printer

1. From within LetterPerfect, call up the Main Print menu by pressing F,P or (Shift-F7). The Main Printer menu will appear (see Figure A.1).

Figure A.1 Main printer menu.

```
Print

     1 - Full Document
     2 - Multiple Pages
     3 - View Document
     4 - Initialize Printer

Options

     5 - Select Printer                   HP LaserJet III
     6 - Binding Offset                   0"
     7 - Number of Copies                 1
     8 - Graphics Quality                 Medium
     9 - Text Quality                     High

Selection: 0
```

2. Press 5 or S to choose the Select option. You will be presented with the Printer Selection menu shown in Figure A.2.

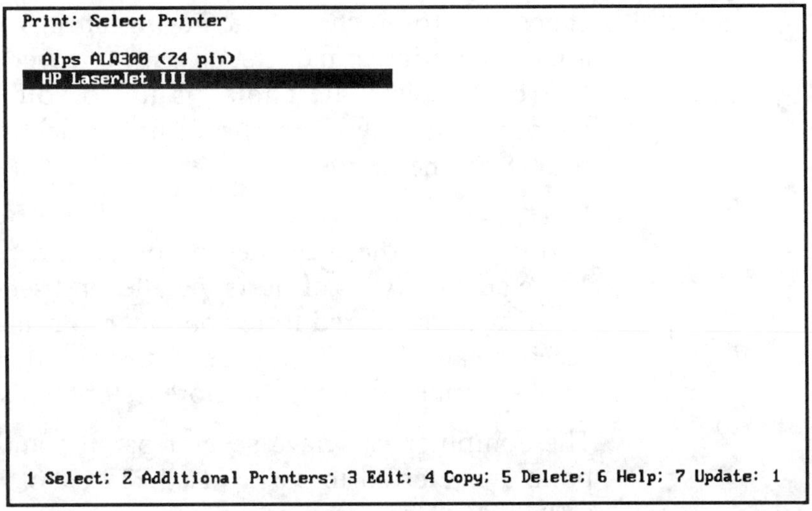

Figure A.2 Printer selection menu.

3. Select 3 for Edit. This displays the Edit screen shown in Figure A.3. There are seven basic options, each of which has several sub-options under it. These are discussed in the sequence in which they appear on the screen. If you don't need to use a certain option, skip it and move on to the next.

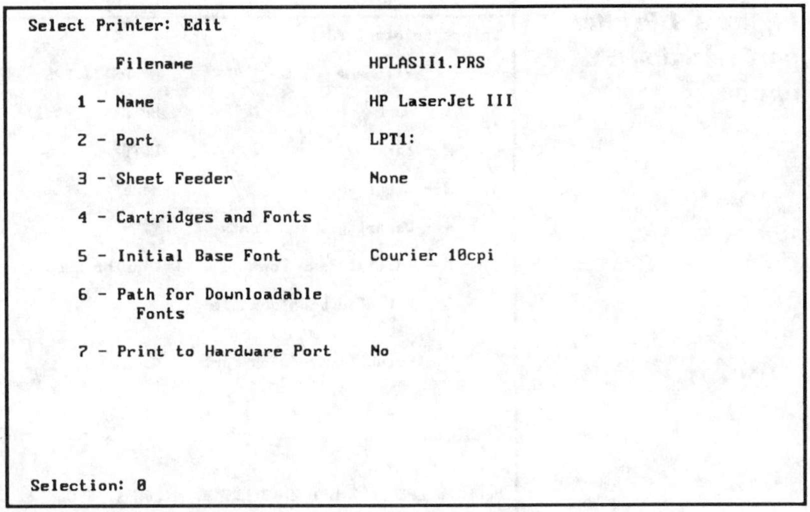

Figure A.3 Printer edit screen.

Name

LetterPerfect supplies a default name for your printer when you first install it. In the case of the LaserJet, the name is "HP LaserJet Series II" or "LaserJet III." You can edit it or insert any name you choose, up to 36 characters. For instance, you may want to supply a more descriptive name such as "My Laser Printer" or "Phil's Dot Matrix Printer." The choice is up to you. Whatever name you choose is displayed on the Printer Selection menu when select printers in the future.

Port

Port refers to the way the computer and printer are connected. There are two types of ports: parallel and serial. Parallel means that the data is transferred from computer to printer eight bits at a time; serial means that the data is transmitted one bit after another. Parallel connections are therefore faster than serial connections.

The computer can have several parallel and serial ports. Parallel ports are referred to as LPT1:, LPT2:, etc. Serial ports are called COM1:, COM2:, and so on. If you don't instruct the computer otherwise, it assumes that your printer is connected to LPT1:, which makes LPT1: the default port. If, however, your printer is connected to LPT2: or COM1: or COM2:, you must inform LetterPerfect of the change. If you're not sure, check your printer manual, or contact your dealer or the person who sets up computers in your company. Select 2 while in the editing menu, and the Printer Port Menu shown in Figure A.4 will be displayed.

Figure A.4 Printer port selection options.

```
Select Printer: Edit

        Filename                        HPLASIII.PRS

    1 - Name                            HP LaserJet III

    2 - Port                            LPT3:

    3 - Sheet Feeder                    None

    4 - Cartridges and Fonts

    5 - Initial Base Font               Courier 10cpi

    6 - Path for Downloadable
          Fonts

    7 - Print to Hardware Port          No



Port: 1 LPT 1: 2 LPT 2: 3 LPT 3: 4 COM 1: 5 COM 2: 6 COM 3: 7 COM 4: 8 Other: 0
```

Enter the number corresponding to the desired port. If the printer is connected to a parallel port such as LPT2:, you don't have to do anything more than enter the number. The screen then redisplays the Edit Menu (Figure A.3). If the printer is connected to a serial port, however, you also have to provide LetterPerfect with additional information. Figure A.5 shows the Serial Port Parameters menu, including the default values for the HP LaserJet Series II and LaserJet III (see your LaserJet manual for details).

Figure A.5 Serial port parameters.

```
Select Printer: COM Port

     1 - Baud                              9600

     2 - Parity                            None

     3 - Stop Bits (1 or 2)                1

     4 - Character Length (7 or 8)         8

     5 - XON/XOFF                          No






Selection: 0
```

You should refer to your printer manual for information about your printer's serial port parameters. When you are satisfied with the Serial Port parameters, press (F7), the Exit key, to save the changes and return to the Edit menu.

Caution: If you press the (Esc) key, you will not save the changes you have made.

Sheet Feeder

If you are using a sheet feeder, which automatically loads individual sheets of paper or envelopes into the printer, you have to enter certain information about the device. Select the appropriate device from whatever list is displayed. Once the sheet feeder has been selected, you will be shown a Help and Hints Screen that describes the assignment of paper bins (see Figure A.6). Make a note of the bin assignments, as you will need it later. You can always review this screen by selecting the Edit option under the Printer Selection menu and asking for Help.

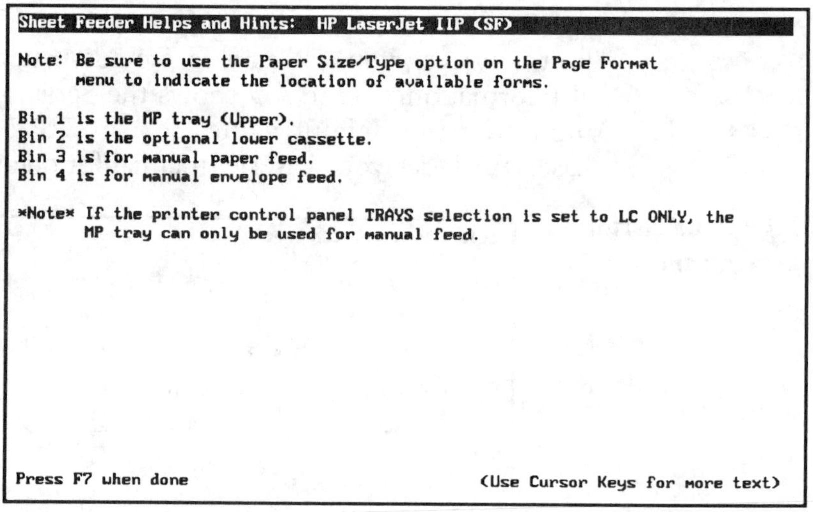

Figure A.6 Sheet feeder bin assignments (for LaserJet IIP).

Press (F7) to exit the Sheet Feeder Selection submenu and return to the Edit menu.

Cartridges and Soft Fonts

If you have optional font cartridges or soft fonts, you must tell LetterPerfect what they are. LetterPerfect not only needs to know which fonts are available, but also how to handle the complex task of character spacing associated with different sized proportional fonts. Here's how to give LetterPerfect the necessary information.

To install a cartridge, you must first select the Cartridges and Soft Fonts option from the Printer Edit menu. You will then be presented with the Cartridge and Fonts Selection Menu shown in Figure A.7.

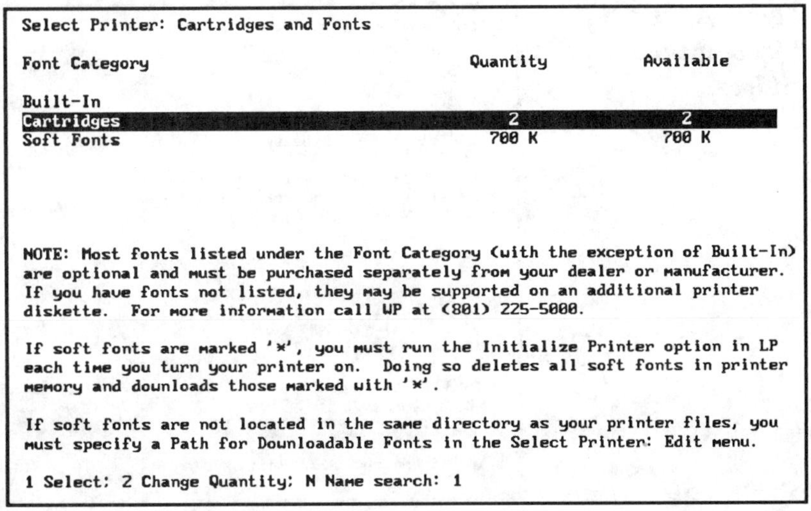

Figure A.7 Cartridge and soft font selection menu.

Note that you can change the number of available cartridge slots and printer memory. Unless you have added additional memory, however, or you are installing a compatible laser printer with more than two cartridge slots, you needn't change either quantity.

Use the cursor to highlight the Cartridge Font option and choose 1 for Select Fonts. You will be presented with the menu of font cartridges available for the H.P. LaserJet Series II or LaserJet III (see Figure A.8). The list of available fonts is determined by the fonts LetterPerfect selects to support. If you are using a font cartridge that is not on the list, call LetterPerfect to determine the best method for either using another driver, obtaining a special driver, or altering one of the existing drivers.

Highlight the cartridge you wish to install and enter an asterisk by pressing (Shift-8). The asterisk indicates that the font cartridge will be ready for use when the print job begins.

Figure A.8 Partial List of available cartridges.

```
Select Printer: Cartridges                              Quantity
                                               Total:      2
                                           Available:      1

                                                         Quantity Used

   HP Polished Worksheets                                       1
   HP Q Memo 1                                                  1
   HP R Presentations 1                                         1
   HP S1 Courier Document 1                                     1
   HP S2 TmsRmn/Helv Report 1                                   1
   HP T Tax 1                                                   1
   HP TextEquations                                             1
   HP U Forms Portrait                                          1
   HP V Forms Landscape                                         1
   HP W 3-of-9 / OCR A                                          1
   HP W1 3-of-9 / OCR-A                                         1
   HP WordPerfect                                               1
   HP X EAN/UPC / OCR-B                                         1
   HP Y PC Courier 1                                            1
   HP Z Microsoft 1                                             1
*  HP Z Microsoft 1A                                            1

Mark:  * Present when print job begins              Press F7 to save
                                                 Press Cancel to cancel
```

You must have the cartridge properly installed before attempting to print. Note that the available quantity of cartridge slots has dropped by one, indicating that you only have one left to select. See Figure A.9.

Figure A.9 Cartridge availability after installing one cartridge.

```
Select Printer: Cartridges and Fonts

Font Category                              Quantity          Available

Built-In
Cartridges                                     2                 1
Soft Fonts                                   700 K             700 K




NOTE: Most fonts listed under the Font Category (with the exception of Built-In)
are optional and must be purchased separately from your dealer or manufacturer.
If you have fonts not listed, they may be supported on an additional printer
diskette.  For more information call WP at (801) 225-5000.

If soft fonts are marked '*', you must run the Initialize Printer option in LP
each time you turn your printer on.  Doing so deletes all soft fonts in printer
memory and downloads those marked with '*'.

If soft fonts are not located in the same directory as your printer files, you
must specify a Path for Downloadable Fonts in the Select Printer: Edit menu.

1 Select; 2 Change Quantity; N Name search: 1
```

Here's where things get a bit tricky. You can actually increase the number of cartridges beyond the two slots available on the Series II and III if you have more than two cartridges, and you can select all of them as being present when the job begins. In that case, though, you are responsible for ensuring that you only use fonts from two cartridges in any single document, and that the correct pair of cartridges are inserted in the printer prior to starting a print job that calls for them (i.e., prior to printing the document in which the particular font cartridges were specified).

When you are done marking all the cartridges, press (F7) twice to get back to the Edit menu. You may have to wait a moment while LetterPerfect updates its available font file.

Initial Base Font

Although you have installed a new font cartridge, your documents will still print in Courier 10 until you tell the printer to either change the Base Font for a particular document, or you reset the Initial Font. To do this, select 5 for the Initial Font option from the Printer Edit menu, use the (Up Cursor) or (Down Cursor) to highlight the font you want to become the new default (Base) font and press 1. The next time you print a document, it will print with whatever Base Font you selected.

Path for Downloadable Fonts and Printer Command Files

If you are going to use soft fonts (fonts that are stored on disk files and downloaded into the printer's memory before use), you must tell LetterPerfect where to find the soft font files. You must also install the soft fonts in a directory on your hard disk according to the manufacturer's directions; each manufacturer uses a different techniques for creating and storing fonts. LetterPerfect is not shipped with soft font drivers—to use any soft fonts, you will have to order the drivers by contacting WordPerfect Corporation.

At this point, you have a fully installed HP LaserJet, and you can print in a variety of fonts, as well as on envelopes fed one-at-a time through the manual paper feed.

Appendix B

Major Function Summary

Feature	Menu Keystrokes	Function Keys
Add Password	F,A	(Ctrl-F5,2,1)
ASCII Text file (Save as)	F,D	(Ctrl-F5,1)
Backspace (Erase)	Backspace	
Backup Files, Automatic	F,T,M	(Shift-F1,2)
Backward Search	S,B	(Shift-F2)
Base Font	O,F	(Ctrl-F8,4)
Block	E,B	(Alt-F4)
Bold	O,B	(F6, or
Bottom Margin	L,F,M	(Shift-F8,3)
Cancel	Esc	
Cancel Print Job	L or C or F7 (If Printing)	
Cartridges and Fonts (select)	F,P,S,E,C	(Shift-F7,5,3,4)
Center		
Page (top to bottom)	L,F,C	(Shift-F8,9)
Text	L,C	(Shift-F6)
Copy		
Block (Block on)	E,C	(Ctrl-F4,2)
File(s)	F,L,Enter,C	(F5,Enter,5)
Paragraph		(Ctrl-F4,2,2)
Sentence		(Ctrl-F4,1,2)
Date		
Text	T,T	(Shift-F5,1)
Code	T,C	(Shift-F5,2)
Define Printer	F, P, S	(Shift-F7,5)
Delete		
Block (Block On)	E,D	(Ctrl-F4,3)
Character Left	Backspace	
Current Character	Del	
Directory	F,L,Enter,D	(F5,Enter,2)
File	F,L,Enter,D	(F5,Enter,2)
Endnote		(Ctrl-F7)
Create	L,R	(Ctrl-F7,1)
Edit	L,E	(Ctrl-F7,2)
Exit	F,X	(F7)
Figure Box	G,C	(Alt-F9,1)

Flush Right	L,L	(Alt-F6)
Font (Base)	O,F	(Ctrl-F8,4)
Footer	L,F,H,F,C	(Shift-F8,6,2)
Create	L,F,H,F,C	(Shift-F8,6,2,2)
Discontinue	L,F,H,F,D	(Shift-F8,6,2,1)
Edit	L,F,H,F,E	(Shift-F8,6,2,3)
Suppress	L,F,H,S,F	(Shift-F8,6,3,2)
Format	L,F	(Shift-F8)
Forward Search	S,F	(F2)
Graphics	G	(Alt-F9)
Create	G,C	(Alt-F9,1)
Edit	G,E	(Alt-F9,2)
Quality	F,P,G	(Shift-F7,8)
Header	L,F,H	(Shift-F8,6)
Create	L,F,H,H,C	(Shift-F8,6,1,2)
Discontinue	L,F,H,H,D	(Shift-F8,6,1,1)
Edit	L,F,H,H,E	(Shift-F8,6,1,3)
Suppress	L,F,H,S,H	(Shift-F8,6,3,1)
Indent		
Left and Right	L,N	(Shift-F4)
Left Only	L,I	(F4)
Initial Codes	F,T,I	(Shift-F1,5)
Initialize Printer	F,P,I	(Shift-F7,4)
Italics Print	O,I	(Ctrl-F8,5)
Justification	L,F,J	(Shift-F8,1)
Center	L,F,J,C	(Shift-F8,1,2)
Full	L,F,J,F	(Shift-F8,1,4)
Left	L,F,J,L	(Shift-F8,1,1)
Right	L,F,J,R	(Shift-F8,1,3)
Left and Right Margins	L,F,R	(Shift-F8,4)
Left Margin Release	L,M	(Shift-Tab)
Line Draw	T,L	(Ctrl-F3)
Line Spacing	L,F,L	(Shift-F8,2)
List Files	F,L	(F5)

Mail Merge	T,M	(Ctrl-F9)
Margin Release	L,M	(Shift-Tab)
Margins		
Left and Right	L,F,R	(Shift-F8,4)
Top and Bottom	L,F,M	(Shift-F8,3)
Menu Bar	Alt or Alt-=	
Merge	T,M	(Ctrl-F9)
Merge Codes	T,E	(Shift-F9)
Move		
Block (Block On)	E,M	(Ctrl-F4)
File	F,L,M	(F5,3)
Paragraph	E,G	(Ctrl-F4,2)
Sentence	E,N	(Ctrl-F4,1)
Text	E,M	(Ctrl-F4,3)
Number Pages	L,F,P	(Shift-F8,7)
Outline		
Off	T,U	(Shift-F5,4)
On	T,O	(Shift-F5,3)
Page Break	L,H	(Ctrl-Enter)
Page Numbering	L,F,P	(Shift-F8,7)
Paper Size/Type	L,F,S	(Shift-F8,8)
Paste Block	E,P	(Ctrl-F4,4)
Preview	F,P,V	(Shift-F7,3)
Print	F,P	(Shift-F7)
Block (Block On)	F,P	(Shift-F7)
Full Document	F,P,F	(Shift-F7,1)
Multiple Pages	F,P,M	(Shift-F7,2)
Preview	F,P,V	(Shift-F7,3)
Recover Text	E,U,R	(Esc,1)
Remove Password	F,E	(Ctrl-F5,2,2)
Rename File	F,L,Enter,M	(F5,Enter,3)
Replace	S,R	(Alt-F2)
Restore Deleted Text	E,U,R	(Esc,1)

Retrieve		
Block (Move)	E,P	(Ctrl-F4,4)
Document	F,R	(Shift-F10)
DOS Text File	F,R	(Shift-F10)
Reveal Codes	E,R	(Alt-F3)
Save Text	F,S	(F10)
Search	S,F	(F2)
Search and Replace	S,R	(Alt-F2)
Select Printer	F,P,S	(Shift-F7,5)
Setup	F,T	(Shift-F1)
Spell	T,S	(Ctrl-F2)
Stop Printer	S	
Tab	Tab	
Align	L,T	(Ctrl-F6)
Set	L,F,T	(Shift-F8,5)
Type	L,F,T,T	(Shift-F8,5,T)
Thesaurus	T,H	(Alt-F1)
Undelete	E,U	(Esc,F1)
Underline Text	O,U	(F8)
Units of Measure	F,T,U	(Shift-F1,3)
View Document	F,P,V	(Shift-F7,3)

Appendix C

Summary of LetterPerfect Codes

Code	Definition
[ ]	Hard Space
[-]	Hyphen Character
-	Soft Hyphen
-	Hard Hyphen
[Block]	Beginning of Block
[Bold]	Bold
[Center]	Center
[Center Pg]	Center Page Top to Bottom
[Cntr Tab]	Centered Tab
[CNTR TAB]	Hard Centered Tab
[Date]	Date Function
[Dec Tab]	Decimal Aligned Tab
{Decml/Algn Char]	Decimal Character
[Dorm HRt]	Dormant Hard Return
[DSRt]	Deletable Soft Return
[DEC TAB]	Hard Decimal Aligned Tab
[Endnote]	Endnote
[Fig Box]	Figure Box
[Fig Opt]	Figure Box Options
[Flsh Rgt]	Flush Right
[Font]	Base Font
[Footer A]	Footer
[Header A]	Header
[HPg]	Hard Page Break
[HRt]	Hard Return
[Hrt-SPg]	Hard Return-Soft Page
[->Indent]	Indent
[->Indent<-]	Left/Right Indent

[ISRt]	Invisible Soft Return
[Italc]	Italics
[Just]	Justification
[L/R Mar]	Left and Right Margins
[Lang]	Language
[Ln Spacing]	Line Spacing
[<-Mar Rel]	Left Margin Release
[Mrg]	Merge Code
[Note Num]	Endnote Number
[Outline Off]	Outline Off
[Outline On]	Outline On
[Paper Sz/Typ]	Paper Size and Type
[Par Num]	Paragraph Number
[Pg Numbering]	Page Numbering
[Rgt Tab]	Right-Aligned Tab
[RGT TAB]	Hard Right-Aligned Tab
[SPg]	Soft Page Break
[SRt]	Soft Return
[Subscpt]	Subscript
[Suppress]	Suppress Header/Footer
[Suprscpt]	Superscript
[T/B Mar]	Top and Bottom Margins
[Tab]	Left-Aligned Tab
[TAB]	Hard Left-Aligned Tab
[Tab Set]	Tab Set
[Und]	Underline

Index

D

L

N

O

R

S

About the Author

Steven J. Bennett is a full-time author specializing in business managament and computing books. He has co-authored the following Brady titles: *1-2-3 Ready-to-Go, dBASE III Plus To Go, dBASE IV Plus To Go, The HAL Handbook, 1-2-3 Power Pack, WordPerfect 4.2/5.0 Power Pack, WordPerfect 5.1 Power Pack, Simply WordPerfect, Instant Byline Publishing, Instant PageMaker/IBM, Instant Ventura Publisher, Hewlett-Packard Laser Printer Power Pack, The LaserJet Handbook, Total 1-2-3: Release 3,* and *Total 1-2-3: Release 2.2.*

"Rhyder McClure has written the first book about computer software that does not appear to have been translated from the Japanese."

—Andy Rooney,
About the original *Fast Access/WordPerfect*

Don't lose valuable time and productivity learning the new features of WordPerfect 5.1. *Fast Access/WordPerfect 5.1* provides crucial information to get you started and keep you going without overwhelming you with irrelevant detail.

Written in plain English with keystroke-by-keystroke instruction. You'll find ready help with:

- All new features of Version 5.1
- Block Manipulation
- Search and replace functions
- Sorting and merging features
- Macros
- Paragraph and outline numbering
- And much more!

Brady's *Fast Access* series of unique reference guides gives you immediate mastery of the key features of many popular software programs. Regardless of the software's complexity or your experience, *Fast Access* books give you clear explanations and precise advice right away! For information that's both thorough and convenient, look no further than Brady's *Fast Access*!

ISBN: 0-13-307646-6

Price: $16.95

Brady